Dear Ch[...]
Happiest o[...]
to you! [...]
rest of your year is
as stunning as you
are. And that you get
lots of joy out of this
book!
Thanks for always
being a friend I can
count on. For all these
years, and many more.
You are truely a
beautiful person - inside
and out!
I have endless love
for you.
Happy 21st birthday!
Love Jess xxx

tashas®

tashas®

NATASHA SIDERIS

photography by David Ross

JONATHAN BALL PUBLISHERS
JOHANNESBURG & CAPE TOWN

All rights reserved.
No part of this publication may be reproduced or
transmitted, in any form or by any means, without prior
permission from the publisher or copyright holder.

© Text Natasha Sideris 2015
© Photographs tashas 2015

Originally published in South Africa in 2015 by
JONATHAN BALL PUBLISHERS (PTY) LTD
A division of Media24 Limited
PO Box 33977
Jeppestown
2043

Reprinted once in 2015

ISBN 978-1-86842-266-1

The right of Natasha Sideris to be identified as the author
of this work has been asserted by her in accordance with the
copyright law of 1978.

The right of David Ross to be identified as the
photographer of this work has been asserted by him in
accordance with the copyright law of 1978.

Twitter: http://www.twitter.com/JonathanBallPub
Facebook: http://www.facebook.com/JonathanBallPublishers
Blog: http://jonathanball.bookslive.co.za/

Edited by Kathleen Sutton
Cover by Alexandra Ross
Design and typesetting by Alexandra Ross
Proofreading by Gudrun Kaiser
Index by Derika van Biljon
Reproduction by Resolution Colour, Cape Town (Pty) Ltd
Printed and bound by Craft International Ltd

For my dad – for all the Mondays, miracles and milkshakes.

natasha sideris is the creator and founder of the successful tashas restaurants. Natasha opened the first tashas in Atholl, Johannesburg in 2005. Since partnering with Famous Brands in 2008, another twelve tashas have opened countrywide and more recently, one in Dubai. Each tashas has its own 'inspired by…' menu and style, which range from a New York deli-style menu in cosmopolitan Rosebank, a Dutch Huguenot-based menu in Pretoria, a sophisticated French-style menu in chic Hyde Park, to a Spanish tapas-inspired menu at the V&A Waterfront in Cape Town. Natasha is a passionate cook with a talent for interior design, reflected in her beautiful, diverse restaurants. This is her first cookbook.

contents

from tasha with love	11
breakfast	16
sandwiches & burgers	54
salads	82
pasta	104
easy eats	126
desserts	162
drinks	188
cocktails	204
acknowledgements	217
index	223

from tasha with love

This book has been years in the making. I began dreaming it up almost a decade ago when I opened the first tashas in 2005. It is a celebration of my heritage and the easy-going, generous Mediterranean way of eating and living that I grew up with and love. It also pays homage to you, the countless, wonderful people who have helped to make tashas the success story that it is today.

the tashas history

It all begins with my father, Harry Sideris, a great chef and successful restaurateur. All his life he worked long and hard hours in his restaurants. But despite his warnings about the pitfalls of the business, my brother Savva and I weren't put off. His passion for food and for feeding people inspired us. My dad could make sauces and season dishes like no one else I've ever met, except perhaps Savva, who is also a brilliant cook. My dad may have been a trained chef but his gift for combining flavours came naturally. He cooked instinctively and he cooked from the heart.

I grew up, first at his knee, later by his side, in his restaurants and cafés, enveloped in the warm, steamy aromas emanating from pots and pans, the clatter and crash in the kitchens, the bustling and banter of the front-of-house staff, and the chatter of the customers. Savva and I learned early on in life the sweet anticipation of dad's after-school 'milkshake Monday' treats. We also learned to appreciate the simple pleasure of a good steak grilled to juicy pink perfection, and new potatoes boiled and buttered.

My father loved people but every now and then he would fend everyone off by telling them we were going away for the weekend and then slip out to the deli instead. He would return home laden with cheeses, exotic cold cuts, fat imported olives and freshly baked bread. We would camp out for the weekend in the lounge and picnic on the carpet, just us.

His passion for food was matched only by his passion for people and he got a thrill, as I do, from feeding them. Maybe it's a Greek thing, but his conversations usually began with, "Have you eaten?" Regardless of the answer you could be sure you'd be eating again soon. The most important value I learned from my parents is that good food is about so much more than just flavour. It's really about how it makes us feel. Both my father the chef, and my mother the home-cook, made wonderful food but each had their own approach. From my father I learned the importance of sharing food with loved ones. From my mother, the importance of caring about where you eat as much as what you eat.

the tashas philosophy

The tashas philosophy is all about generosity and abundance. Our passion for people and the belief that enjoyable eating is about more than just food has been at the heart of tashas since we opened our doors in Atholl, Johannesburg nine years ago. The first restaurant, and each of the twelve that have followed, were inspired by my idea to transform daytime eating in South Africa. I wanted to create an environment where food and conversation go hand in hand. I wanted to evoke the warm feeling of the little cafés in Moçambique where my father grew up and where we spent our holidays. Like the little cafés, I wanted to serve fresh, made-to-order meals.

Unlike many other restaurants, we don't precook anything at tashas. I insist on freshness. Logistically, this is very tricky. It means that our menu has to focus on uncomplicated, unfussy dishes and that we have to use only the freshest and the best ingredients. Informal café-style food tastes better when shared with good company, a glass of wine, in a relaxed environment; I always intended tashas to be a sociable, informal place where you are welcomed and served with a smile. A place where you feel at home and the food is simple and delicious. It has to be both comfortable and sophisticated, kind of like putting your feet up on an insanely expensive couch. It's a philosophy based on generosity, and is at the heart of the Greek and Mediterranean way of life. This is where I come from, these are my roots.

Of course, good food also relies on good ingredients, well cooked. No matter how fancy your dressing or elaborate your sauce, it won't miraculously resurrect a plate of wilted veg, nor will it make frozen fish smack of the sea. Even the most experienced chef sometimes messes up by over-complicating things. I agree with Nigel Slater when he says that ingredients should speak louder than cooks.

That's not to say you shouldn't bring your individual style and personality into the kitchen. Once you understand flavours and have mastered a few basic cooking skills, you should follow your instincts. Cooking is a lot like life. There is no rulebook; we make it up as we muddle along. No cream, no potatoes, or only a single chicken breast and some green beans to feed four? Substitute, invent! Add a bit of this and a pinch of that, experiment with your favourite flavours and textures, present your dish with a flourish and you will be rewarded with plates licked clean. Inspired cooks make food that celebrates great ingredients but they are also creative, inventive and most of all, passionate.

the tashas classics

The recipes in this book come from the original tashas menu, some of which have now been replaced with newer ones. All of them are based on the timeless café classics we know and love so well. If nothing will do but good old-fashioned comfort food, you'll find it in the creamy Chicken Pot Pie (page 149). Light and breezy summer elegance? It's in the eternally popular Salmon Fish Cakes (page 133).
Old school classics are still around because they're the people pleasers that continue to satisfy us after all these years. It may not be as exhilarating as a fierce Tom Yum but sometimes nothing hits the spot like a steaming bowl of minestrone (page 147). We love the classics and welcome them like old friends. Don't get clever with Harry's Roadhouse Steak Sarmie (page 65). And don't mess with mom's Spaghetti Bolognaise (page 113) because in this case, my mother really does know best. These recipes work because they've stood the test of time.

But people's tastes evolve. Over time and through experience, my team of wonderful cooks and I have introduced new ingredients and tweaked traditional flavours. We've added a touch of spice or a dash of cream here, a bit of crunch and a micro green there. We've left out the bland and boring bits that don't suit our modern, more experienced palates. You should also feel free to ad-lib and adapt according to your mood and what's available in your cupboard and fridge. This is a cookbook, not a rulebook.

When you're feeding others, remember that long before we dive in for our first eager bite, lick or hungry slurp, good food is tempting. It's mouth-watering, imaginative and lovely to look at. The beautiful photography in this book should stimulate your senses and your appetite, make you want to cook up a storm and inspire you to present your food creatively. And an easy recipe doesn't mean a meal has to be unsophisticated. A simple supper can be transformed into an elegant dinner just through presentation, both on the plate and at the table. Dig out granny's white linen napkins, crack open an extra special bottle of wine or add just one inspired ingredient to take your basic meal from 'whatever' to 'wow'.

Some people prefer to cook by-the-recipe-book and that's good too, but if you do, be warned – your dish will never taste exactly the same as ours. No, I haven't left out any secret ingredients. Food just tastes different according to your mood, where and when you eat it, and who you share it with.
Take these recipes and make them just as we do or take them and make them your own.
Make them even better by sharing them with the people you love.

Part of the success of our breakfast menu is that we are open early enough to accommodate early birds. It's a huge part of our business. We also cater for a wide variety of tastes from healthy and light to big and greasy. We should all make breakfast more of an occasion. There is so much you can do with breakfast; hot or cold, smoothies and juices, fry-ups and traditional grills. The options are endless, which is why we serve breakfast all day.

breakfast

eggs	18
good intentions	23
granny smith	25
health breakfast	27
syrups for fruit salad	28
breakfast royale	31
pea & fennel bruschetta	33
jett & luke's breakfast	35
bacon rösti	37
pimp my toast	39
mushroom ciabatta	41
livers on toast	45
12 o'clock breakfast	47
millionaire's breakfast	49
lazy smoked salmon frittata	51
grandma goes french	53

eggs

poached
Use a deep pot, fill it about two-thirds of the way with water and bring it to simmering point. We use a dash of vinegar, but not more or it makes your eggs smell sour. Crack the egg into a small cup. Start swirling the water to create a whirlpool and drop the egg from the cup right into the middle of the vortex. Keep swirling until the egg white is solid. The longer you stir, the firmer the yolk will be. If you're not eating the egg immediately, keep it in ice-cold water. The egg will firm up immediately. Before serving, reheat in boiling water.

scrambled
We add only salt and pepper to our scrambled eggs, but we cook them in a big knob of pure butter. We use between one and three eggs per portion. You can add cream or milk to make them more decadent. The trick to good scrambled eggs is in the cooking. It is important to gently fold the egg as it cooks and not to mix or beat it.

boiled
Just in case you don't know how to do this. Put the eggs in a pot of cold water with a splash of white wine vinegar and a pinch of salt. Bring the water to the boil. Once the bubbles break the surface of the water, start timing. Cooking times vary, so leave them for as long as you like. The yellow should be bright. Experiment with the timings but I have found that the following work well: soft – 3 minutes; medium – 5 minutes; hard – 7 minutes.

fried
My mom makes these using only butter, my granddad used only olive oil. Butter makes them creamier, oil makes them crispier. For best results, I use both. Heat your pan on medium heat and add oil, then butter. Break the eggs into the pan, cover the pan with a lid and let them cook for a bit. Remove the lid and tilt your pan to spoon the oil or butter over the eggs. Cook to your liking.

good intentions

This is the healthiest breakfast imaginable: no wheat, no gluten, no fat, no sugar, no problem. Just delicious goodness in a bowl. The milk can be substituted with water or soya milk to make it lactose free.

SEED MIXTURE
40 g linseeds
40 g sunflower seeds
40 g almond shavings

PORRIDGE
500 ml milk
500 ml coconut milk
250 ml seed mix
2 bananas, sliced
4 dried figs, diced
pinch cinnamon
1 tsp vanilla essence

4 dried figs, diced
16 almonds, halved
2 bananas, sliced
120 ml honey

To make the seed mixture, grind the linseeds, sunflower seeds and almond shavings in your food processor. The mixture should look like coarse flour, but most of the linseeds will still be whole. Be careful not to overgrind or it will become a paste.

Make the porridge by mixing the milk, coconut milk and seed mix in a pot. Add the sliced bananas, diced dried figs, cinnamon and vanilla essence. Bring the mixture to the boil. Allow it to boil for 4 minutes only, stirring often to avoid lumps. The mixture must still be slightly runny. Don't let it become too thick.

Once the porridge is cooked, pour it into 4 bowls and garnish with the diced figs and halved almonds. Serve with sliced bananas and honey on the side.

SERVES 4

granny smith

This is a wonderful way to start the day. It's a bit like Bircher muesli (the original overnight oats, developed around 1900 by a Swiss doctor). The muesli should soak for two or three hours, so you need to plan ahead. Our recipe adds a secret ingredient, which is condensed milk. Not the healthiest option, but absolutely worth it.

ROLLED OATS MIXTURE
30 g dried apple rings
30 g dried mango strips
60 g dried cranberries
300 g rolled oats
30 g coconut flakes
30 g pumpkin seeds
350 ml apple juice

200 ml double cream Greek yoghurt
60 ml condensed milk (optional)

4 Granny Smith apples
half a lemon
maple syrup for garnish
4 strawberries, sliced

Make the rolled oats mixture by first dicing the 3 dried fruits and then mixing with the next 3 ingredients. Drench the mixture with the apple juice and allow to soak for 2–3 hours in the fridge. Then fill 4 teacups with about 150 g of the mixture and press down firmly.

Mix together the cream, yoghurt and condensed milk.

Cut off the cheeks of the unpeeled apples and slice into thin discs, discarding the cores. Stack and slice into thin matchsticks. Squeeze a little lemon juice over the apple to prevent it from going brown.

Invert the cups onto a plate. The rolled oats mixture should slide out easily. Top with the cream and yoghurt mixture, the apple matchsticks, drizzle with syrup and garnish with strawberries.

SERVES 4

health breakfast

I use yoghurt in a lot of recipes. You can use low fat or fat free yoghurt, but full fat Greek yoghurt is the best. For this dish you need to make your own fresh fruit salad. Use a variety of interesting fruit. If you can get starfruit, it adds whimsy to your salad and has a delicious sweet-tangy flavour.

GRANOLA
300 g rolled oats
100 g raw almonds, halved
100 g pecan nuts, roughly chopped
40 g sunflower seeds
40 g linseeds
2 tbsp chia seeds
80 g honey
2 tsp fresh ginger, grated
150 g dates, roughly chopped
2 tsp orange zest
2 tsp cinnamon powder
2 tbsp dessicated coconut

FRUIT SALAD
apples, bananas, pears, oranges, kiwis, pawpaw, pineapple, strawberries, figs, berries, peaches

FRUIT SALAD DRESSING
fruit juice
OR syrup (page 28)

720 g Greek yoghurt

Preheat the oven to 150 °C.

To make the granola, mix the oats, nuts and all the other ingredients together and bake for 20 minutes. Set aside to cool.

To make the fruit salad, cut your fruit and layer in your bowl. I use everyday fruit like apples, pears and oranges as the base. Softer fruit goes in the middle – kiwis, peaches and bananas. Prettier fruit like berries goes on top where they are visible. Dress with some fruit juice or make a syrup (page 28) to flavour it.

Serve the granola, fruit salad and yoghurt in separate bowls or layered in one large glass bowl.

SERVES 4

syrups for fruit salad

mint & sesame seed

125 ml honey
125 ml hot water
small handful fresh mint, chopped
20 g sesame seeds

In a pot, melt the honey in the hot water. Add the mint and sesame seeds. Let the mixture boil and reduce. Then strain, and allow the syrup to cool before adding it to the fruit salad.

orange zest

125 g sugar
1 orange, zested
125 ml fresh orange juice
1 stick of cinnamon
1 vanilla pod

Bring a pot of water to the boil and add all the ingredients. Once the mixture has reduced, strain and allow to cool before adding to the fruit salad.

lemongrass, lime & ginger

100 ml water
125 g sugar
3 limes, juice and zest
1 stick lemongrass
20 g ginger, grated

Bring the water to the boil and add all the remaining ingredients. Allow the liquid to reduce. Strain and allow to cool before adding to the fruit salad.

breakfast royale

I don't like pre-making sauces, especially hollandaise. This sauce cannot stand. It must be made fresh, so I rely on this cheat's version, which is healthier and lighter than its buttery counterpart. The consistency of the sauce is very important. It shouldn't be too runny or too thick. You can serve this breakfast with crispy Parma ham or smoked salmon, whichever you like best.

8 slices Parma ham
OR 8 slices smoked salmon

LEMON SAUCE
800 ml cream
juice of 4 lemons
salt and pepper

32 asparagus spears
OR 280 g spinach

8 eggs
8 slices toast

If you are using Parma ham, roast it in the oven at 180 °C until it is dry and crispy.

Make the lemon sauce by slowly bringing the cream to the boil in a pan. Add the lemon juice a little at a time, until the cream starts to thicken. Season with salt and pepper. The sauce shouldn't be too thick or too runny.

If you're serving asparagus, blanch the spears for 2–3 minutes in a pot of rapidly boiling salted water. Shock them in ice-cold water to stop the cooking process and to preserve their colour, drain and set aside.

If you're serving spinach, wilt it in a pan with a small knob of butter. Cover the pan with a lid and let it steam for a moment or two.

Scramble the eggs.

To assemble, top the toast with scrambled eggs, lemon sauce, asparagus or spinach, and the Parma ham or smoked salmon.

SERVES 4

pea & fennel bruschetta

I'm obsessed with fennel. It adds a distinct flavour to any meal. This is my favourite way to prepare it. The liquorice taste of the fennel and the saltiness of the Parmesan and bacon work perfectly together. Visually it's also very appealing. The sweet green peas create a beautiful contrast with the golden yellow of the egg yolk. It's like eating art.

1 large fennel bulb
320 g frozen peas
16 slices back bacon, chopped
olive oil
butter
1 red onion, chopped
3 tbsp water
salt and pepper

4 eggs
4 slices of ciabatta
olive oil

120 g Parmesan shavings

Slice the fennel bulb into paper-thin slices and roughly chop the leaves. Defrost the peas. Chop the bacon. Heat the olive oil in a pan, then add the butter. Sauté the onion and add the bacon. When the bacon is almost crisp, add the fennel and sauté until it is soft. Deglaze the pan by adding 3 tablespoons of water while the pan is still on the heat. Add the peas and 2 tablespoons of chopped fennel leaves to the pan until they are heated through. Don't overcook the peas or they will lose their colour. Squash them a little with the back of a fork and season to taste with salt and pepper.

Poach the eggs (page 18) and toast the ciabatta.

Spoon the fennel, pea and bacon mixture over the ciabatta toast. Top with poached eggs, drizzle with a little olive oil and Parmesan shavings.

SERVES 4

jett & luke's breakfast

Jett and Luke are my best friend Candice's sons. I've been on holiday with them to Cape Town, Greece, Turkey, Spain and the South of France. They called me early one morning after a rather late night and invited me to breakfast. When I got there, they were cooking up a storm all by themselves. The only thing more awesome than their breakfast is the fact that at the time, Jett was eight and Luke was six. This is one of our best sellers and I can't thank them enough.

24 baby potatoes
salt
sunflower oil for deep frying

1 onion, sliced
1 tbsp olive oil

16 rashers streaky bacon
8 eggs
8 mini burger rolls
16 slices Cheddar
handful rocket

Preheat the oven to 180 °C.

Boil the unpeeled baby potatoes in salted water. They should be cooked, but still slightly firm. Cut a shallow cross into the top of each potato and squeeze the sides so that the skin breaks and the flesh pops out a little. The potatoes should remain whole. Deep-fry them in very hot sunflower oil until they are brown and crisp.

While the potatoes are frying, sauté the sliced onions in a separate pan in a little olive oil.

Start cooking the bacon and frying the eggs. Cut the rolls open and place a slice of cheese on each half. Bake them in the oven until the cheese has just melted. Assemble the rolls in this order: rocket, bacon, egg, onion, Serve with the fried baby potatoes on the side and some tomato sauce.

SERVES 4

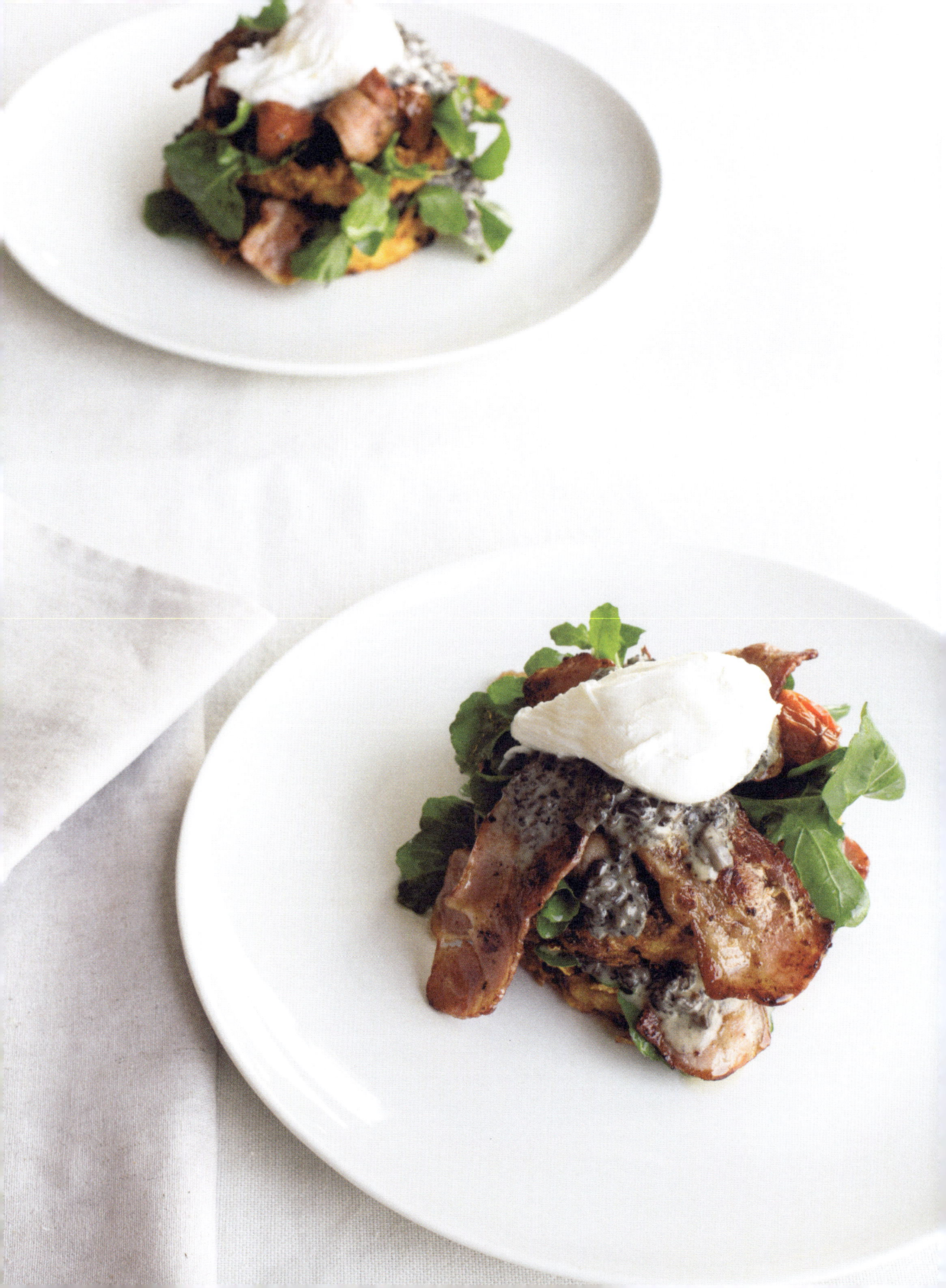

bacon rösti

My mom grew up in Highlands North. It was an area with a strong Jewish influence. She made excellent *latke*, Jewish potato cakes and my granddad made *patates me avga*, the Greek version. I grew up with both. We serve them with a forestière sauce – a creamy mushroom sauce that's also good on toast or pasta.

OVEN-ROASTED TOMATOES
500 g cherry tomatoes
olive oil
salt and pepper
4 sprigs rosemary

RÖSTI
8 medium potatoes
2 eggs, whisked
onion flakes
salt and pepper
100 g butter
16 rashers streaky bacon
4 eggs

FORESTIÈRE SAUCE
12 large brown mushrooms, diced
250 ml cream
salt and pepper

olive oil
small handful rocket

Preheat the oven to 180 °C.

Place the tomatoes on a baking tray, drizzle with olive oil, season with salt and pepper and scatter with rosemary. Roast for about 45 minutes, or until the tomatoes have wrinkled.

To make the rösti, first parboil the potatoes. When they are cool enough to handle, peel and then grate them on the coarse side of a grater. Mix a handful of the grated potato with a small amount of the whisked egg, the onion flakes and season with salt and pepper. Compact the mixture into 4 patties and pan-fry in a little olive oil and a knob of butter. The rösti should be golden brown and crisp. Drain on kitchen paper and keep warm in the oven until serving.

Fry the streaky bacon until it is crispy.

While the rösti and the bacon are cooking, poach the eggs (page 18) and start making the forestière sauce. Dice the mushrooms. Fry them over a medium heat in the remaining butter. When they are soft, add the cream. Season to taste and simmer to reduce the cream. The sauce will thicken naturally.

Stack the rösti with rocket, bacon and the oven-roasted tomatoes. Top with a generous spoon of forestière sauce and a poached egg.

SERVES 4

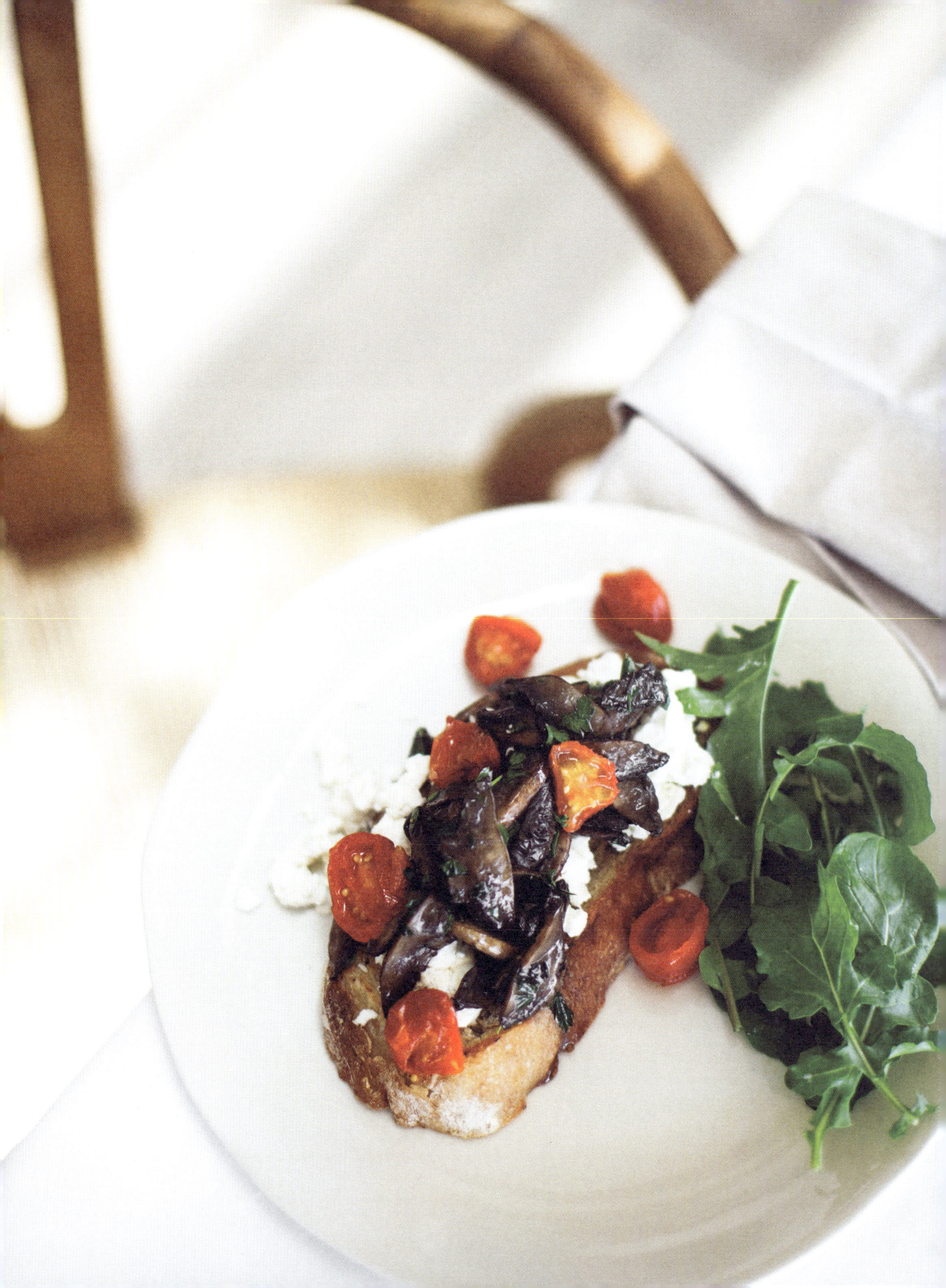

pimp my toast

The name of this dish says it all. This is the vegetarian version but it is an amazingly versatile recipe. Use the toast as the base and then get creative. If you're having a brunch party, make different savoury toppings and lay them all out separately, then let your guests pimp their own.

OVEN-ROASTED TOMATOES
500 g cherry tomatoes
40 ml olive oil
salt and pepper
pinch rosemary

MUSHROOMS
8 large brown mushrooms
100 g butter
salt and pepper
lemons
pinch flat leaf parsley, chopped

200 g chevin (soft goat's cheese)
4 slices ciabatta, toasted
olive oil
4 handfuls rocket

Preheat the oven to 180 °C.

Place the tomatoes on a baking tray, drizzle with olive oil, season with salt and pepper and scatter with rosemary. Roast for about 45 minutes, or until the tomatoes have wrinkled.

Thinly slice the mushrooms and fry over a medium heat in the butter until soft. Season with salt and pepper. When the mushrooms are cooked, squeeze in some lemon juice and add the parsley.

Divide the chevin into 4 and crumble onto each slice of toast. Top with the mushrooms and drizzle with olive oil.
Serve with roasted tomatoes and rocket.

SERVES 4

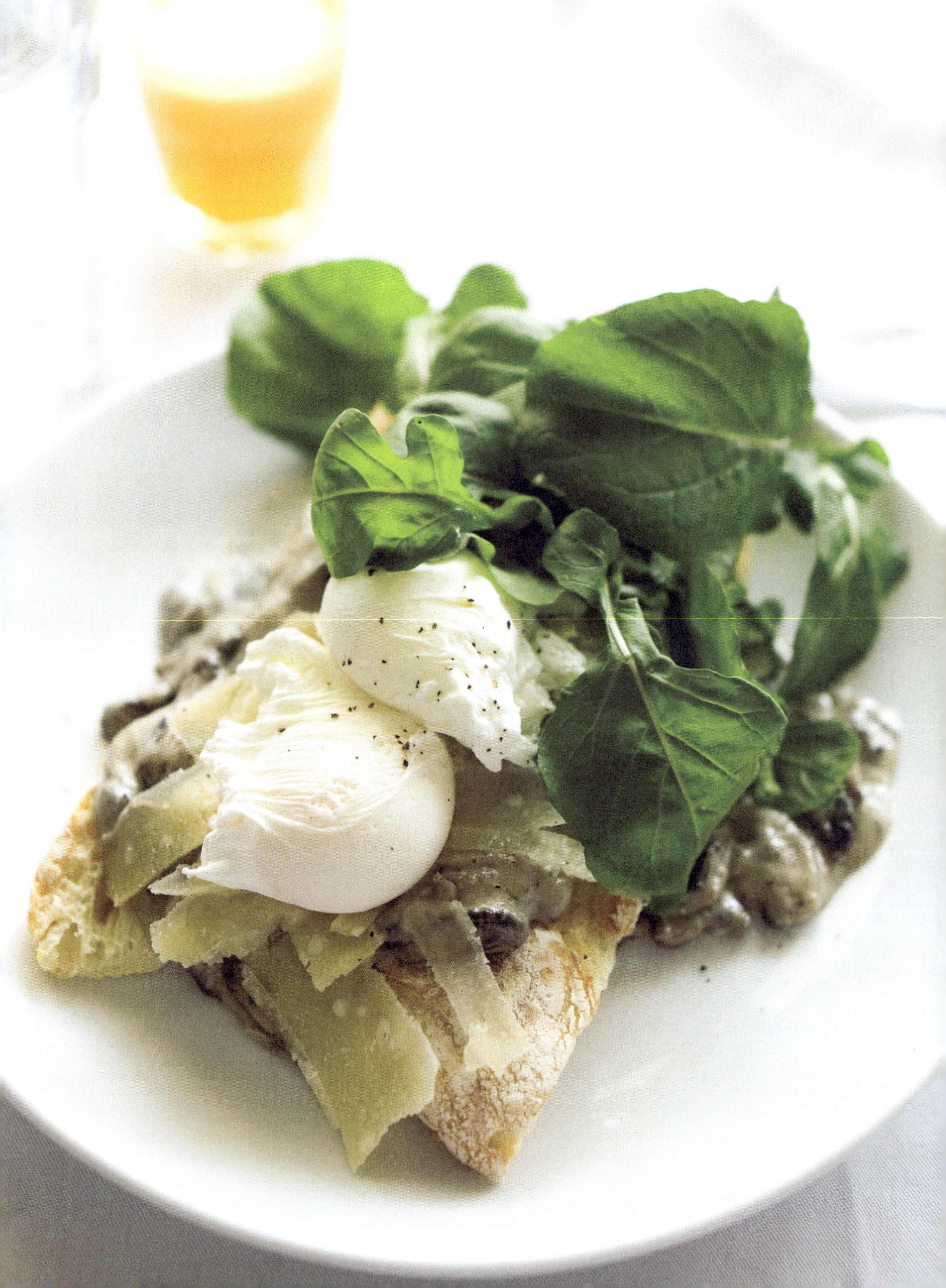

mushroom ciabatta

This is the ultimate indulgence after a night of overindulgence. My inbox was so swamped when we took it off the menu that we just had to put it back on. Everybody has a version of this dish; the French and the English use less cream than we do. We also add cheese so it is very rich and filling. Few people manage to finish an entire helping, but you can try.

MUSHROOM SAUCE
800 g large brown mushrooms
80 g butter
500 ml whipping cream
120 g Parmesan, finely grated
salt and pepper

8 eggs
4 ciabatta rolls

4 handfuls rocket
80 g Parmesan shavings

To make the sauce, slice the mushrooms and fry in butter over medium heat until they are soft. Add the cream and when it begins to boil, add the grated Parmesan. Let the cream reduce and thicken for a couple of minutes. Season with salt and pepper.

Poach the eggs (page 18).
Cut the ciabatta rolls open and toast.

Spoon the mushroom sauce over the ciabatta, leaving the corners of the bread showing. Top with the eggs and garnish with Parmesan shavings and rocket.

SERVES 4

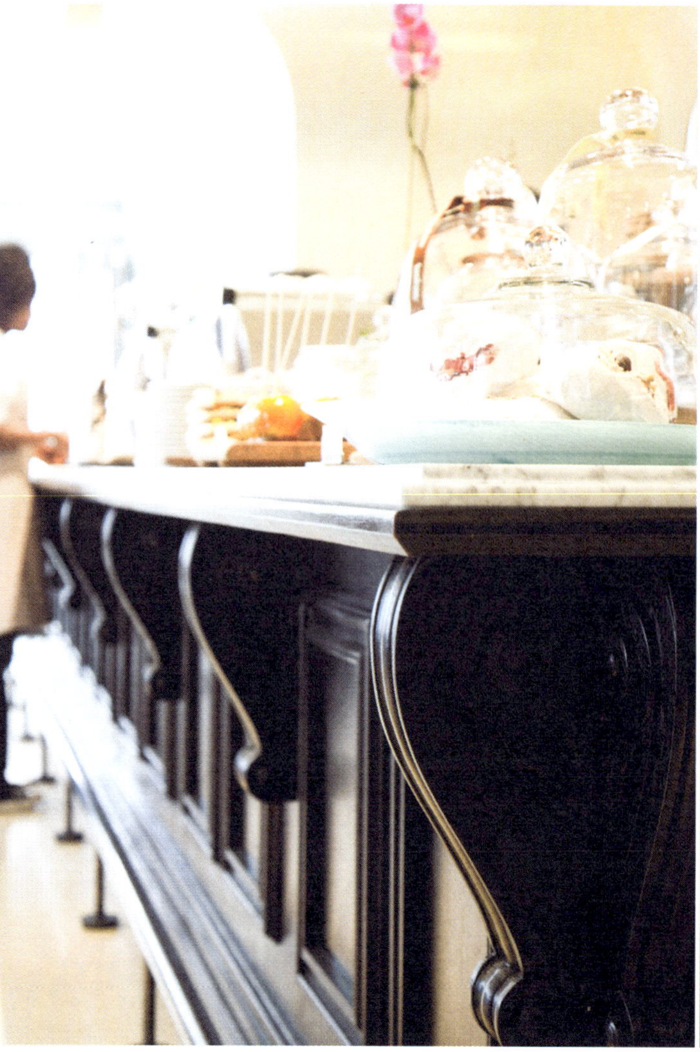

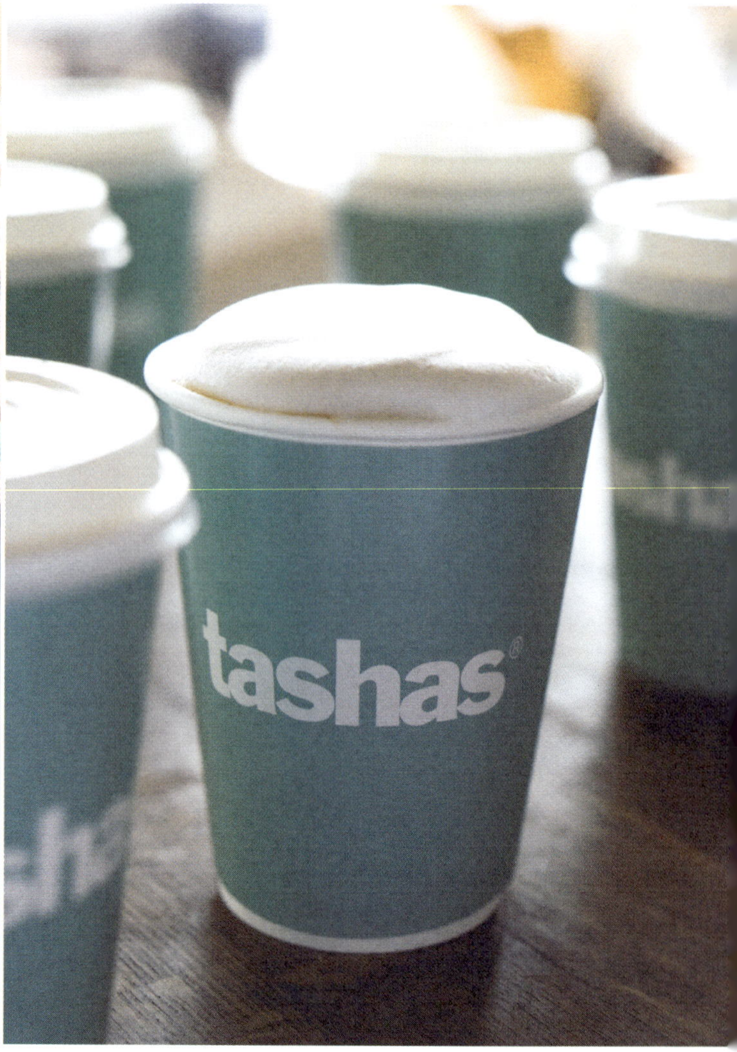
tashas

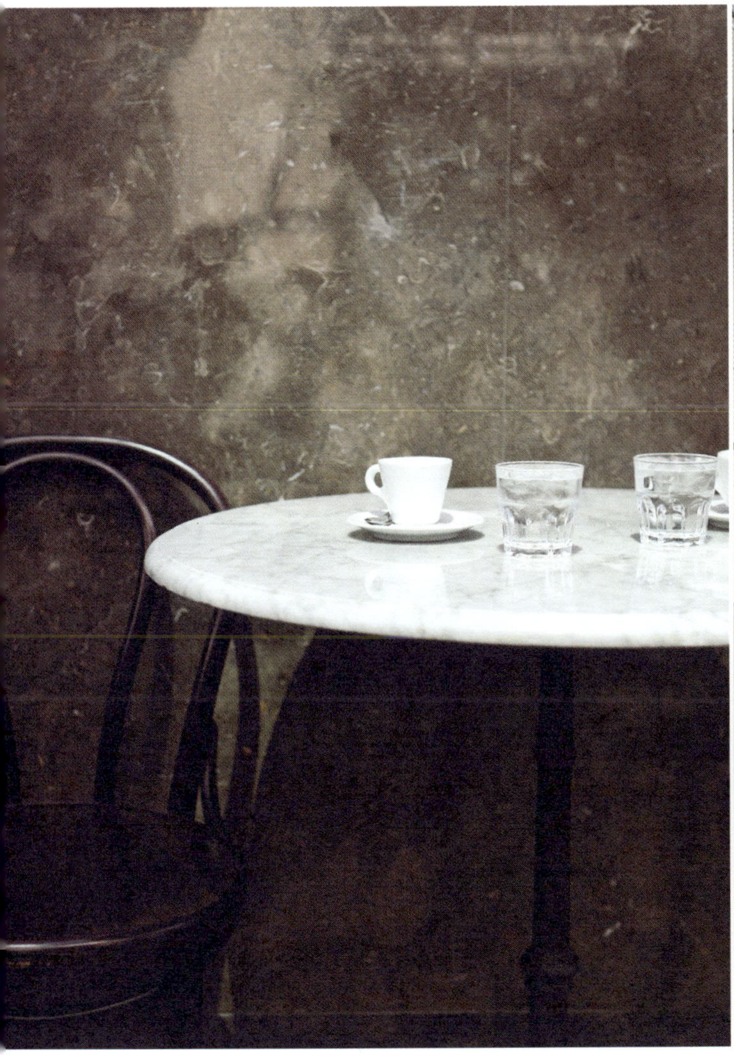

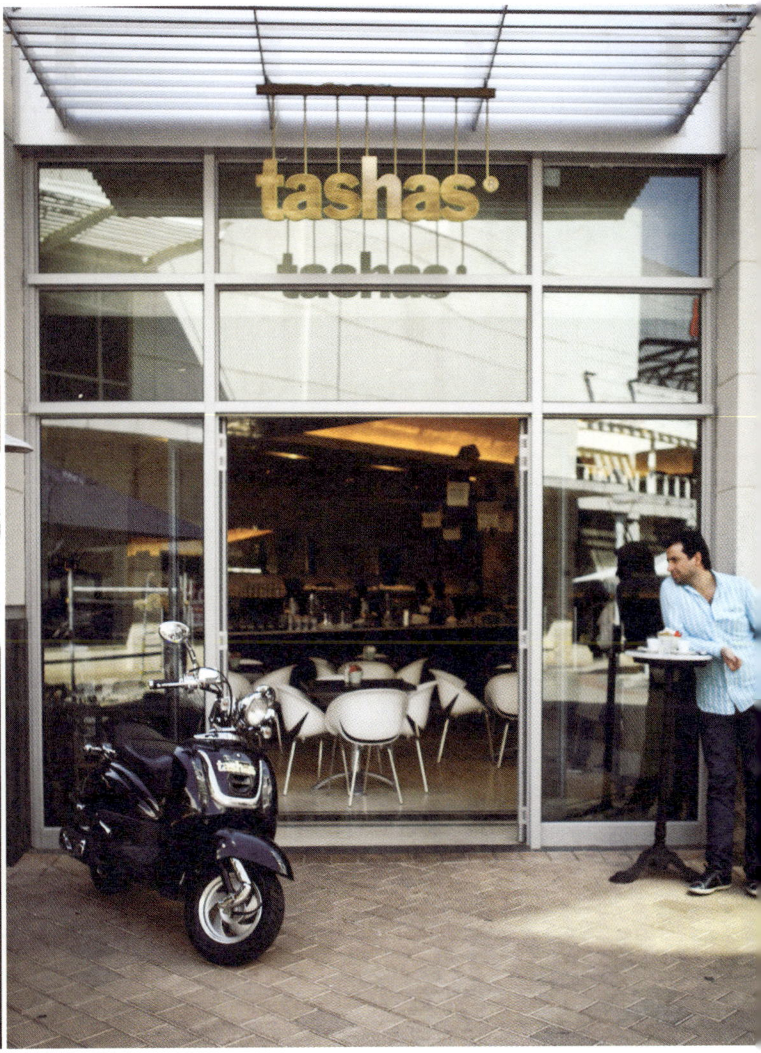
tashas

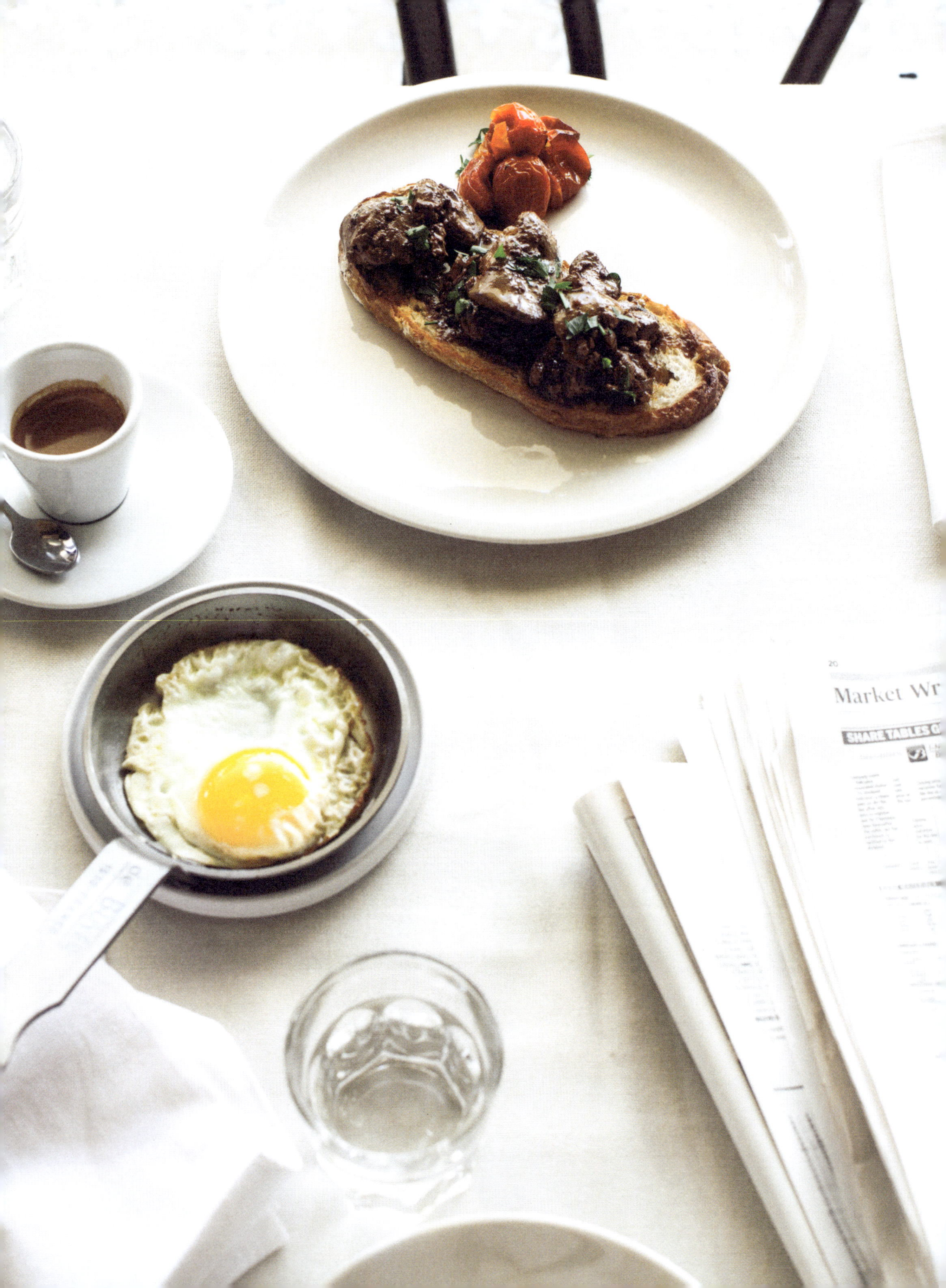
20
Market Wr
SHARE TABLES

livers on toast

This is an old family favourite that reminds me of happy mornings. Oven-roasted tomatoes and a fried egg are great additions to the iron-rich livers. It's a hearty breakfast that easily doubles up as a quick but filling brunch.

olive oil
butter
1 small white onion
2 cloves garlic
500 g chicken livers
1 tsp beef stock powder
1 tsp dried thyme
salt and pepper
1 tsp flour
lemon juice
150 ml water
30 g butter
flat leaf parsley, chopped

4 eggs, fried (optional)
4 slices ciabatta toast, buttered

Heat a little olive oil in a pan and add a knob of butter. Fry the finely chopped onion and when it begins to soften, add the garlic, chicken livers, beef stock powder and thyme. Season with salt and pepper to taste. Sprinkle the flour over the livers in the pan, add a squeeze of lemon juice and the water. Cook on medium heat until the sauce has thickened. Stir in the extra butter to glaze the sauce. When it has melted, add the parsley.

Fry the eggs to your liking and toast the ciabatta.

Top the ciabatta toast with the livers and cover with the sauce. The egg can be served either on top or on the side.

SERVES 4

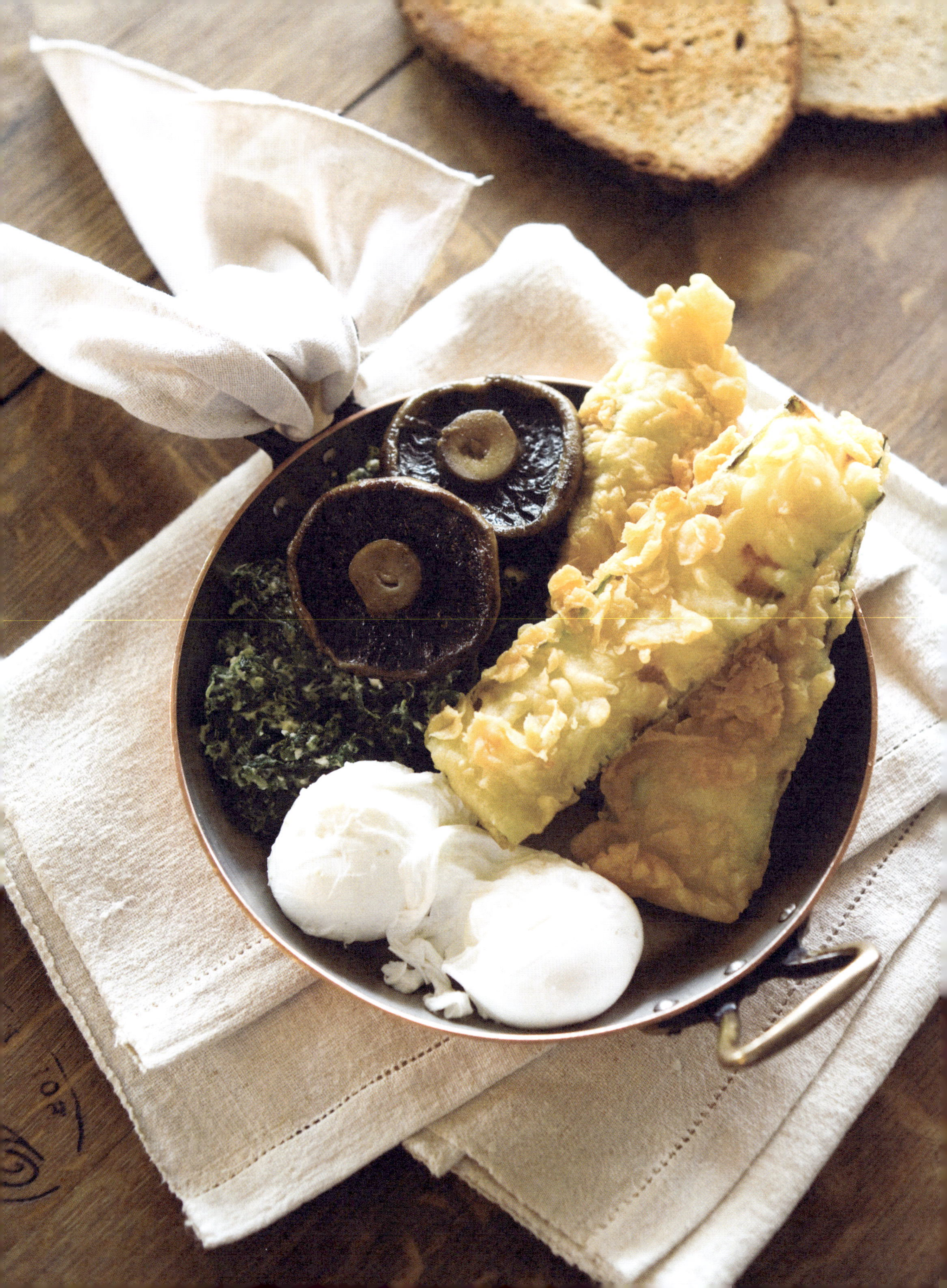

12 o'clock breakfast

This is a wonderful vegetarian breakfast full of flavour and texture: crispy battered courgettes, wilted spinach with creamy feta and fried mushrooms. A perfect way to end the morning and to begin the afternoon. Add poached eggs if you want some protein.

BATTER
115 g flour
200 ml soda water
salt and pepper

8 medium courgettes

8 brown mushrooms
8 eggs

480 g baby spinach
butter
200 g Danish feta, crumbled

To make the batter, mix the flour and soda water until smooth. Season with salt and pepper. Slice the courgettes lengthways and dip them into the batter. Deep-fry in very hot oil until golden brown and crispy.

Sauté the mushrooms whole in a pan until they are cooked but still firm. Poach the eggs (page 18).

Wilt the spinach in a pan with a knob of butter. Cook until the water has evaporated. Crumble the feta into the spinach and mix well. Serve with poached eggs.

SERVES 4

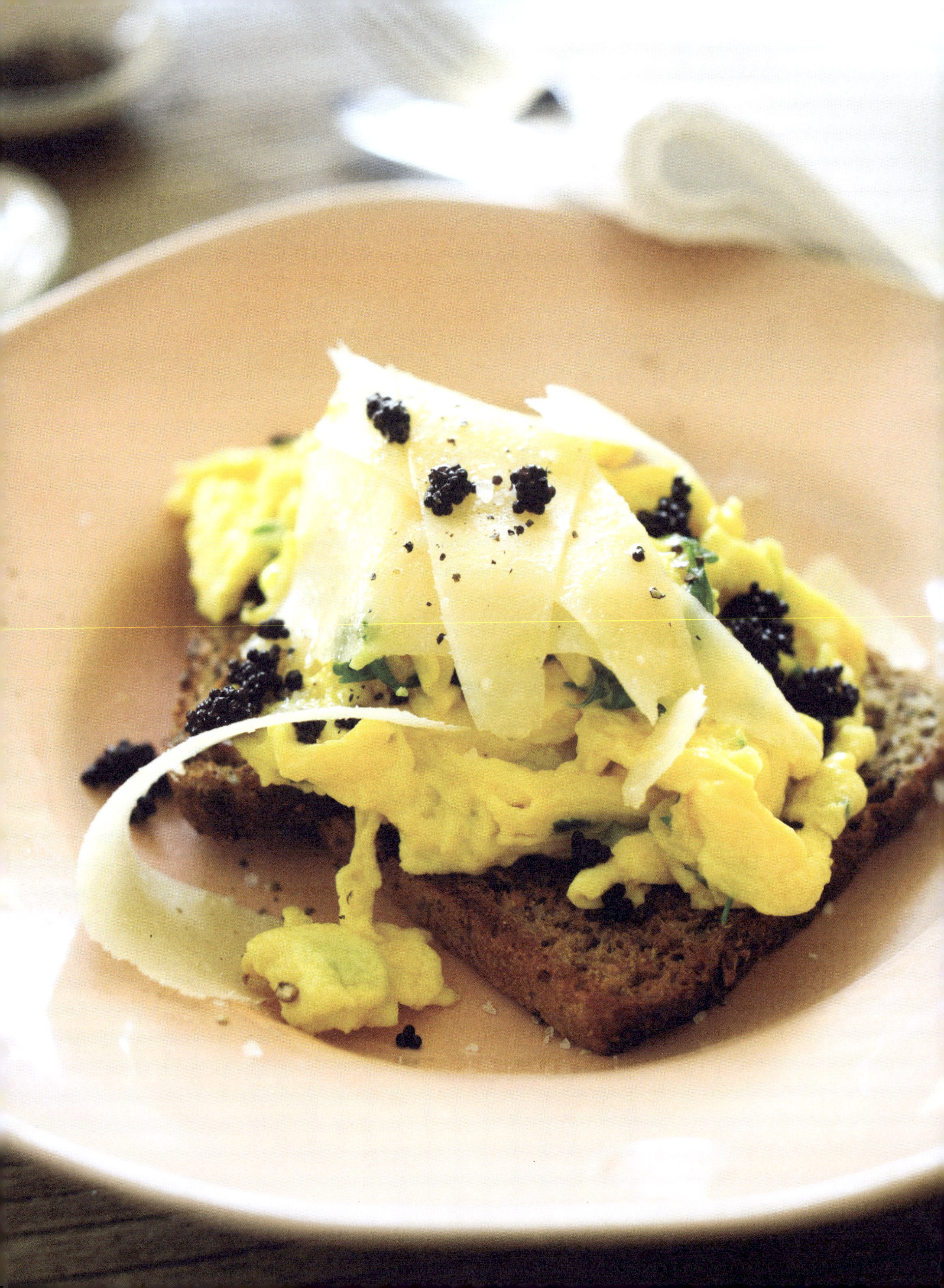

millionaire's breakfast

I was introduced to these decadent scrambled eggs by my childhood friend Nicky. The first time he made them for me was when we were on a yacht in Monaco – where else would you have a millionaire's breakfast? This breakfast is his invention and he's justifiably famous for it. When we put it on the menu at tashas, it was an instant success.

butter
12 eggs
salt and pepper
handful flat leaf parsley, chopped

4 slices toast (rye or seeded)
16 drops truffle oil
80 g Parmesan shavings
4 tsp caviar (optional)
truffle shavings (optional)

Heat the butter in a pan. Whisk the eggs in a bowl and season with salt and pepper. Pour the eggs into the pan and scramble. When they are almost ready, add the parsley.

Put the eggs on the toast, top with truffle oil, Parmesan shavings and, if you choose, caviar and truffle shavings.

SERVES 4

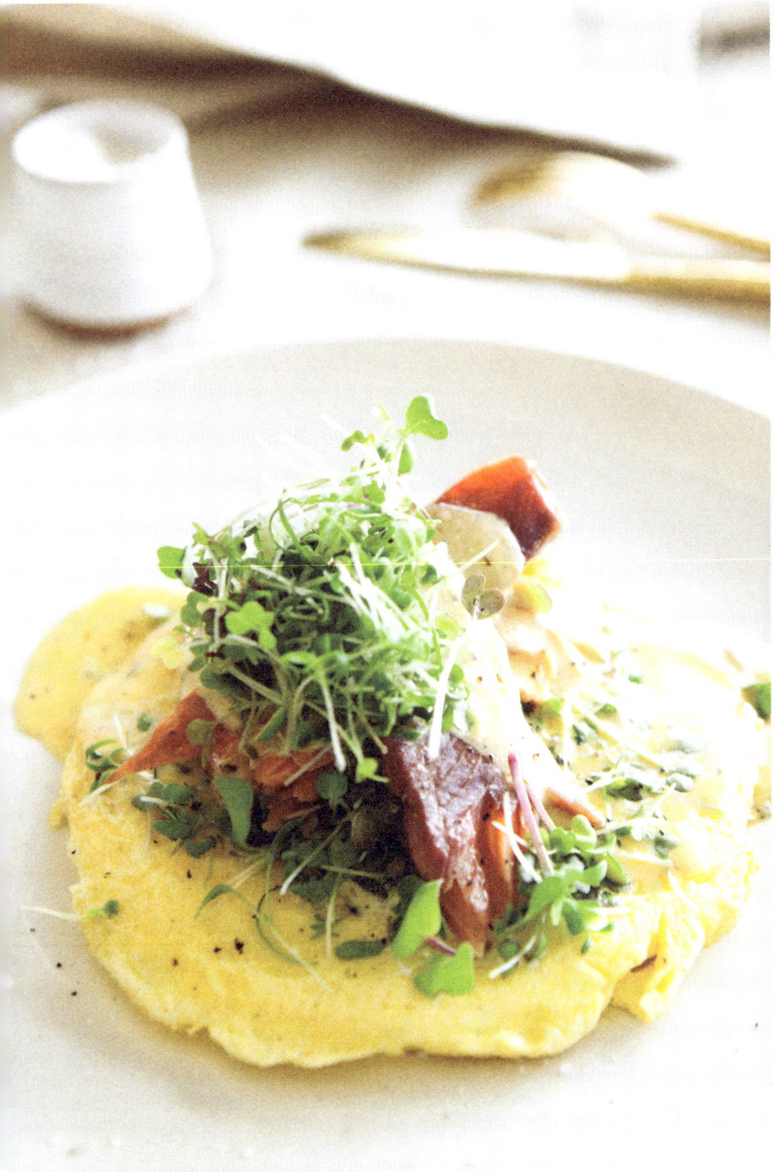
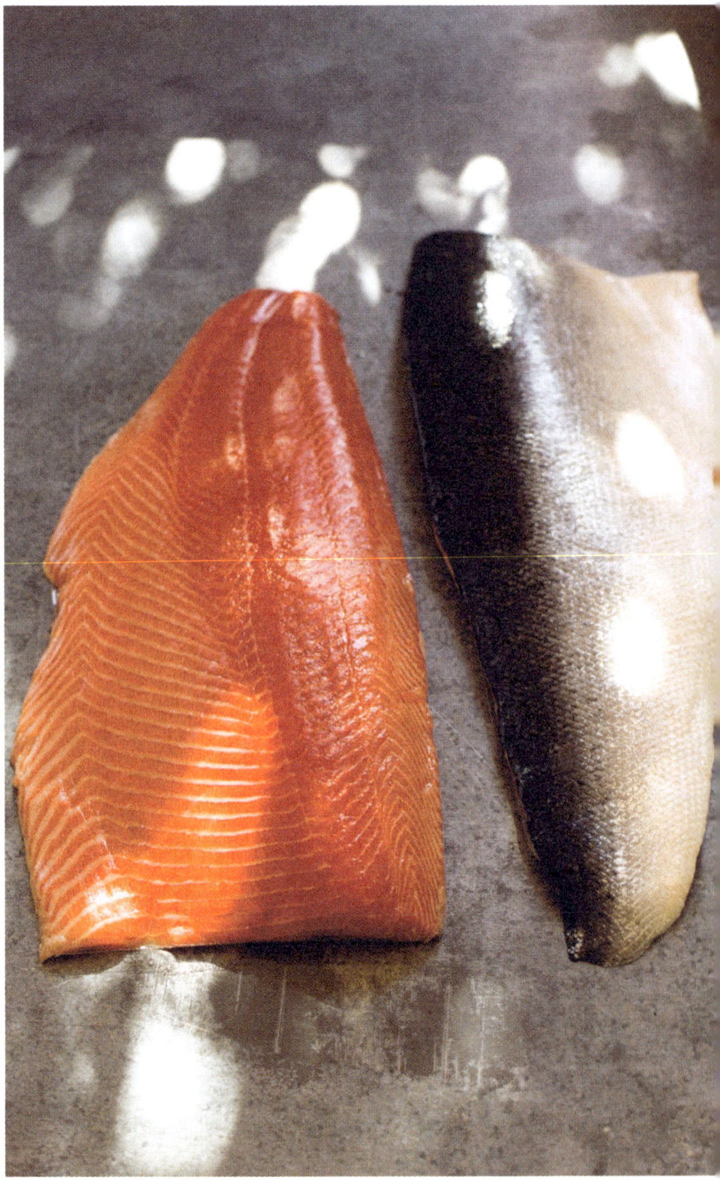

lazy smoked salmon frittata

A frittata is simply a thick, open omelette, or a quiche without the crust. You can make individual portions, which is more of an effort, or make one large frittata. You can serve it at room temperature in summer or hot from the pan in winter. Make it as rich or as light as you like. Be inventive with the toppings; this is a very versatile dish that goes well with a lightly dressed, crisp herb salad.

SAUCE
300 ml cream
100 g Cheddar cheese, grated
2 tsp English mustard
pinch dried oregano

OMELETTE
12 eggs (3 per omelette)
salt and pepper
small handful chives, chopped

320 g hot-smoked salmon
60 g micro greens

salad ingredients of your choice

To make the sauce, heat the cream in a pan. The cream should be hot, but don't let it boil or the sauce will split. Add the cheese, mustard and oregano, then season with salt and pepper to taste. Keep stirring until the cheese has melted.

Whisk 3 eggs at a time and season with salt and pepper. Make 4 thick, individual omelettes in a small 15-cm pan or one large pan.

To serve, top the omelette with salmon and the cheese sauce. Garnish with micro greens and serve with a salad.

SERVES 4

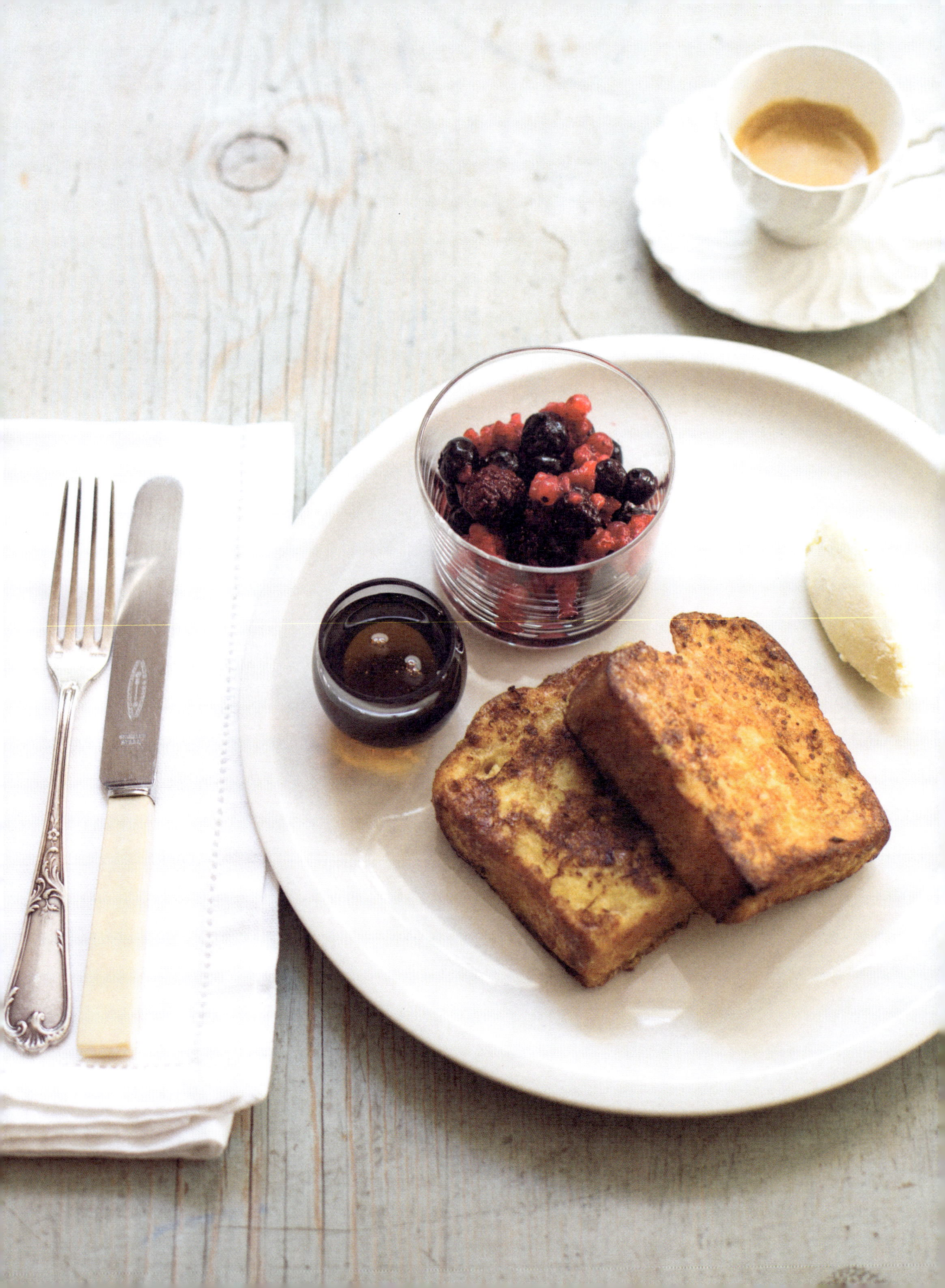

grandma goes french

My grandmother used to make preserves in the traditional Greek way. They are very sweet and syrupy. I remember eating cherries, watermelon rinds and citrus fruits with syrup dripping down my chin. Every time I see a plate of French toast with preserved cherries it takes me back to my childhood. In the restaurants, we make our French toast with brioche, but bread works very well too if you sprinkle it with a little sugar while frying to make it sweet and crispy. Croissants also do the trick.

8 eggs
60 ml cream
8 slices bread
oil
sugar (optional)

160 g mascarpone
100 ml golden syrup
240 ml fresh mixed berries or preserved fruit

Whisk the eggs with the cream. Soak both sides of the bread in the egg mixture and then fry in a lightly oiled pan until golden brown. If you are using bread, not brioche, remember to sprinkle the bread with sugar when it is in the pan.

Per portion, serve 2 slices of bread with a dollop of mascarpone, a drizzle of golden syrup and either mixed berries or preserved fruit.

SERVES 4

Sandwiches are special in my world. They were the most sought-after object of my childhood.
I spent lunch breaks in hiding, terrified that someone would see what my mother had packed for lunch. The Sideris children never got sandwiches for school. We got everything but. We got spaghetti bolognaise, prawns and rice, chicken with sauces. We even got ribs wrapped in tinfoil that were so big they didn't fit into our school bags. In short, we got leftovers. And, of course, I should not have complained. Which person in their right mind complains about a lunch box filled with delicious food? Well, this ten-year-old apparently. I got prawns and all I wanted was sarmies.

I have done all I can at tashas to pay homage to my sandwich-less youth and have made sure they are present. In abundance.

Sandwiches are all about showing off the filling. Make sure you spread it evenly and right up to the edges. If you have to toast the bread make sure it is toasted perfectly. Adjust your toaster until you get the setting right to neither over or under toast the bread. Using olive oil or a spread makes a great alternative to butter. A beautifully layered sandwich is a pleasure to look at and a pleasure to eat.

sandwiches & burgers

jimmy's lamb sandwich	59
king, queen & i	61
madame & monsieur	63
harry's roadhouse steak sarmie	65
mini beef burgers	69
harry's burger basting sauce	70
mini salmon burger	73
healthy salmon bite	75
classic caesar sarmie	77
the brazilian	79
falafel pockets	81

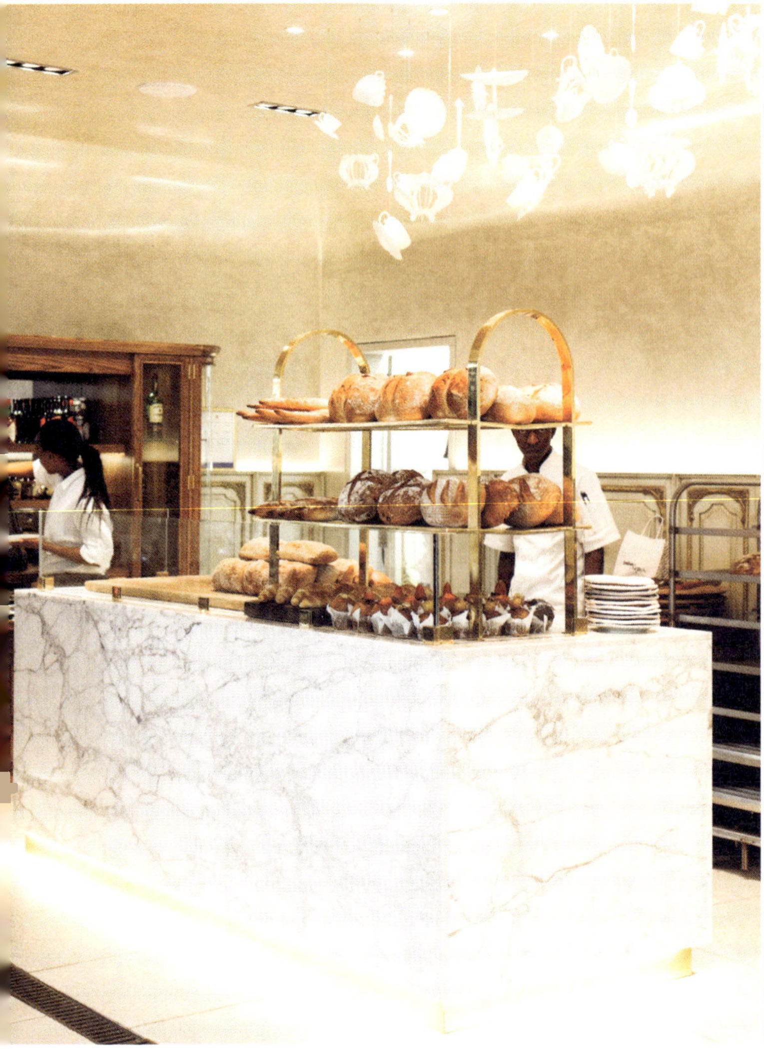

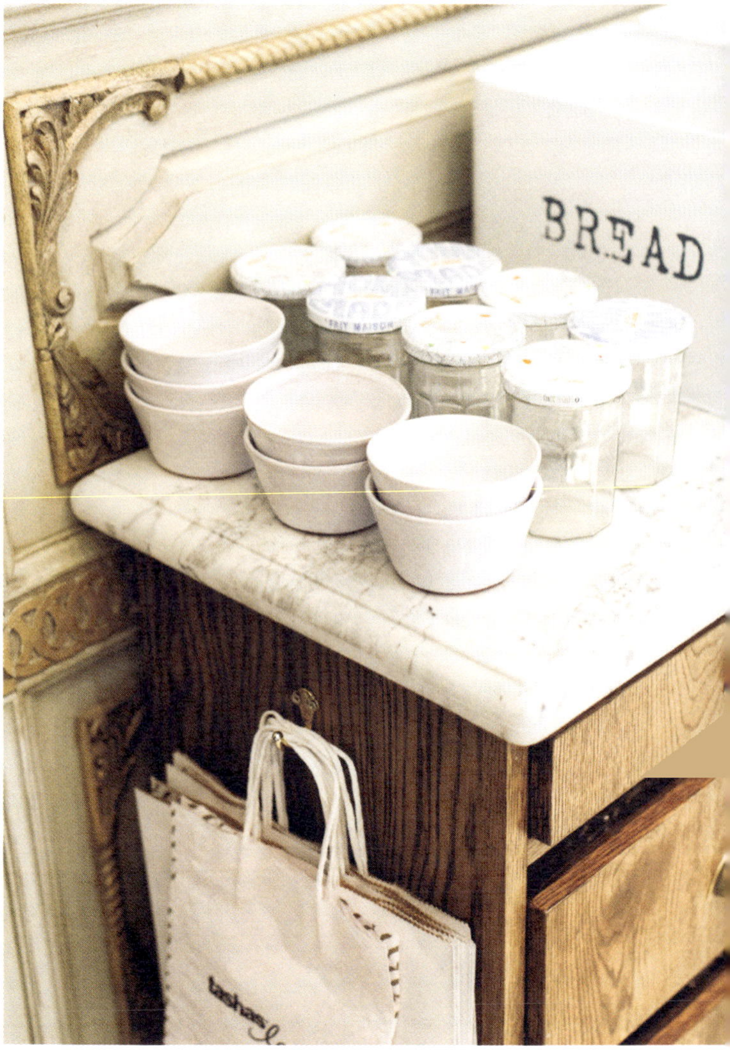
BREAD
tashas

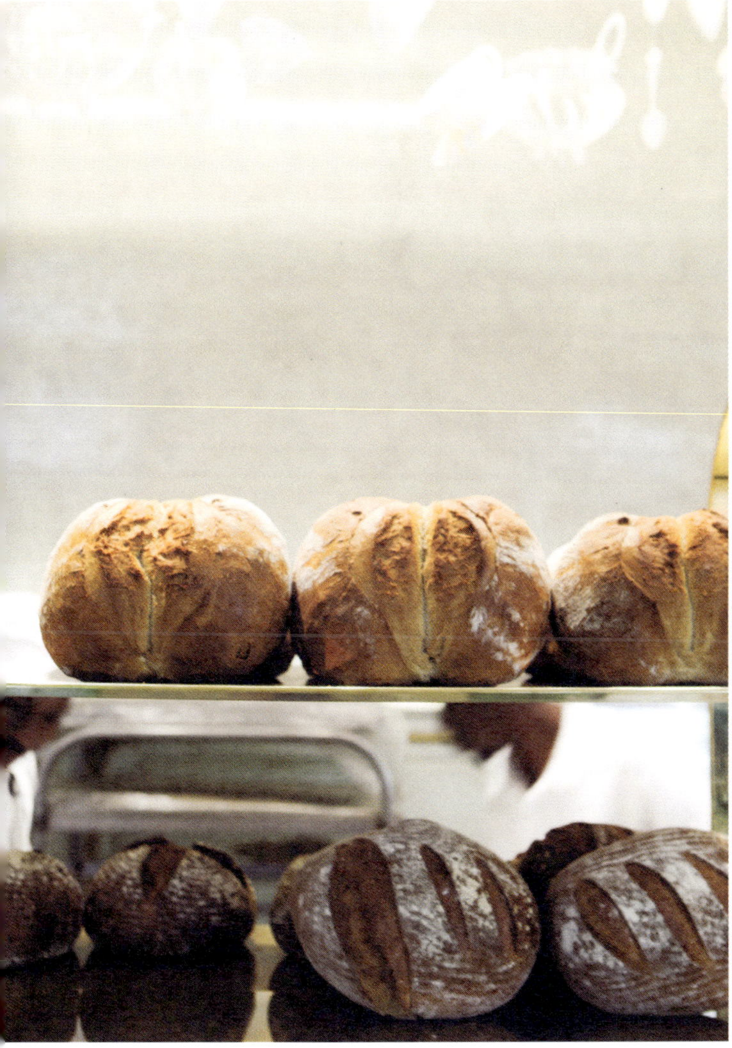
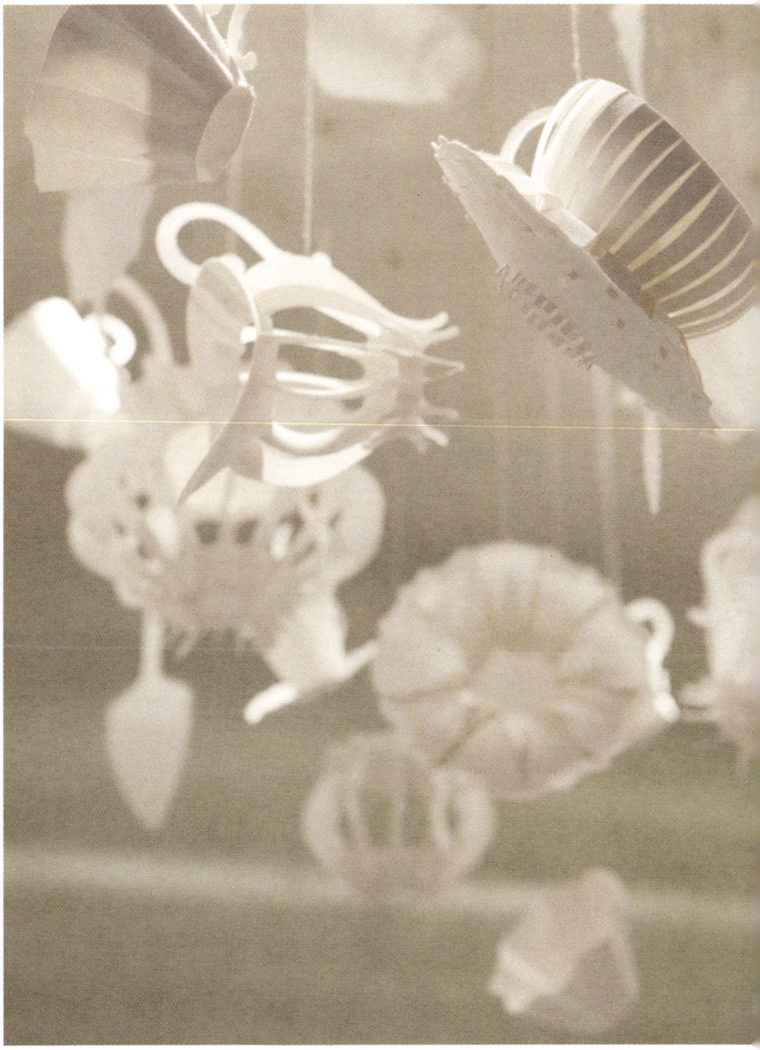

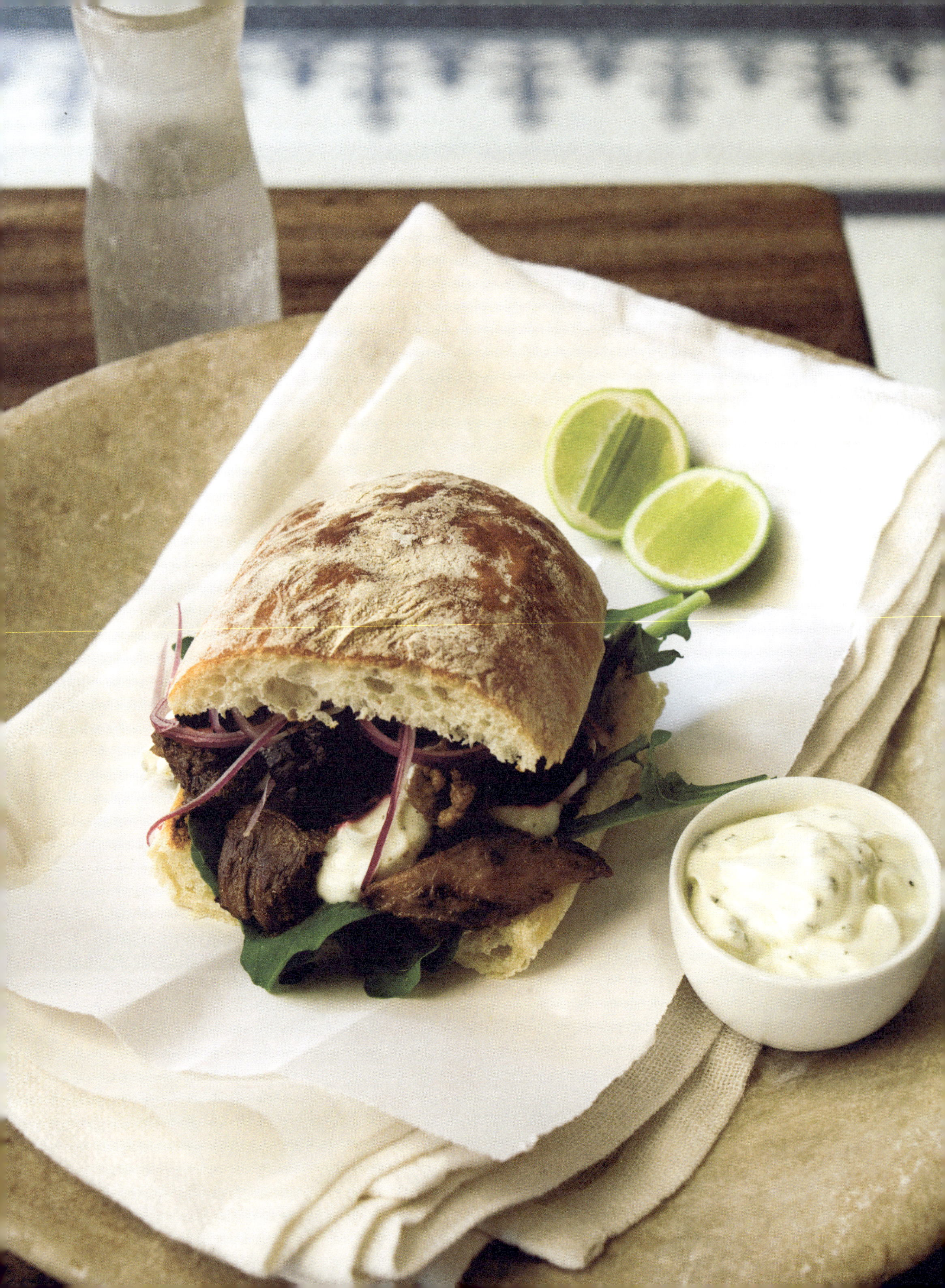

jimmy's lamb sandwich

Jimmy is the head chef at Hyde Park. He has opened every tashas with me and does all the initial kitchen training. He and my father worked together for 20 years. This is my father's lamb recipe, which Jimmy makes every day. He suggests choosing a piece of lamb that is not too fatty and keeping it in the oven for a long time. This sandwich is another leftover special from my childhood. Sunday roast became Monday's school sandwiches.

8 baby beetroots, roasted
olive oil
balsamic vinegar
salt and black pepper

ROAST LAMB
2 kg lamb leg, bone in
OR 1,5 kg, deboned
5 bay leaves
5 g black pepper
2 medium carrots, roughly chopped
2 celery sticks, roughly chopped
3 whole garlic bulbs, cut in half
2 medium red onions, quartered
6 rosemary sprigs
5 ml salt
100 g butter
3 large potatoes, quartered
100 ml olive oil
350 ml red wine

TZATZIKI
160 g cucumber, very finely grated
15 ml olive oil
pinch dried oregano
2 garlic cloves, finely chopped
salt and pepper
360 g yoghurt

4 ciabatta rolls
handful rocket

Preheat the oven to 180 °C.

Peel and cut the beetroot into quarters. Place on a baking tray and drizzle with olive oil, a touch of balsamic, salt and pepper and roast for about 20 minutes, or until soft.

Place the lamb in a roasting tray with the ingredients as listed. Cover with foil and roast for 3 hours at 180 °C. When the lamb is cooked, remove from the oven, but do not remove the foil. Allow the meat to rest for 30 minutes. It should be very soft and pull apart easily. Remove all the vegetables except the onions, garlic and rosemary, and save the juices. Pull the meat off the bone and tear into small pieces. Return the lamb pieces to the pan, mixing them with the onions, garlic, rosemary and meat juices.

To make the tzatziki, grate the cucumber very finely and squeeze it to remove excess water. Stir the cucumber and the next 3 ingredients into the yoghurt. Season with salt and pepper to taste.

Cut the ciabatta rolls in half and layer with rocket, lamb and tzatziki. Top with the beetroot quarters.

SERVES 4

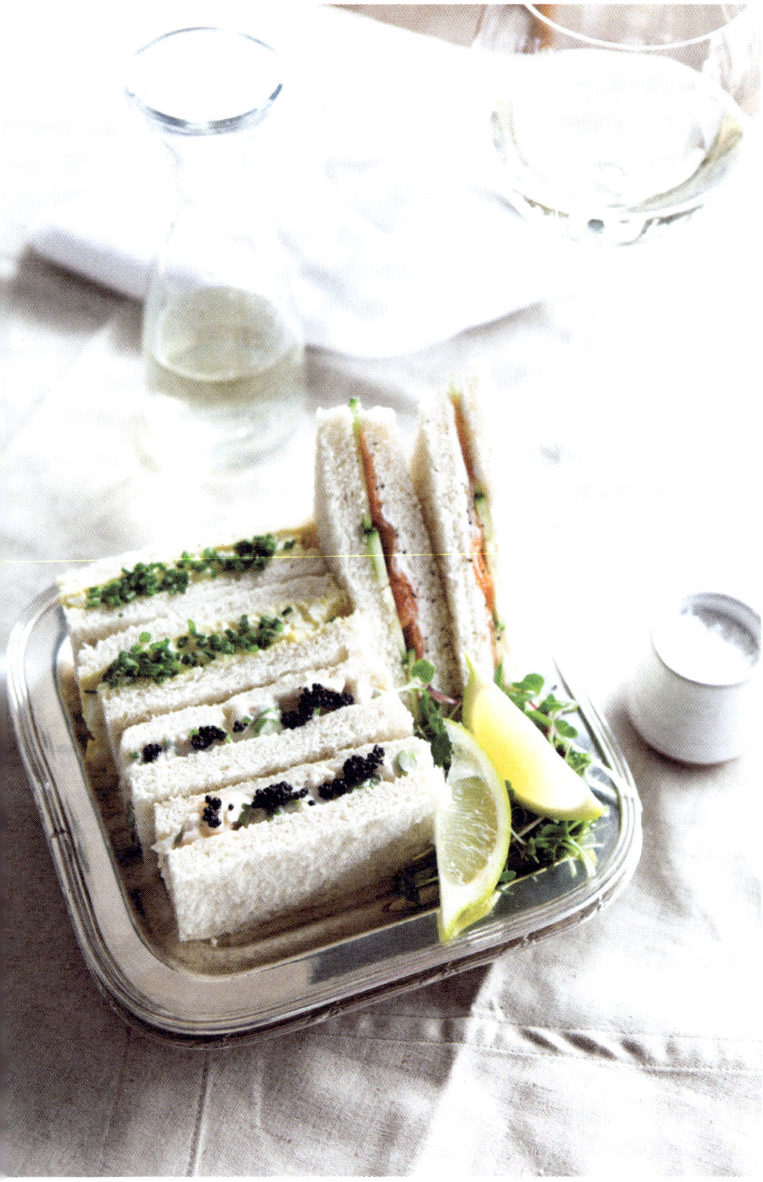

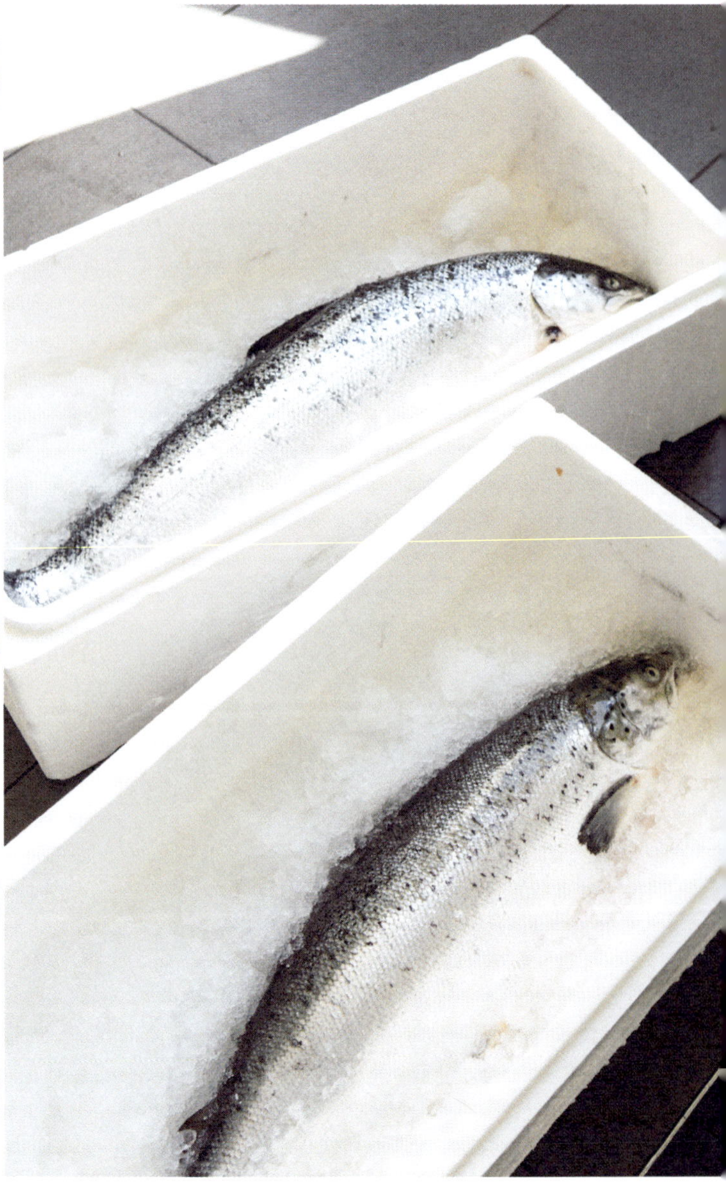

king, queen & i

Long before Jason and Maria owned tashas Melrose, they were my friends. They once asked if I could help them with the food for a party; they wanted something special and glamorous, definitely not boring tea sandwiches. I couldn't resist the temptation. I arrived with platters of the sexiest little sandwiches, and they were a hit.

CUCUMBER & SALMON
120 g cream cheese
15 ml lemon zest
8 slices fresh white bread
32 paper-thin cucumber slices
160 g smoked salmon trout

Mix the cream cheese with the lemon zest. Layer 4 slices of the bread with cream cheese, then cucumber slices and salmon. Close the sandwiches, remove the crusts and cut diagonally into triangles.

EGG MAYONNAISE
8 eggs, hard-boiled and chopped
8 ml olive oil
120 ml tangy mayonnaise
4 tsp chives, chopped – plus extra for garnish
salt and pepper
8 slices fresh white bread

Mix the chopped, hard-boiled eggs with olive oil, mayonnaise and most of the chives. Season with salt and pepper. Spread on 4 slices of the bread, then close the sandwiches, remove the crusts and cut into rectangles. Garnish with the extra chives.

PRAWN & ASPARAGUS
12 asparagus spears, blanched
400 g prawn tails, cleaned
big squeeze of lemon
60 ml French-style mayonnaise
5 ml olive oil
5 ml lemon juice
salt and pepper
4 tsp black caviar (optional)
8 slices fresh white bread
handful micro greens to garnish
lemon wedges

Blanch the asparagus, cool and slice lengthwise. Cook the prawns in boiling water with a big squeeze of lemon until they turn pink and firm, 5–10 minutes. Drain and allow to cool on ice. Chop the prawns and the asparagus roughly, mix with the mayonnaise, olive oil, lemon juice and season. Top with caviar and spread onto 4 slices of the bread, close and trim the crusts. Cut the sandwiches into rectangles.

Garnish the platter with micro greens and thin lemon wedges.

MAKES 24 SANDWICHES

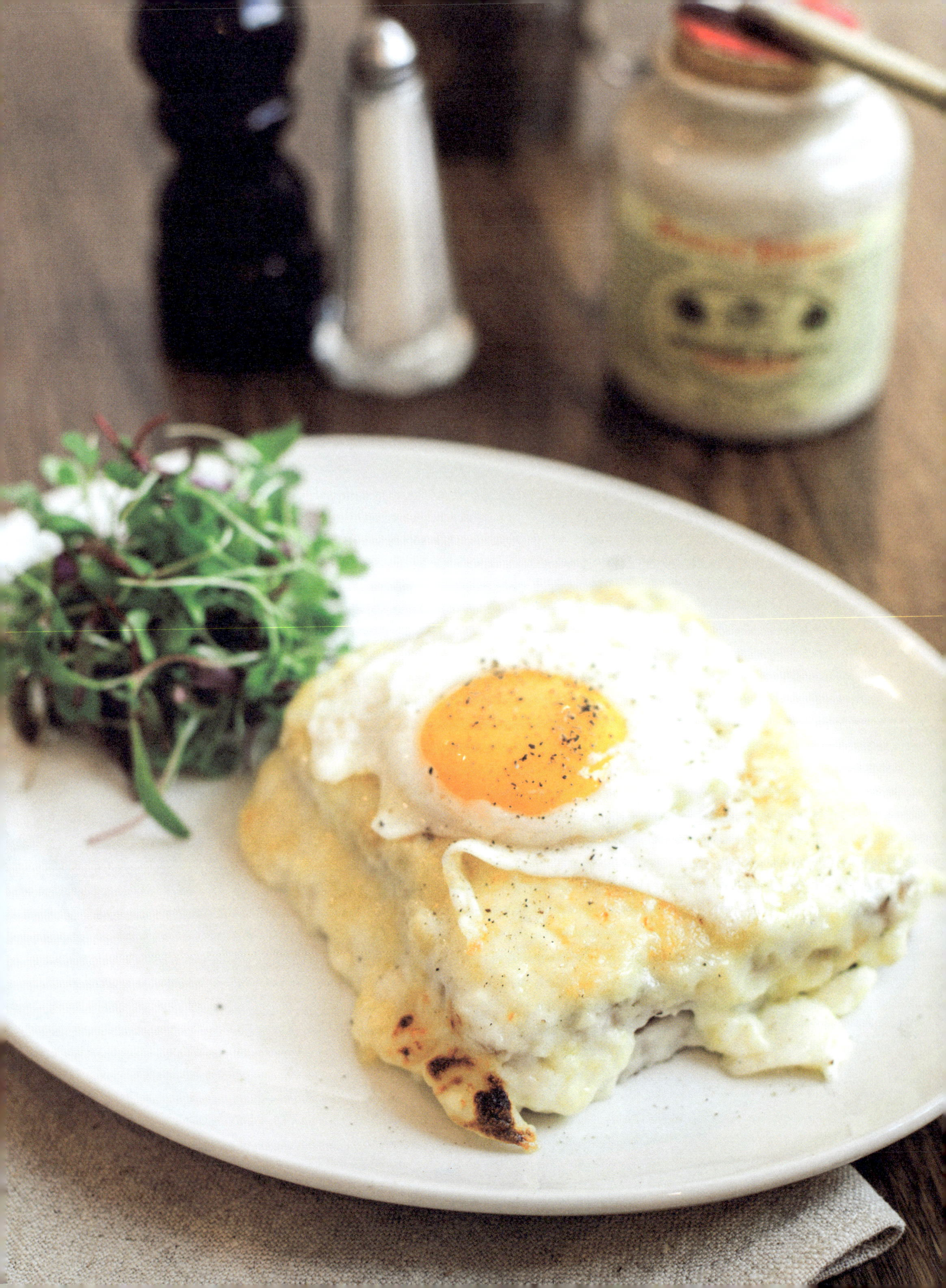

madame & monsieur

When I was in Paris for the first time I had a long list of dishes I wanted to try. Believe it or not, the simple croque monsieur was one of them. As it is shown here, the croque monsieur is actually a croque madame because, of course, madame wears a hat. The egg is her hat.

CHEESE SAUCE
30 g butter
30 g flour
400 ml milk
100 g Gruyère cheese

8 slices bread, toasted
40 ml Dijon mustard
8 slices gypsy ham
2 x 100 g Gruyère cheese, grated
4 eggs, fried (optional)

Preheat the oven to 180 °C.

To make the cheese sauce, melt the butter in a saucepan. When it begins to foam, add the flour to make a paste (we call it a roux). Take the saucepan off the heat and slowly add half the milk. Stir until the roux has mixed well with the milk. It should not be lumpy. Put the saucepan back on the heat and add the rest of the milk, bringing it to the boil slowly. Cook for about 5 minutes, stirring continuously. Remove from the heat and add the cheese.

Spread a small amount of Dijon mustard on the toast. Place a slice of ham and a handful of Gruyère on top, then another slice of ham. Close with the second slice of toast and smother with cheese sauce and the remaining grated cheese. Bake it in the oven until the cheese is bubbling and golden. If you were planning on having a madame, don't forget her hat.

SERVES 4

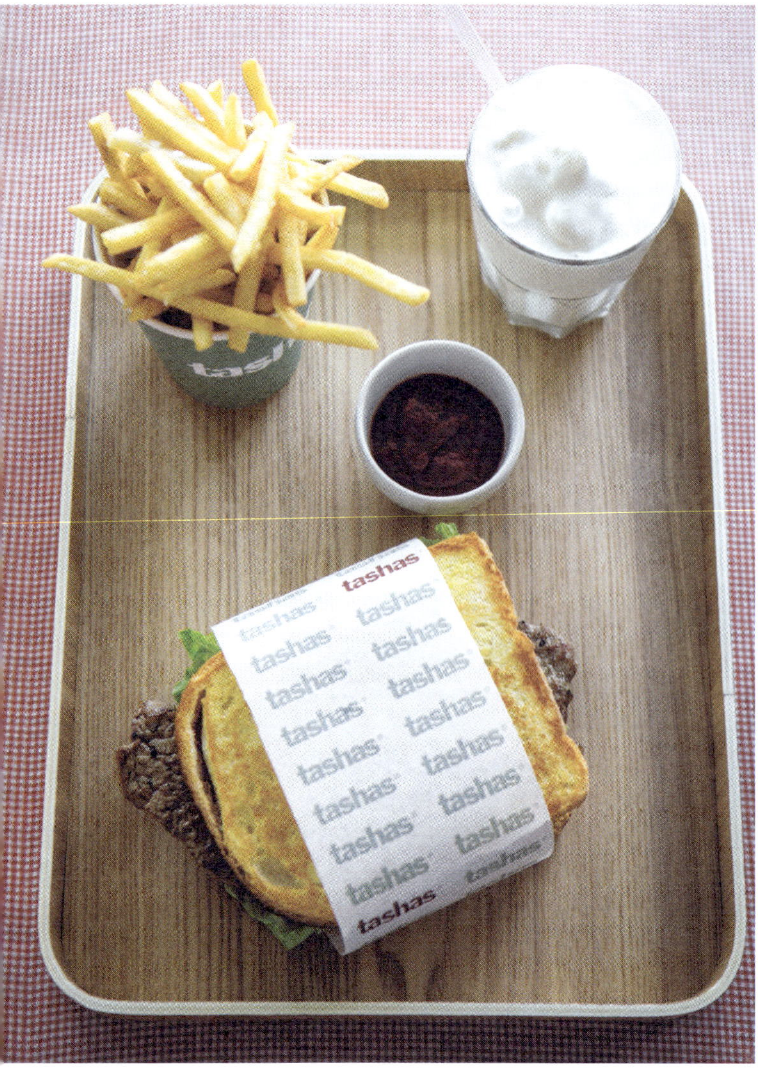
tashas

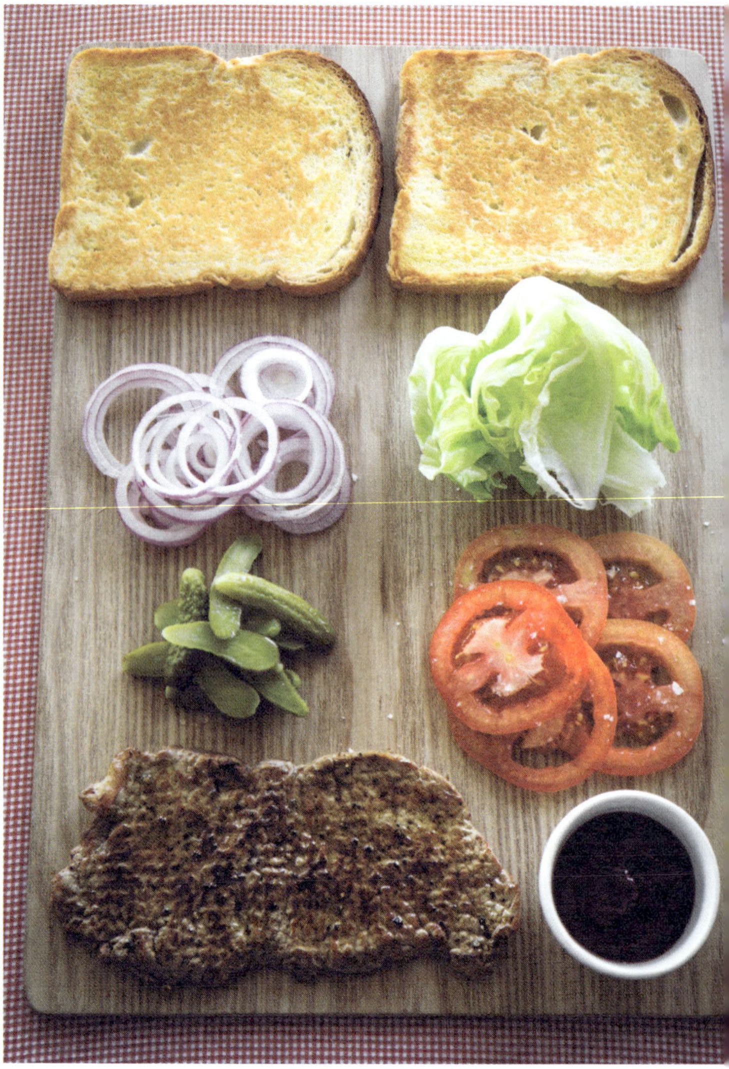

harry's roadhouse steak sarmie

There isn't a part of my life that wasn't influenced by my father. He is in every recipe I cook, in every restaurant I open, in every decision I make. He was in every single Monday. His restaurant would be closed and he'd pick us up from school – just him, me and Savva. He'd take us to the Doll's House. We'd pull up in his big, dusty gold Jag and roll down the window. The order never changed: three steak sandwiches, three portions of chips and three double-thick malts. Six days of the week he ran restaurants, placed orders, grilled, cooked, sliced and kept waiters on their toes, but for that one afternoon a week he was ours.

BBQ SAUCE
75 ml tomato sauce
30 ml Worcestershire sauce
25 ml white vinegar

4 x 150 g sirloin steak
olive oil
salt and pepper
8 slices bread
butter
1 iceberg lettuce
2 tomatoes, sliced
1 red onion, sliced
12 cocktail gherkins, cut in half lengthways

Mix together all the BBQ sauce ingredients.

To flatten the sirloin, give it a good bash with a meat tenderiser. Heat a griddle pan until it is smoking hot. Rub the meat with a little olive oil, salt and pepper and fry to your liking. Put 2 slices of bread together to form a sandwich. Butter the outside of each slice and toast the bread in a sandwich press or a hot pan, as if you are making a toasted sandwich. You can use a regular toaster if you don't have a sandwich press, but do not butter the bread before toasting.

Open the sandwich and place the ingredients on the untoasted side in the following order: start with lettuce, add 4 slices of tomato, then onion slices and gherkin halves. Make sure the ingredients are evenly spaced. Place the steak on top, dress with BBQ sauce and top with the remaining lettuce. Close the sandwich, cut it on the diagonal and wrap it in wax paper.

Serve with a double-thick vanilla milkshake and fries for a proper roadhouse treat. Keep the balance of the BBQ sauce for dipping your chips.

SERVES 4

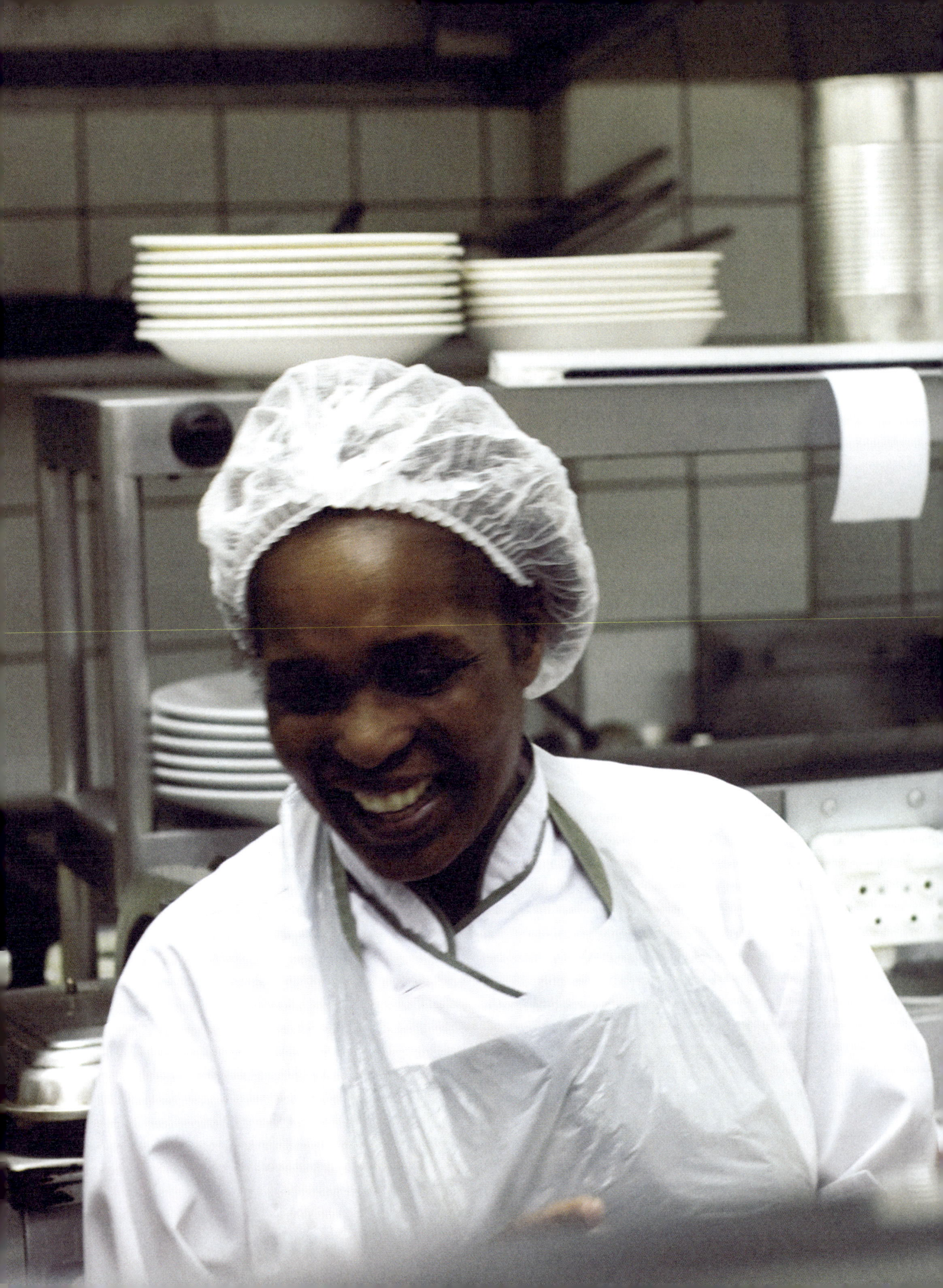

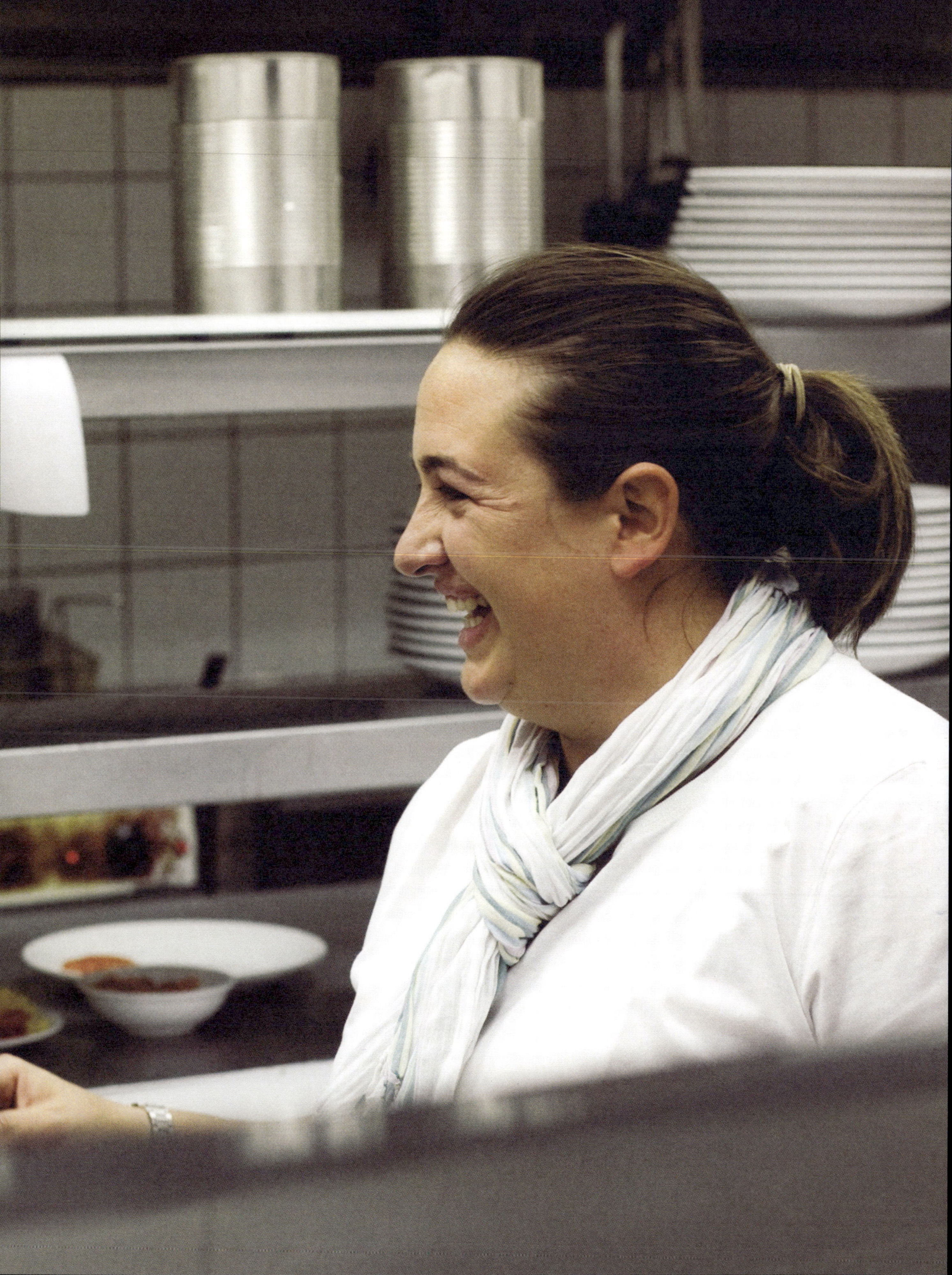

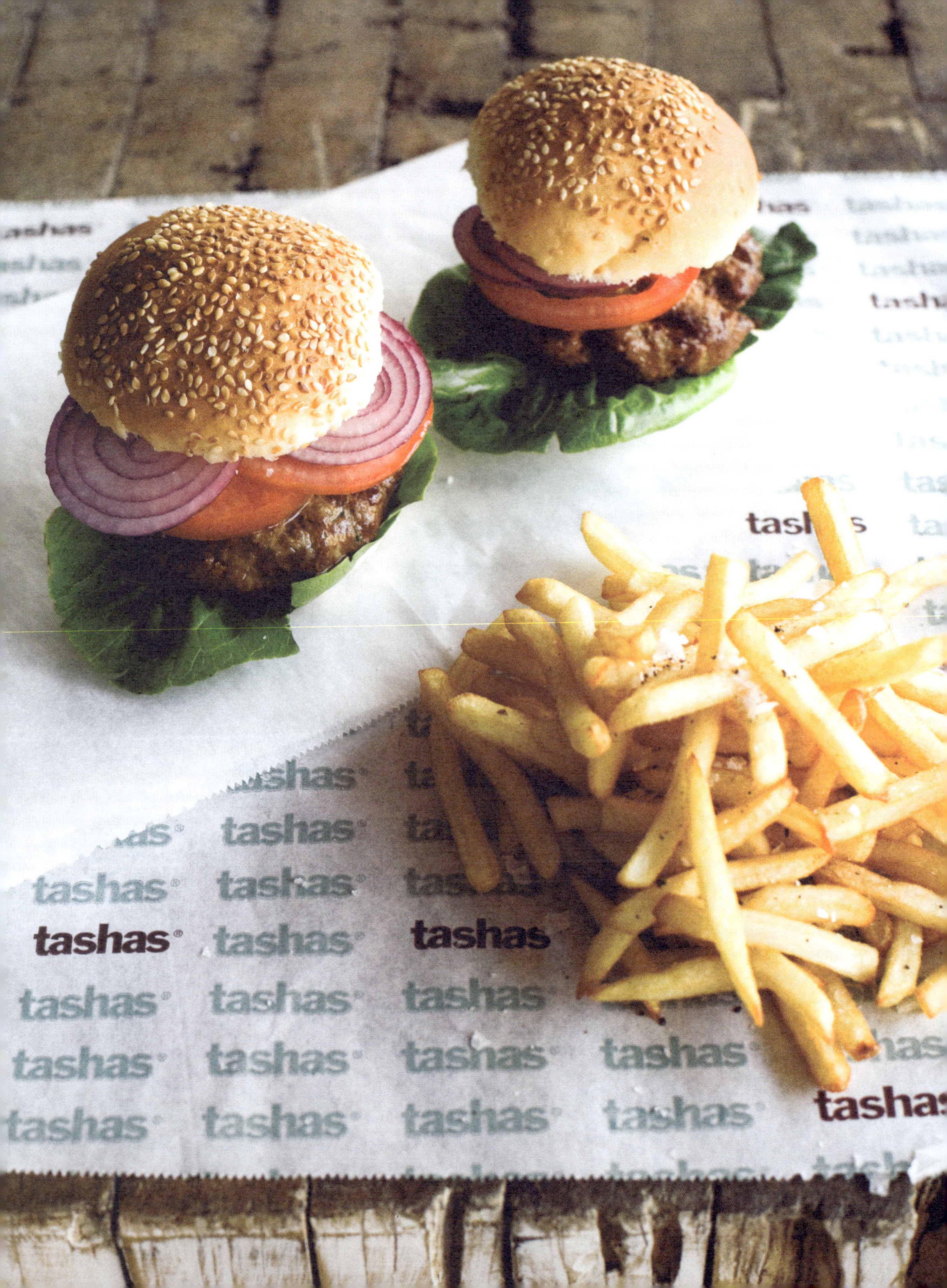
tashas

mini beef burgers

In the early 90s, Ed's Diner was an institution in Pretoria. It was as close to a proper American diner as you could get back then. They had the sugar pot with the spout, the stainless steel napkin holders and curly fries. We begged our parents to take us for 'sliders', which is what their mini burgers were called. I couldn't get enough. I guess I never out grew my fascination for tiny burgers. I just had to have them on the menu so I invented my own.

120 ml Harry's Burger Basting Sauce (page 70)

MINI BURGER PATTIES
1 kg beef mince (with meat:fat ratio 80:20)
2 egg yolks
handful parsley, chopped
salt and pepper

TZATZIKI
80 g cucumber, finely grated
5 ml olive oil
5 ml dried oregano
garlic clove, finely chopped
180 g yoghurt
salt and pepper
melted butter (optional)

8 mini burger rolls
16 baby gem lettuce leaves
8 slices tomato
2 red onions, sliced

Start by making the basting sauce according to the instructions on page 70.

To make the patties, combine all the ingredients for the mini burger patties. Mould the burger mix into 125 g patties. They should be about 1,5 cm thick and should have roughly the same diameter as the rolls.

To make the tzatziki, grate the cucumber very finely and squeeze it to remove excess water. Stir the cucumber and all of the remaining ingredients into the yoghurt. Season with salt and pepper to taste.

Baste the patties with a brush and then grill on an open fire or on a smoking hot griddle until cooked to your liking. Baste each of the patties now and again. Savva's secret last step is to baste them again with melted butter.

Assemble the burgers with lettuce, tomato and onion and serve with chips and tzatziki.

SERVES 4

harry's burger basting sauce

This is my father's basting sauce from The Town Tavern Steakhouse on 101 Market Street in Johannesburg. My mother found this recipe on a piece of paper dated 11 November 1981. When we were testing this recipe for the book, we couldn't read my father's handwriting. We tried it over and over. After the fifth time I called Savva over and he perfected it in one go.

3 garlic cloves, crushed
175 ml tomato sauce
2 tsp paprika
1 tbsp English mustard
10 whole bay leaves, dried
1 tsp black pepper
15 ml white vinegar
2 tbsp dried oregano
1 tbsp salt
5 tbsp white sugar
4 tbsp Worcestershire sauce
250 ml red wine
2 tbsp tomato paste
1 tsp treacle molasses
2 tsp cayenne pepper
125 ml boiling water

First crush the garlic with the back of a knife. Then put it with all the other ingredients into a pot. Boil for approximately 20 minutes until the sauce has reduced. Strain the sauce through a sieve or strainer. Discard the coarse ingredients.

And there you have it, Harry's famous burger basting sauce.

MAKES ABOUT 250 ML

1981 NOVEMBER / WEDNESDAY 11

Tamate Sauce   R5.00   5 Lit ✓
Garlic   4.80   500
Paprika   3.50   500
Mustard   2.15   500
Regui X   2.50   500
   3.40   100
MSG   5.90   250
Bay Leaf   6.00   500
Roggan   Slick   35~   1kg   4×500
Sant   18.00   4×5
Sugar   20.20   100
W Sauce
Wine   800
Cayan Pepper   400
Tamote Paste   75~   100
Citraozu   400
Black Reef low
Musara   45 Lit

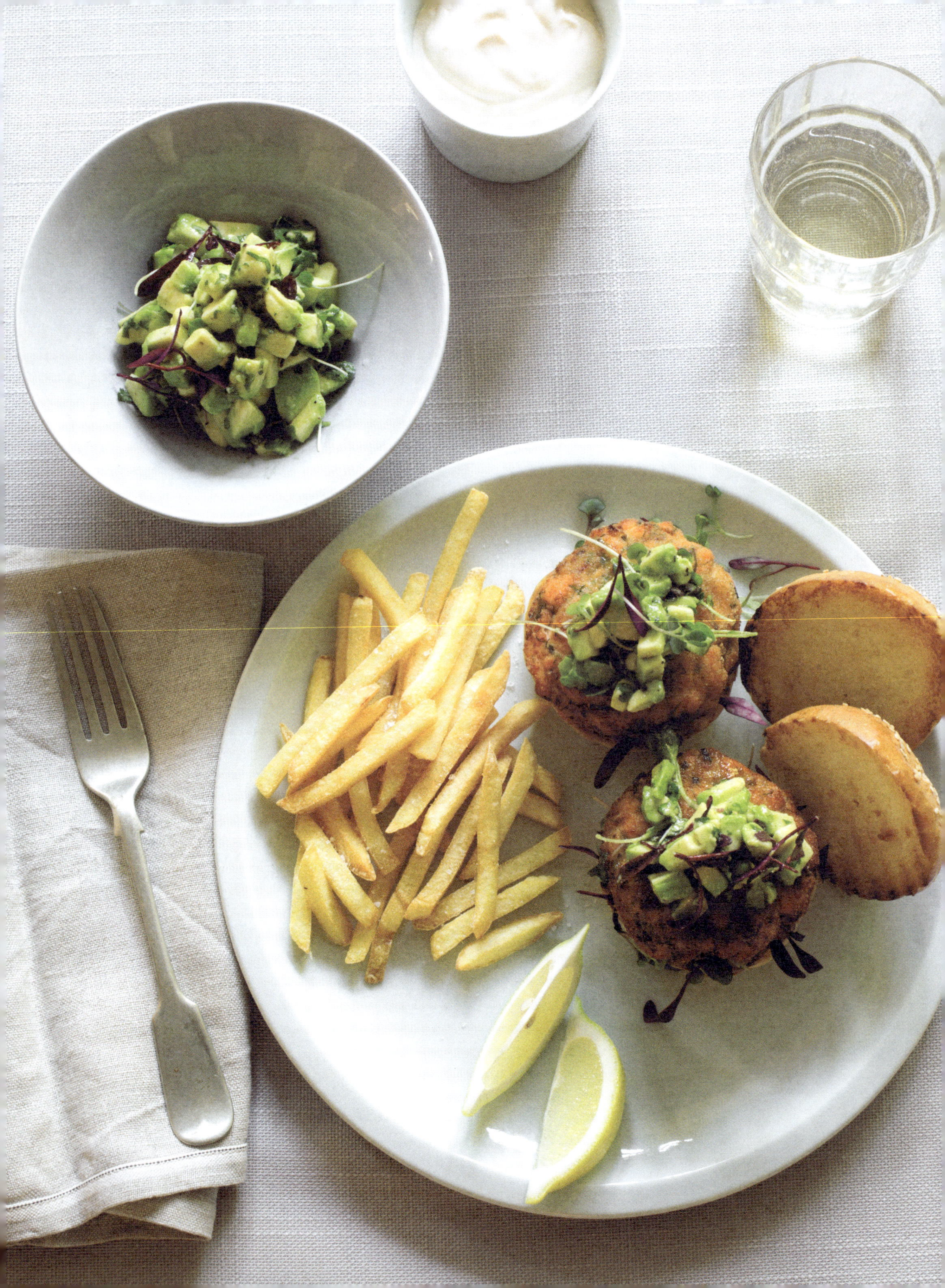

mini salmon burger

The only thing that beats a mini beef burger is a mini salmon burger. These patties are lighter than fish cakes and we use fresh salmon, not tinned. They are great for a late lunch or as a snack with drinks and they'll delight your guests. Make extra salsa; it's a lovely topping for almost anything.

SALMON PATTIES
400 g fresh salmon
4 egg yolks
120 ml mayonnaise
1 red onion, finely chopped
2 tbsp chives, chopped
2 tbsp dill, chopped
180 ml fine breadcrumbs
salt and pepper

AVOCADO SALSA
2 avocados, diced
a small bunch coriander leaves
half a lemon
60 ml olive oil
salt and pepper

8 mini burger rolls
handful baby herbs
lemon wedges to serve

To make the patties, roughly chop the salmon and combine well with the egg yolks and mayonnaise. Add the red onion, chives and dill and mix gently. Add the breadcrumbs a little at a time to bind the mixture. Be careful not to add too much because it will make them dry. Season to taste. Divide the salmon mixture into 8 portions and shape into patties about 3 cm thick, then shallow-fry in hot oil until they are golden brown.

To make the salsa, dice the avocados and tear the coriander leaves into a bowl with a big squeeze of lemon juice, olive oil, salt and pepper.

Cut the rolls in half and toast on the inside. Place equal amounts of baby herbs on each roll and then add a salmon patty. Top each patty with salsa.

Serve the mini burgers with wedges of lemon, accompanied by chips and mayonnaise.

SERVES 4

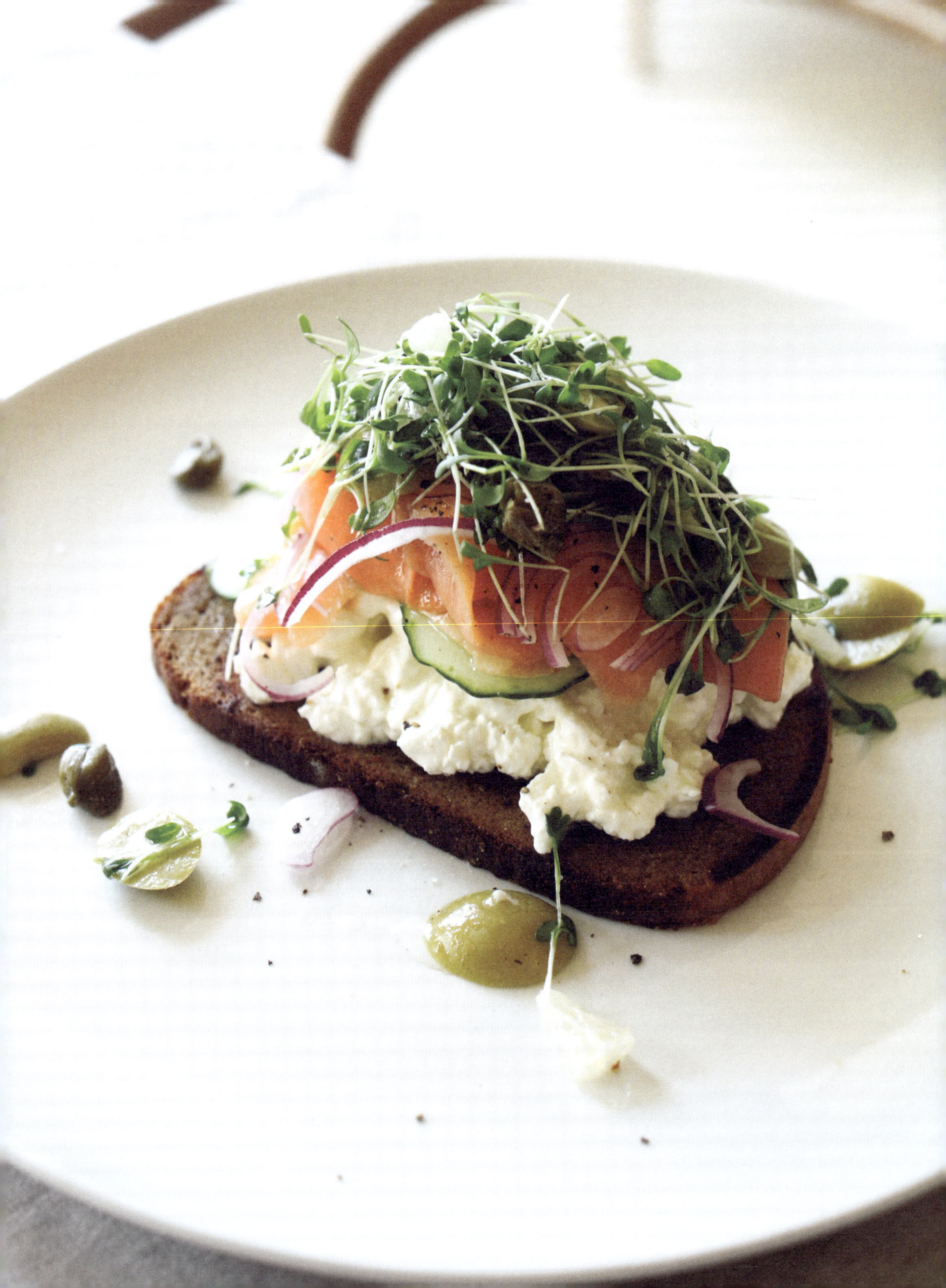

healthy salmon bite

Open sandwiches are lovely and this one is especially so. Choose salmon that is a nice bright pink. The colour varies according to the season, changing from pink to orange depending on what and when the salmon eat. Garnish the sandwich with a fresh, green herb salad for a beautiful contrast with the pink salmon and creamy cottage cheese.

ZESTY HERB SALAD
80 g micro greens
24 capers
4 green olives
olive oil
lemon juice
quarter lemon, segmented
salt and pepper

4 slices seeded bread
250 g chunky cottage cheese
4 x 80 g smoked salmon
1 cucumber, thinly sliced
1 red onion, thinly sliced

To make the herb salad, mix the micro greens, capers and olives together and dress with olive oil, a squeeze of lemon juice and lemon segments. Season with salt and pepper.

This sandwich is served open, so start with a slice of bread. Spread the cottage cheese on the bread, top with thinly sliced cucumber slices, salmon and the red onion slices.

Garnish with the herb salad.

SERVES 4

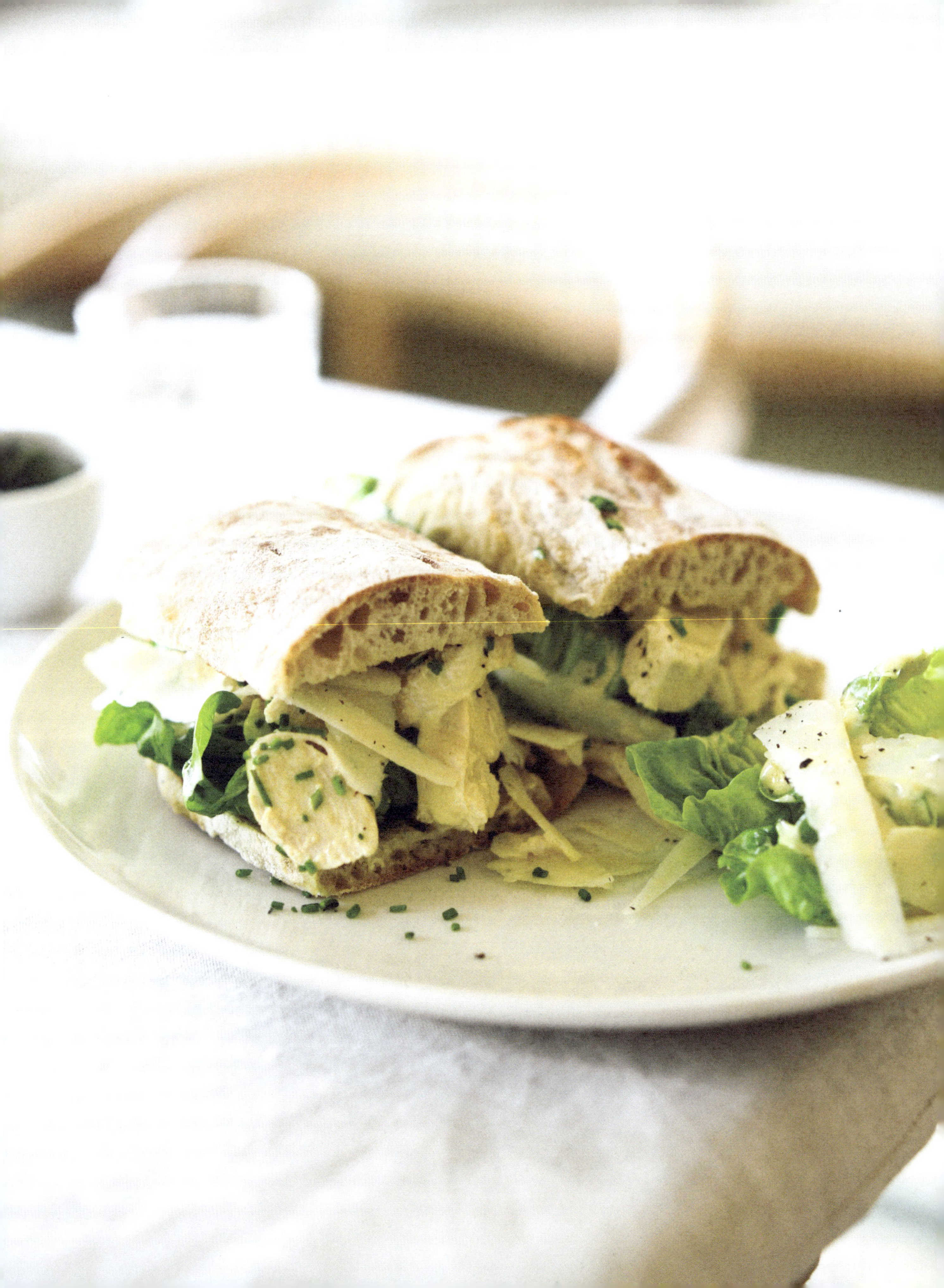

classic caesar sarmie

The Caesar salad is universally popular, as are sandwiches, so the Classic Caesar Sarmie makes perfect sense. In our kitchens we grill the chicken breasts and we add yoghurt to the dressing to lighten it. Gem lettuce, which has both the softness of butter lettuce and the crunch of iceberg, is the best salad leaf for this sandwich.

CAESAR DRESSING
16 g anchovies
quarter clove garlic
1 tbsp Dijon mustard
juice of 1 lemon
2 egg yolks
150 ml olive oil
2 tsp boiling water
4 tbsp double-thick Greek yoghurt
1 handful chives, chopped
1 tbsp flat leaf parsley, chopped
salt and pepper

8 chicken breasts
4 ciabatta rolls, cut lengthways
20 baby gem lettuce leaves
about 120 g Parmesan shavings
avocado slices (optional)

Use a blender to make the Caesar dressing. Blend the anchovies, garlic, Dijon mustard, the juice of half the lemon and the egg yolks. Slowly add the olive oil while the blender is on and then the boiling water. Pour the dressing into a bowl and add the Greek yoghurt, chives, parsley and another squeeze of lemon. Season to taste, but be careful with the salt as anchovies are already salty.

Season the chicken breasts and shallow-fry or grill until golden brown and cooked through. Cut into strips and combine with the dressing.

Cut the ciabatta in half, lengthwise, and toast the inside.

Assemble the sandwiches by placing the lettuce, then the chicken mixture, then the Parmesan on the bottom ciabatta half. You can also add avocado slices if you like. Close with the top half of the ciabatta.

SERVES 4

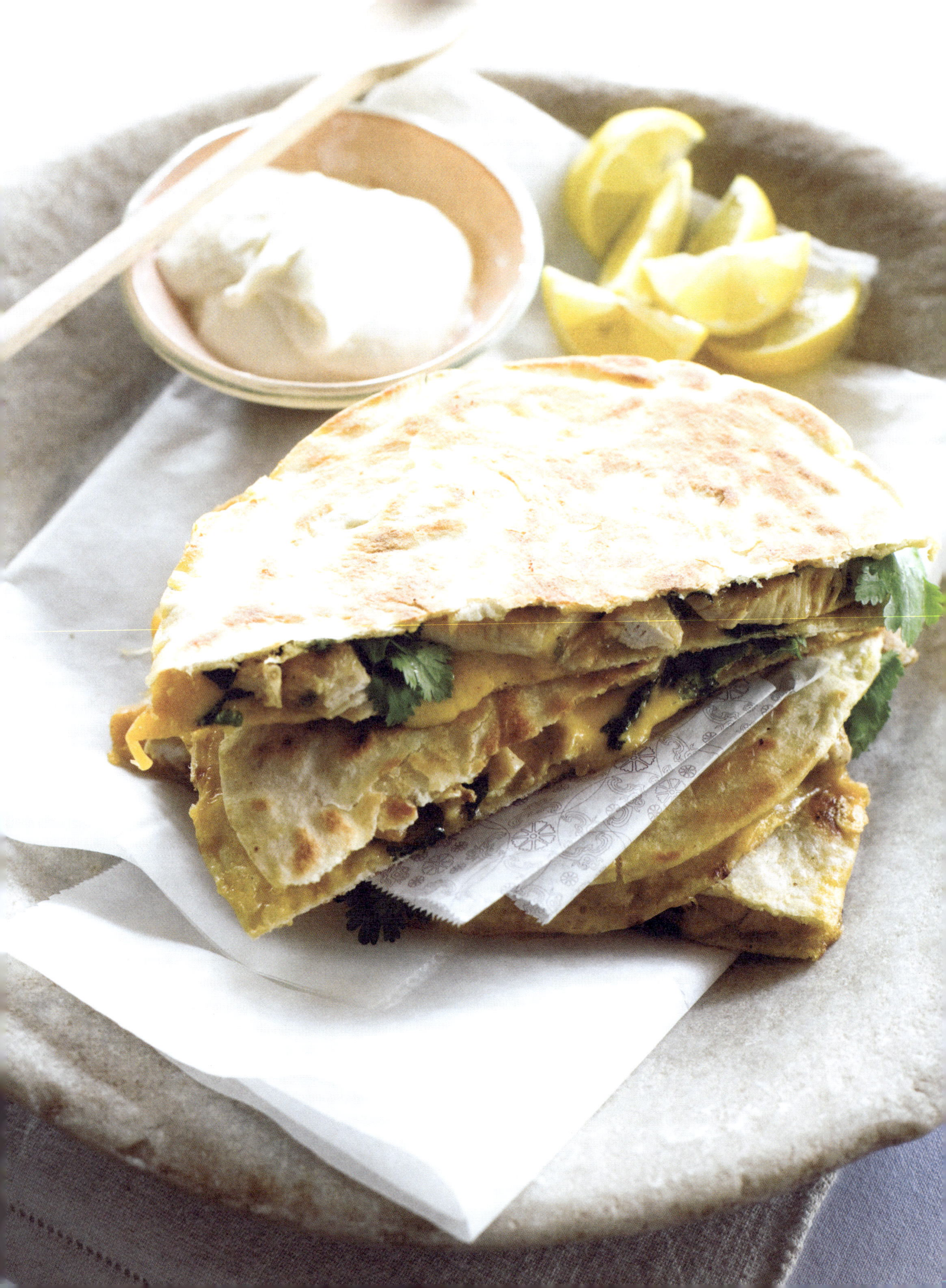

the brazilian

We have a menu committee that meets, tastes, debates and finally decides what dishes make it to the menu. We analyse and pick apart every morsel. We juggle lemons and limes, potato wedges and string fries. It always amazes me how much heated discussion something as innocent as a sandwich can generate. This one almost didn't make it – too similar to a tramezzini I thought. But my friend and self-appointed 'head taster', Melpo, argued that customers would enjoy the filling more when the bread was not the main ingredient. As usual, she was right.

800 g chicken breasts, cubed
salt and pepper
oil for frying
4 red chillies, seeded, thinly sliced
1 large handful coriander leaves
juice of 1 lemon

8 tortilla wraps
240 g Cheddar cheese, grated
300 g double-thick Greek yoghurt
4 lemon wedges

Cut the chicken into thin strips. Season with salt and pepper and shallow-fry or grill in a pan with oil until golden brown. Add the chilli to the pan, and after a minute or two, add a squeeze of lemon and a handful of coriander leaves (no stalks).

Lay half the wraps flat and cover with cheese, chicken and a handful of coriander. Close the wraps with the other halves and heat in a pan until golden brown and crisp.

Serve with yoghurt and lemon wedges. It's also great with a fresh tomato salsa.

SERVES 4

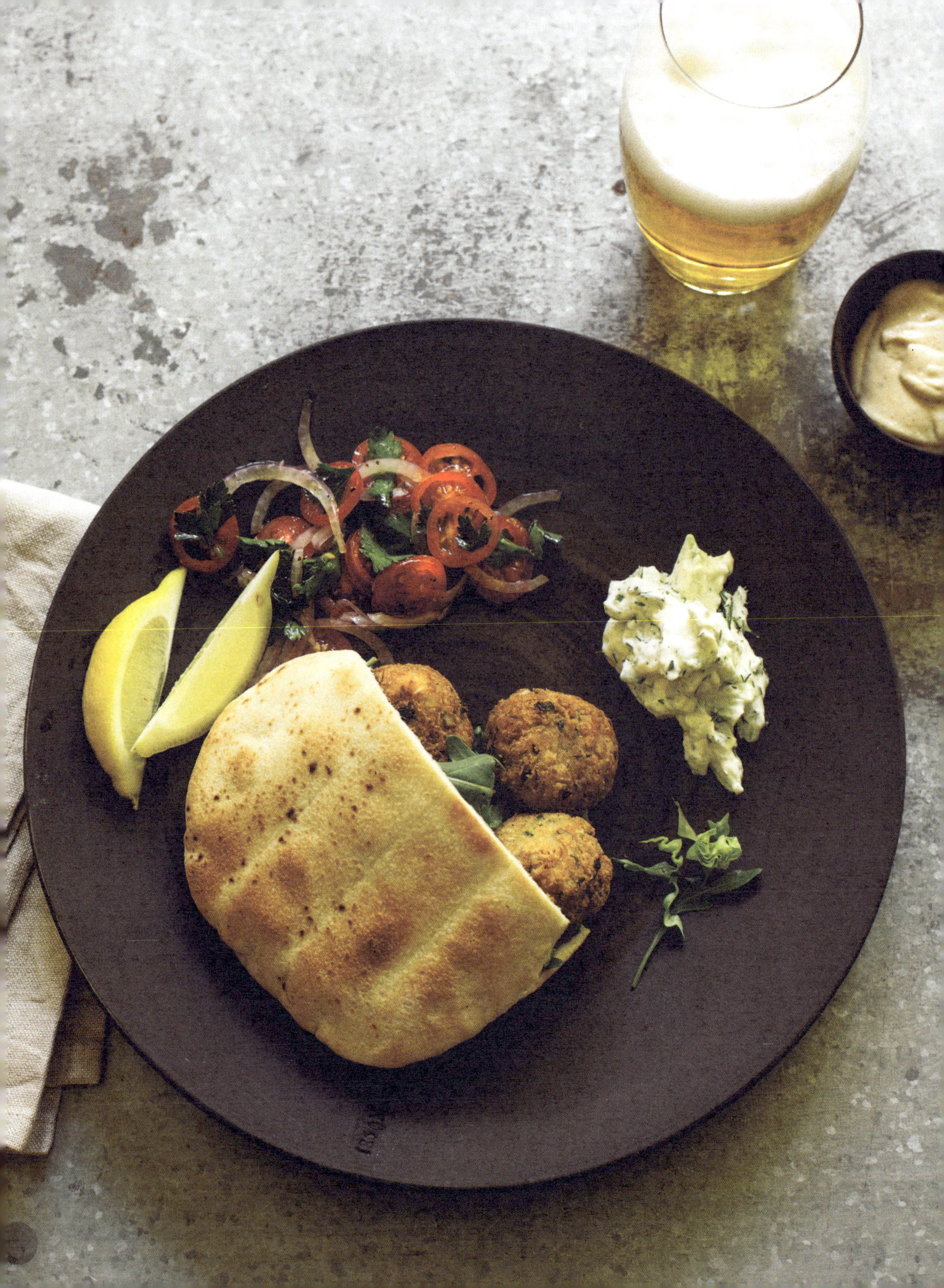

falafel pockets

George, the owner of tashas Morningside, asked me to put a new spin on this favourite classic. These falafels are lighter and creamier than the traditional ones because we combine the chickpeas with chevin, brown rice and lots of fresh herbs. Keep the chickpeas fairly chunky – it helps the falafel to crisp.

FALAFEL
200 ml brown rice, cooked
2 tins chickpeas, drained and crushed
2 spring onions, chopped
handful parsley, chopped
handful coriander, chopped
100 g chevin (soft goat's cheese)
salt and pepper
flour for dusting
sunflower oil for frying

CHUNKY TZATZIKI
100 g cucumber, diced
360 g yoghurt
2 tsp olive oil
1 tsp dried oregano
2 cloves garlic, chopped
salt and pepper

4 pita pockets
120 ml tahini
2 heads gem lettuce, washed and sliced
1 tomato, chopped
1 red onion, sliced
handful parsley, chopped
handful chopped coriander
lemon wedges to serve

Combine the brown rice, chickpeas, spring onions, parsley, coriander and chevin. Season to taste. Divide and roll the mixture into balls, roughly the size of ping pong balls. Dust with flour and shallow-fry in 2 cm of hot oil.

To make the chunky tzatziki, peel, deseed and dice the cucumber. Mix with the remaining ingredients.

Toast the pita pockets. Cut the top quarter off each pocket, open and spread the tahini inside. Fill with lettuce, tomato, onion, herbs and tzatziki but leave space for the falafel.

Serve with lemon wedges and extra tahini.

SERVES 4

One of the most important things I've learnt is that quality is not an option, it's a given.
Every tashas salad has at least five different kinds of leaves including baby leaves and micro greens and each one has to be perfect. When shopping for your salad ingredients select the very freshest ones – bruised, blemished or wilted leaves will not do. Pick a variety of textures and colours and when you wash the baby leaves, especially micro greens, splash or rinse, rather than drown. I wash them in a sieve under a gentle stream of water. They bruise very easily and shouldn't go in a salad spinner.

Toss and dress your leaves in a mixing bowl and then transfer them to a serving bowl. If you're using a heavier dressing, such as one that is mayonnaise-based, toss the leaves with a little olive oil first. This helps to coat the leaves.

salads

the traditional caesar · 87

barley & bocconcini salad · 89

quinoa & edamame salad · 91

texas salad · 93

labne lentil salad · 95

golden pear salad · 97

dakos salad · 99

salad niçoise · 103

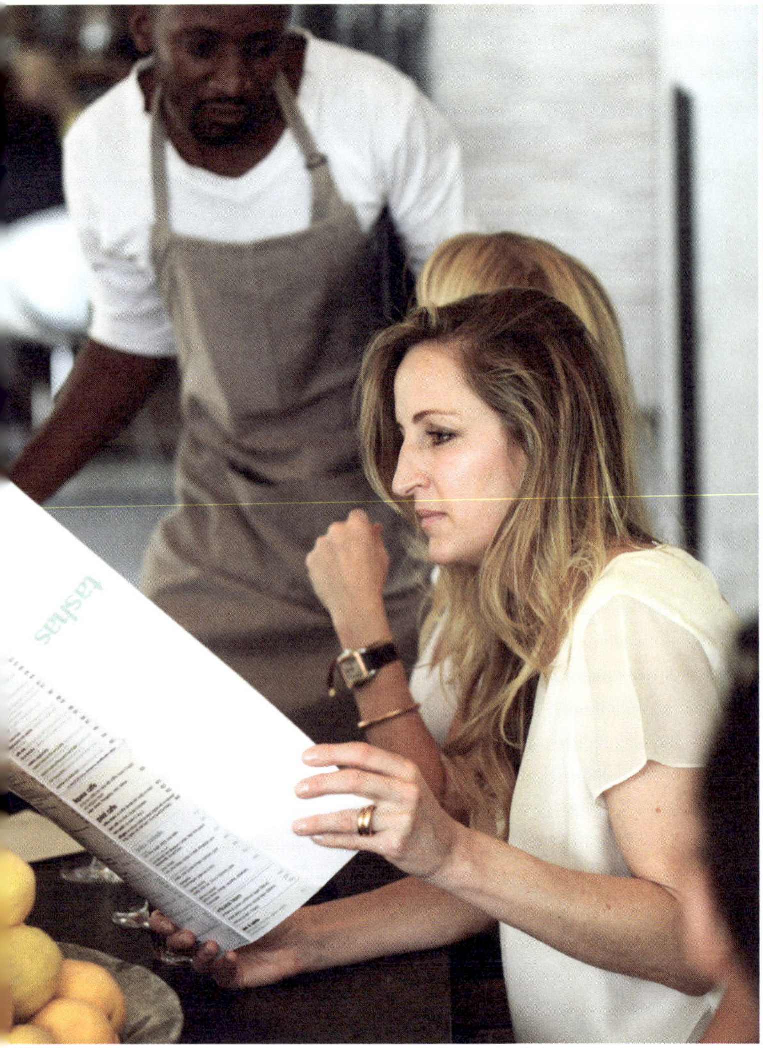
tashas

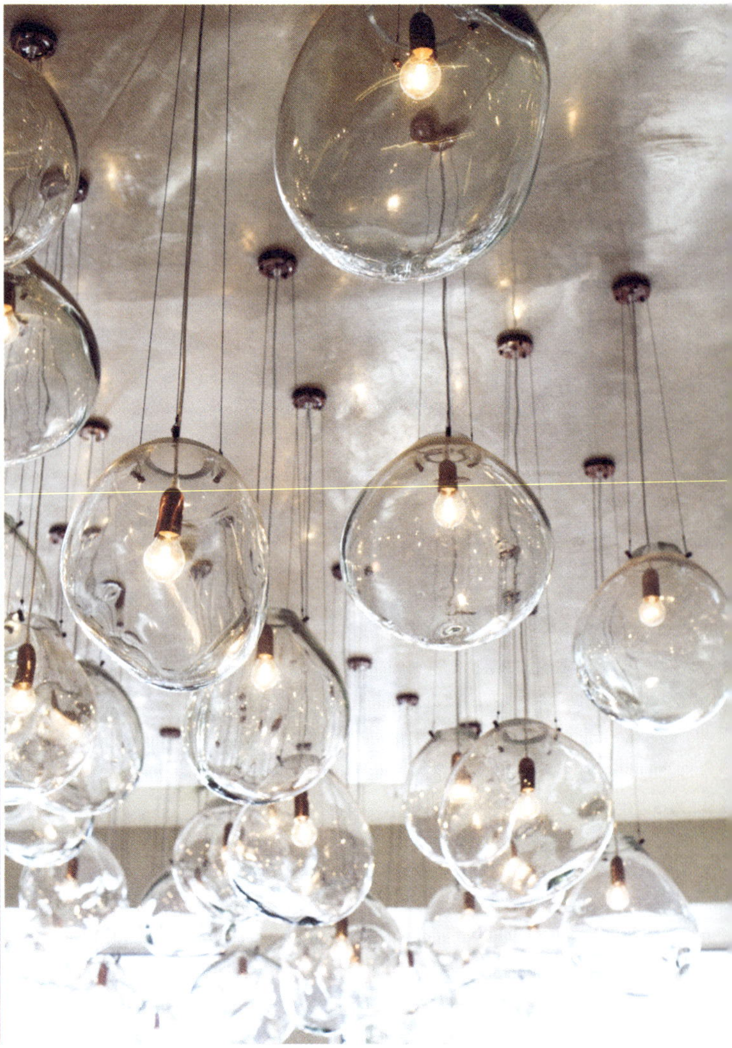

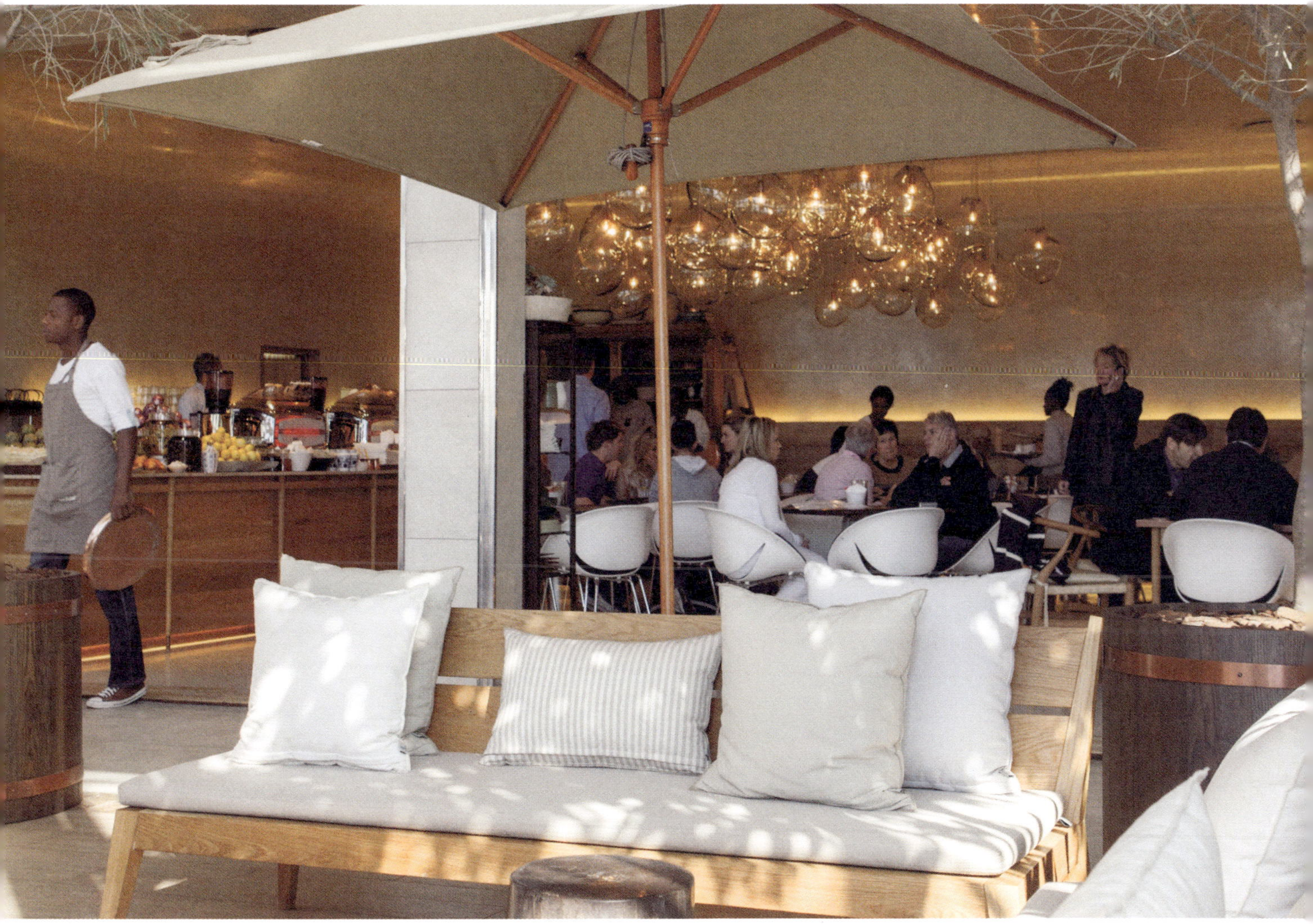

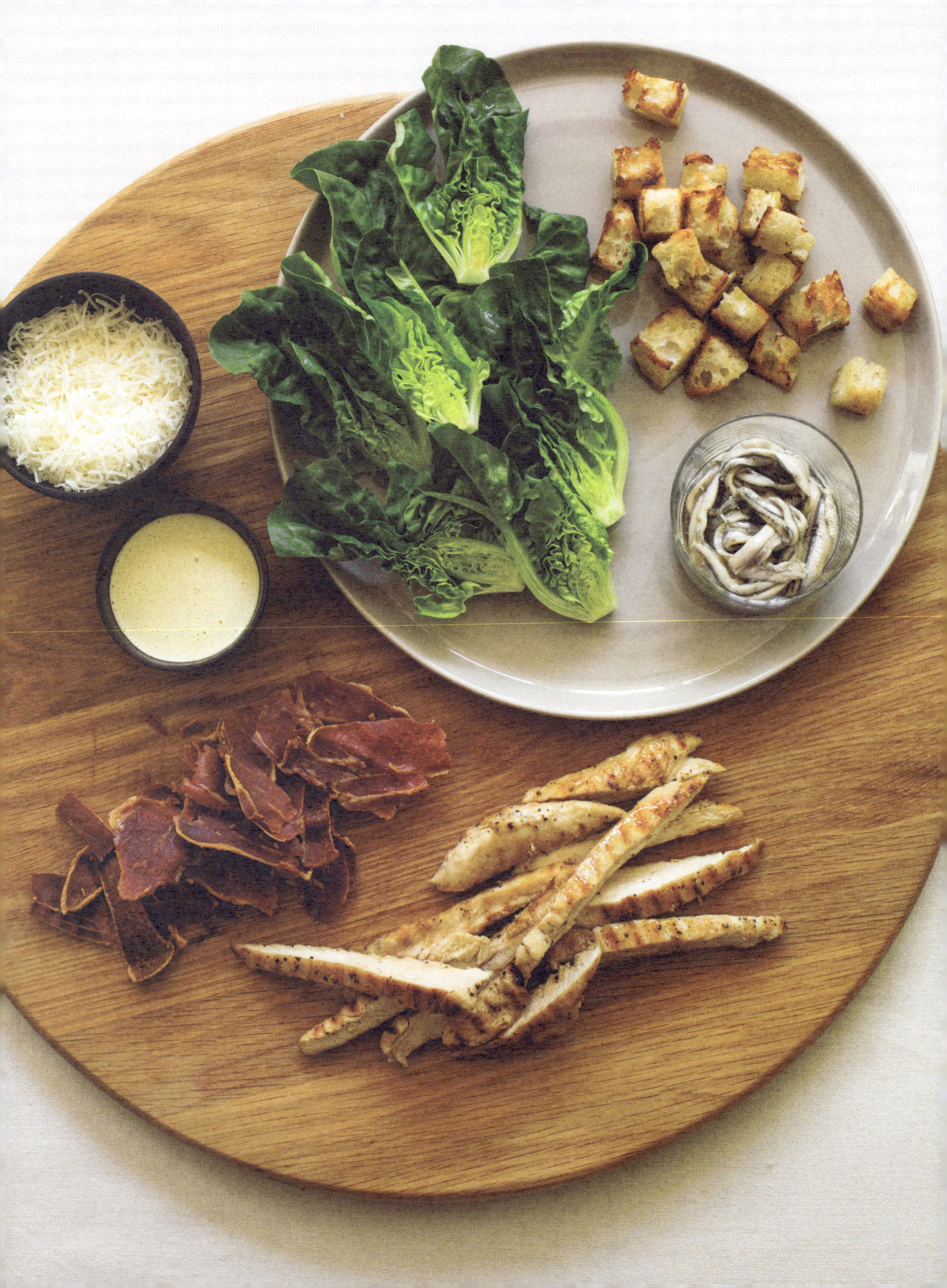

the traditional caesar

This recipe is for the traditional caesar, but if you want to make it a bit different, add tomatoes, cucumbers or spinach leaves. I love serving it as a deconstructed salad so that everyone can choose their favourite ingredients. Add oven-roasted Parma ham for extra crunch and flavour.

70 g Parma ham
4 slices ciabatta, cubed
olive oil

CAESAR DRESSING
16 g anchovies
quarter clove clove garlic
1 tbsp Dijon mustard
juice of 1 lemon
2 egg yolks
150 ml olive oil
2 tsp boiling water
4 tbsp double-thick Greek yoghurt
1 handful chives, chopped
1 tbsp flat leaf parsley, chopped
salt and pepper

8 chicken breasts, slightly flattened to 1 cm in thickness
salt and pepper
olive oil
4–6 heads baby gem lettuce
16 white anchovies
80 g Parmesan, grated

Roast the Parma ham in an oven at 40 °C for about 20 minutes or until it is dry and wafer-like.

To make croutons, drizzle the ciabatta cubes with olive oil and shallow fry in a pan until they are golden brown.

Use a blender to make the Caesar dressing. Blend the anchovies, garlic, Dijon mustard, the juice of half the lemon and the egg yolks. Slowly add the olive oil while the blender is on and then the boiling water. Pour the dressing into a bowl and add the Greek yoghurt, chives, parsley and another squeeze of lemon. Season to taste, but be careful with the salt as anchovies are already salty.

Season the flattened chicken breasts with salt and pepper, cook in a griddle pan in a little olive oil until golden brown.

You can serve everything in separate bowls or in the traditional way by tossing the lettuce with the dressing, anchovies and Parmesan, and garnishing with the croutons, Parma ham and chicken.

SERVES 4

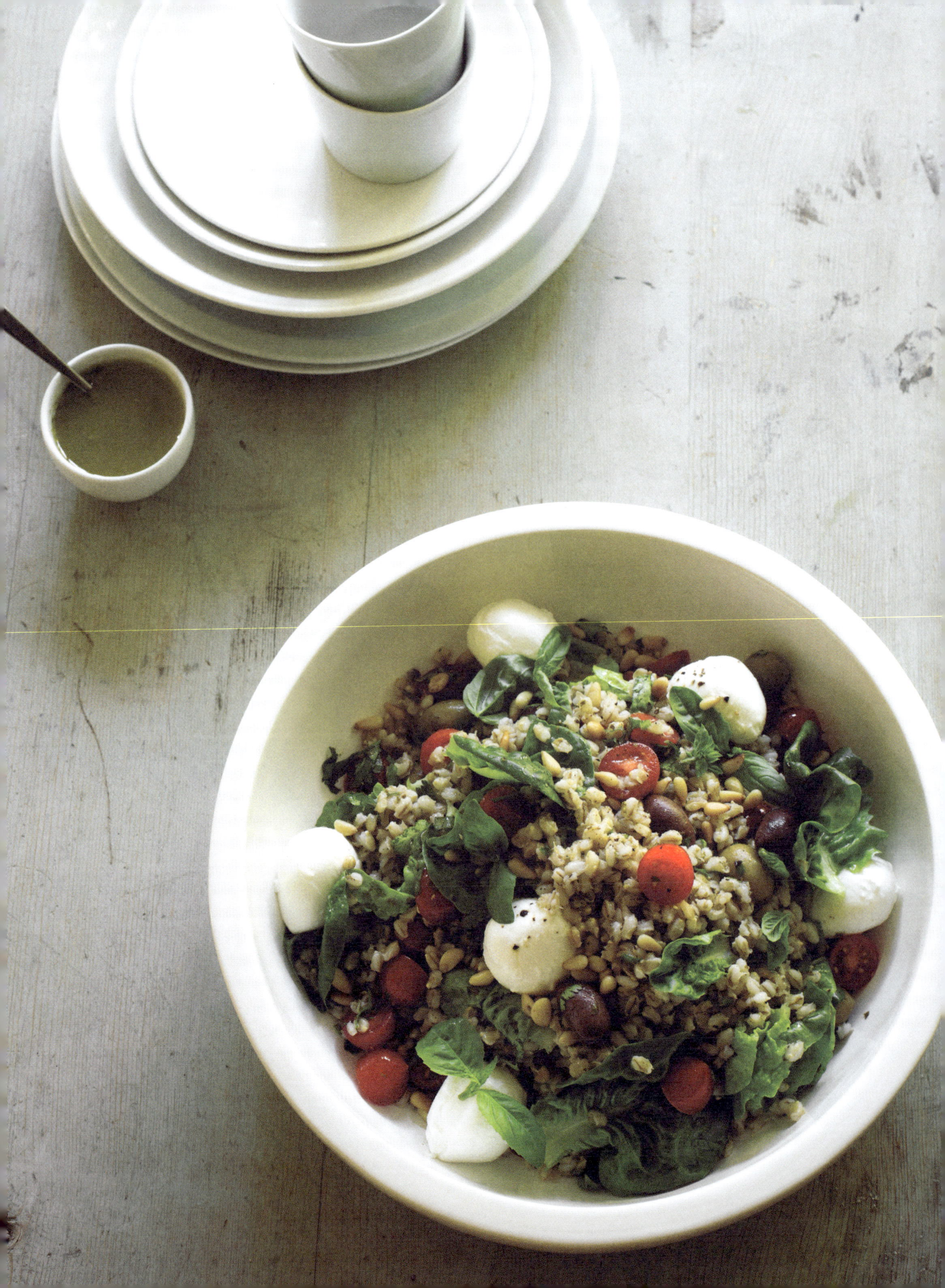

barley & bocconcini salad

My cousin Maria loves this salad. She had a fit when I removed it from our menu. I added this recipe just for her in the hope that I can now take her calls without fearing for my life.

320 g barley
2,5 litres boiling water
2 tsp salt

LEMON BASIL DRESSING
juice of 2 lemons
100 ml olive oil
small handful basil leaves, chopped
10 ml basil pesto
salt and pepper

24 sundried tomatoes, halved
40 g pine nuts, roasted
handful coriander, roughly chopped
24 cherry tomatoes, halved
16 black olives, pitted
16 green olives, pitted
4 heads baby gem lettuce, torn
24 bocconcini (small mozzarella balls)
small handful rocket
small handful micro greens

Cook the barley in salted, boiling water for approximately 90 minutes. Leave the lid on the pot. The barley should be soft but not mushy and all the water should have cooked away. Rinse well to wash off the starch. Allow to cool.

To make the dressing, mix the ingredients in a blender until smooth.

Place the remaining salad ingredients except the micro greens in a mixing bowl and toss gently with the dressing. Transfer the salad to your serving dish.

Top with the micro greens just before serving.

SERVES 4

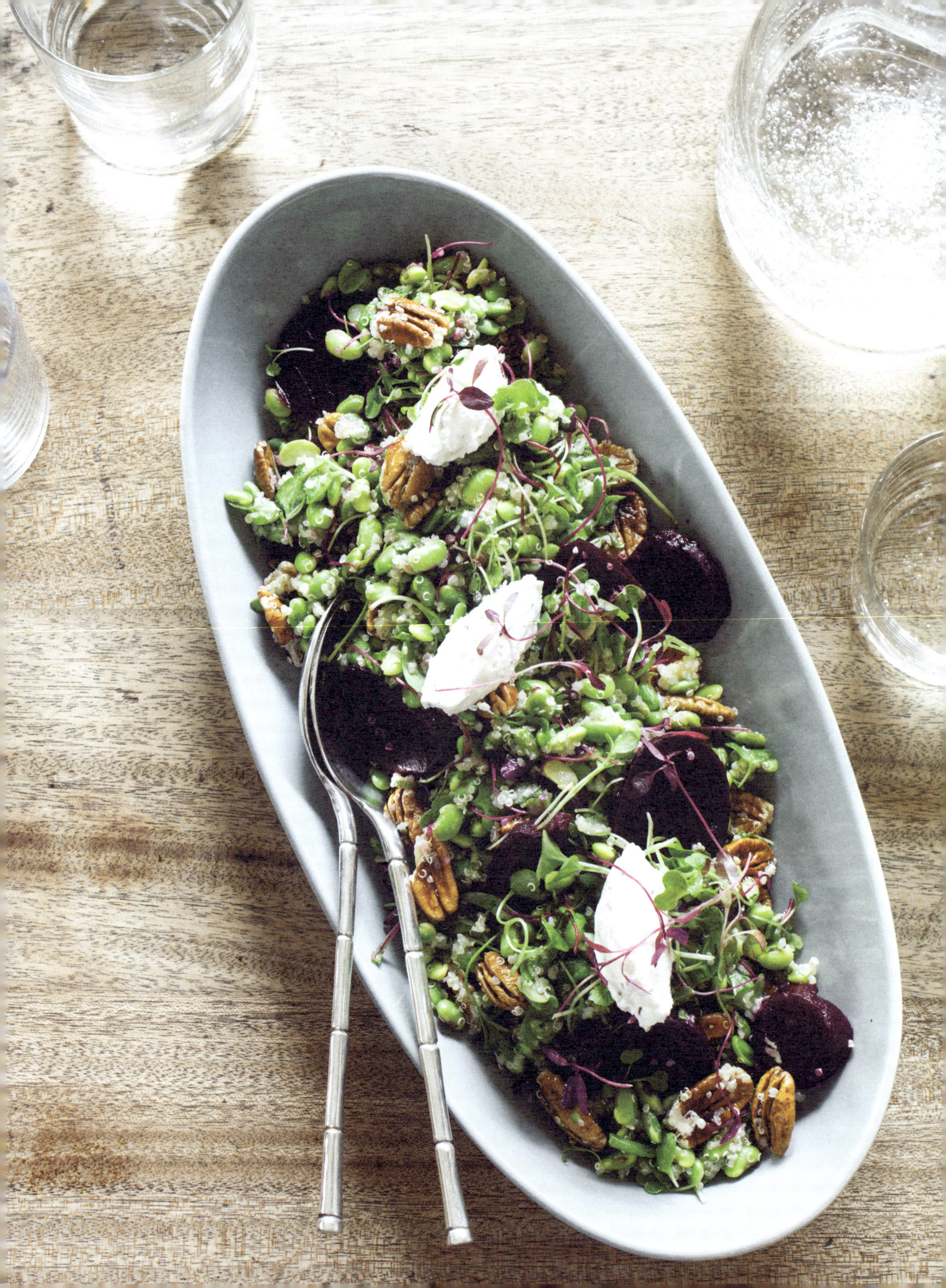

quinoa & edamame salad

And then there was quinoa. In a world that shies away from carbs this is a gift that is as satisfying but far more nutritious. For light, fluffy quinoa, boil it until almost cooked and then steam. I spread it out on a baking tray to dry after I have rinsed it, which keeps the grains from sticking together. If you can't find edamame beans for this recipe, you can substitute with peas.

440 g quinoa
1 litre boiling water
2 medium onions, sliced
olive oil
800 g edamame beans

VINAIGRETTE
120 ml olive oil
1 tbsp red wine vinegar
120 ml fresh lemon juice

FETA SPREAD
80 g Danish feta
2 tbs olive oil
pinch dried oregano
black pepper

24 pickled beetroot, sliced
120 g pecans, dry roasted
2 large handfuls micro greens

Boil the quinoa in a litre of salted, rapidly boiling water. Keep the lid on and cook for about 20 minutes. Most of the water should have evaporated. Remove the pot from the heat and leave the quinoa to steam in the pot with the lid on for 5-10 minutes. Lightly season the onions with salt and sauté on a low heat until they are soft and golden. Boil the edamame beans in a pot of boiling water for 10 minutes or until tender. Rinse under cold running water, drain and set aside.

Make the vinaigrette by whisking the olive oil, red wine vinegar and lemon juice together.

Mix the feta spread ingredients to form a fine paste.

Toss the cooled quinoa, onions, edamame beans, beetroot and pecans together in a large bowl. Transfer to your serving dish and garnish with micro greens.

SERVES 4

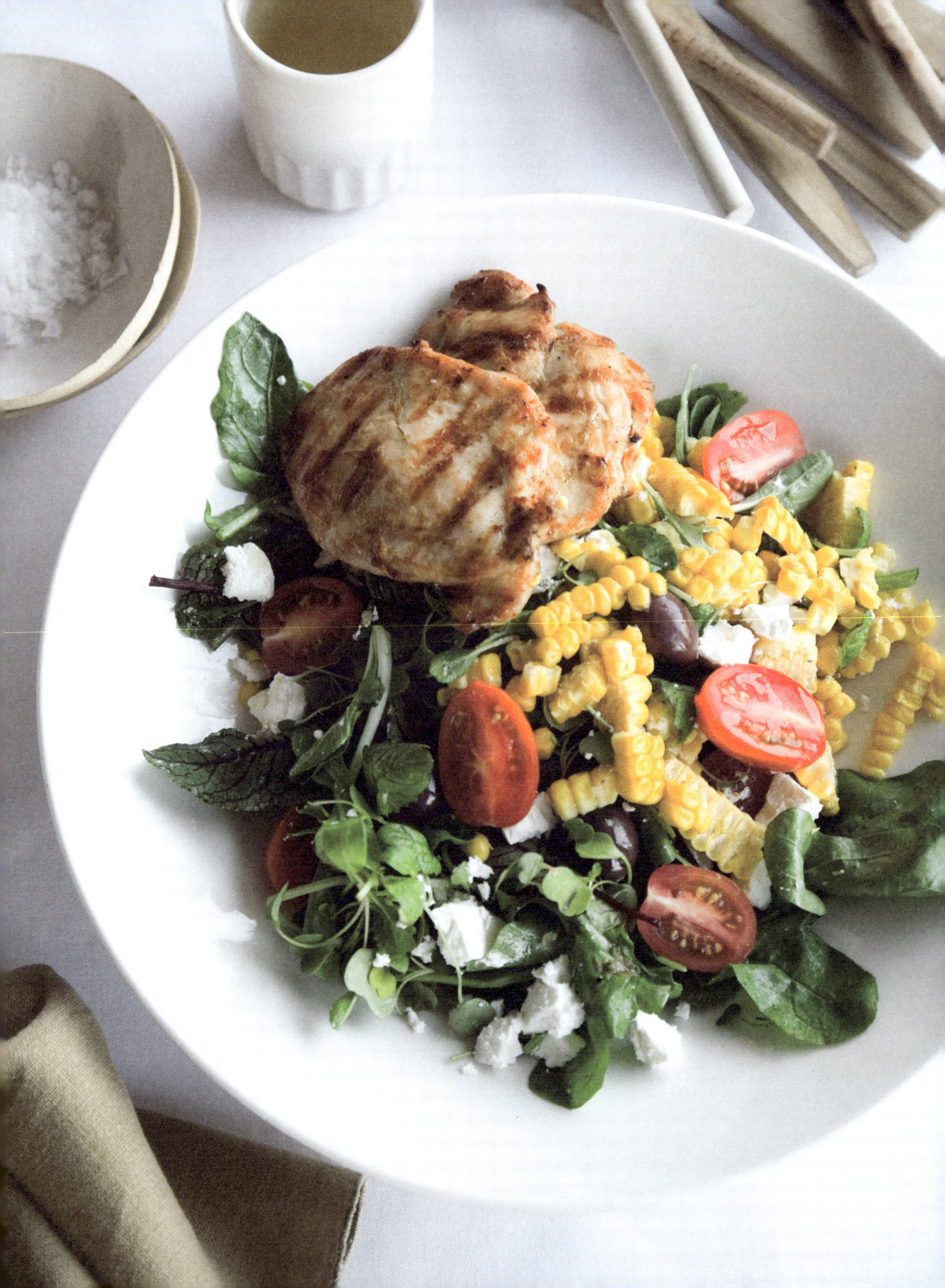

texas salad

This salad was inspired by things we love: chicken, mielies, tomatoes, feta and olives. In hindsight, we wonder why we called it the Texas Salad. There is nothing Texan about a Greek salad with mielies. Despite this, it's one of our best-selling salads and has been on the Classic menu from the start.

8 chicken breasts, flattened
2 tbsp olive oil

LEMON BASIL DRESSING
juice of 2 lemons
100 ml olive oil
handful basil leaves
10 ml basil pesto
salt and pepper

8 sweetcorn cobs
24 cherry tomatoes, halved
32 calamata olives
200 g feta, crumbled
handful basil leaves
2 large handfuls rocket leaves
lemon wedges

Season the chicken breasts and grill in the olive oil in a griddle pan.

To make the dressing, combine all the ingredients in a blender until smooth.

Cook the sweetcorn, cut the kernels off the cob and allow to cool. Toss the corn with the tomatoes, olives and feta. Add a small amount of the dressing and mix again. Combine the corn mixture with the basil and rocket leaves and add the rest of the dressing.

Place the salad mixture into 4 serving bowls and top each with 2 grilled chicken breasts.

Serve with lemon wedges.

SERVES 4

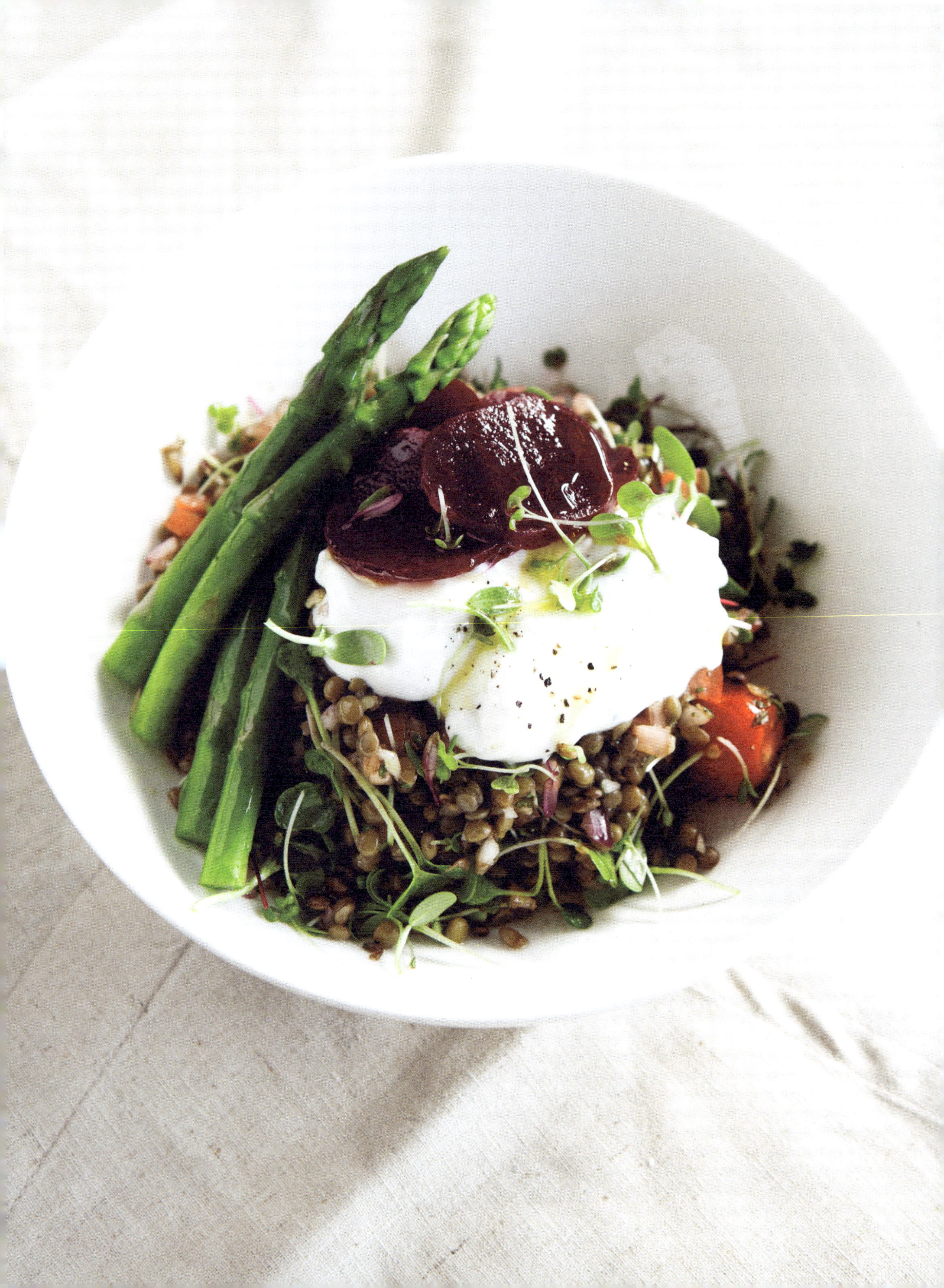

labne lentil salad

My friends Candice and Sarah are forever trying to convince me that just about everything you can think of – from the alphabet to alphabet soup – was invented by the Lebanese before the Greeks. We've spent many nights debating and Googling into the wee hours. For once though, I'll have to give it to them: labne is Lebanese. It's a delicious cheese made from yoghurt and so easy to make. Some say my love for labne is just another excuse to use yoghurt. Maybe, but what I really want to know is, if I use Greek yoghurt, is the labne still Lebanese?

LABNE
ALLOW FOR 24-HOUR PREPARATION TIME
400 g Greek yoghurt
1 tsp salt

LENTIL SALAD
800 g brown lentils, cooked
OR use 2 tins
4 medium tomatoes, diced
6 cherry tomatoes, sliced
2 handfuls mint leaves, chopped
2 red onions, chopped
60 ml olive oil
40 ml balsamic vinegar
salt and pepper

16 pickled beetroot, sliced
20 asparagus spears, blanched 30 ml lemon juice
handful micro greens

Make the labne the day before you want to use it.

Labne is made by straining yoghurt in a muslin cloth. Use a plain white cloth – stripes and prints colour the cheese. Line a colander with the cloth, put the yoghurt in the middle, fold the corners together and tie it to the middle of a wooden spoon. Let it hang from the spoon over a deep bowl for at least 24 hours. The longer you hang it, the thicker it gets. Don't use fat free or low fat yoghurt; the water content is too high. The salt gives the labne a more cheese-like flavour.

To make the lentil salad, combine the freshly cooked or tinned lentils, tomatoes, mint and onion in a bowl. Stir in the olive oil and balsamic vinegar, season with salt and pepper. Divide the salad into 4 serving bowls. Place a dollop of labne on top of each portion and top with the beetroot, asparagus and lemon juice.

Garnish with micro greens.

SERVES 4

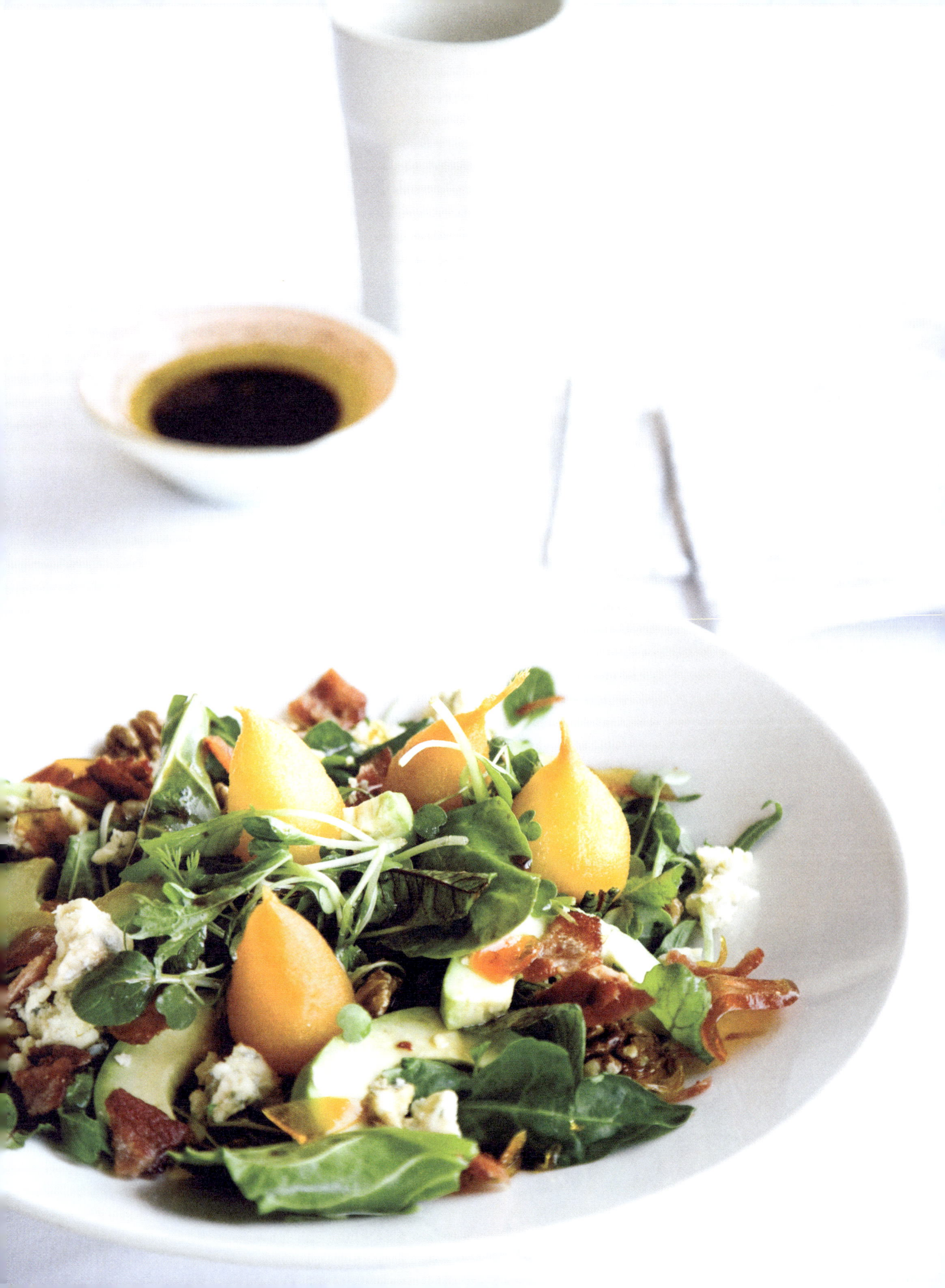

golden pear salad

This is as close as a salad gets to a dessert. Blue cheese and pears are a classic combination. We fell in love with the idea of the pears, designed this dish around them and now it's one of our most popular. You can caramelise the pears about two hours in advance – not more than that though because the sugar dissolves. If pears are not in season, you can get away with tinned ones.

20 rashers crispy bacon, chopped
32 walnuts, dry roasted

GOLDEN PEARS
12 baby pears
300 g sugar

FOR 160 ml BALSAMIC TOFFEE DRESSING
30 g caramelised sugar
130 ml olive oil
30 ml balsamic vinegar
salt and pepper

SALAD
2 large handfuls baby spinach
2 large handfuls baby lettuce leaves
2 large handfuls baby gem lettuce
2 avocados, sliced lengthways

caramelised sugar shards
200 g Gorgonzola cheese

First fry the bacon until crispy and dry roast the walnuts in a pan. Set aside to cool.

Peel the baby pears and pat dry. If you're using tinned pears, drain well before caramelising. Caramelise the sugar in a pot over a high heat. Don't stir it, rather gently shake the sugar in the pan until it has melted. Be careful: caramelised sugar is extremely hot. Tilt the pan slightly and dip each pear into the caramel. Place on a baking tray to harden. Once the pears have all been covered, pour the remaining caramel (less 30 g for the dressing) out onto a baking sheet. It should form a thin pool which you can break into shards when it has cooled and hardened.

To make the dressing, crush the 30 g caramelised sugar that you kept aside, and mix with the rest of the dressing ingredients.

Assemble the salad using the spinach as a base. Scatter with the leaves, avocado slices, bacon and walnuts. Arrange 3 baby pears on top of each serving. Drizzle with the dressing, and garnish with crumbled Gorgonzola and the remaining caramelised sugar shards.

SERVES 4

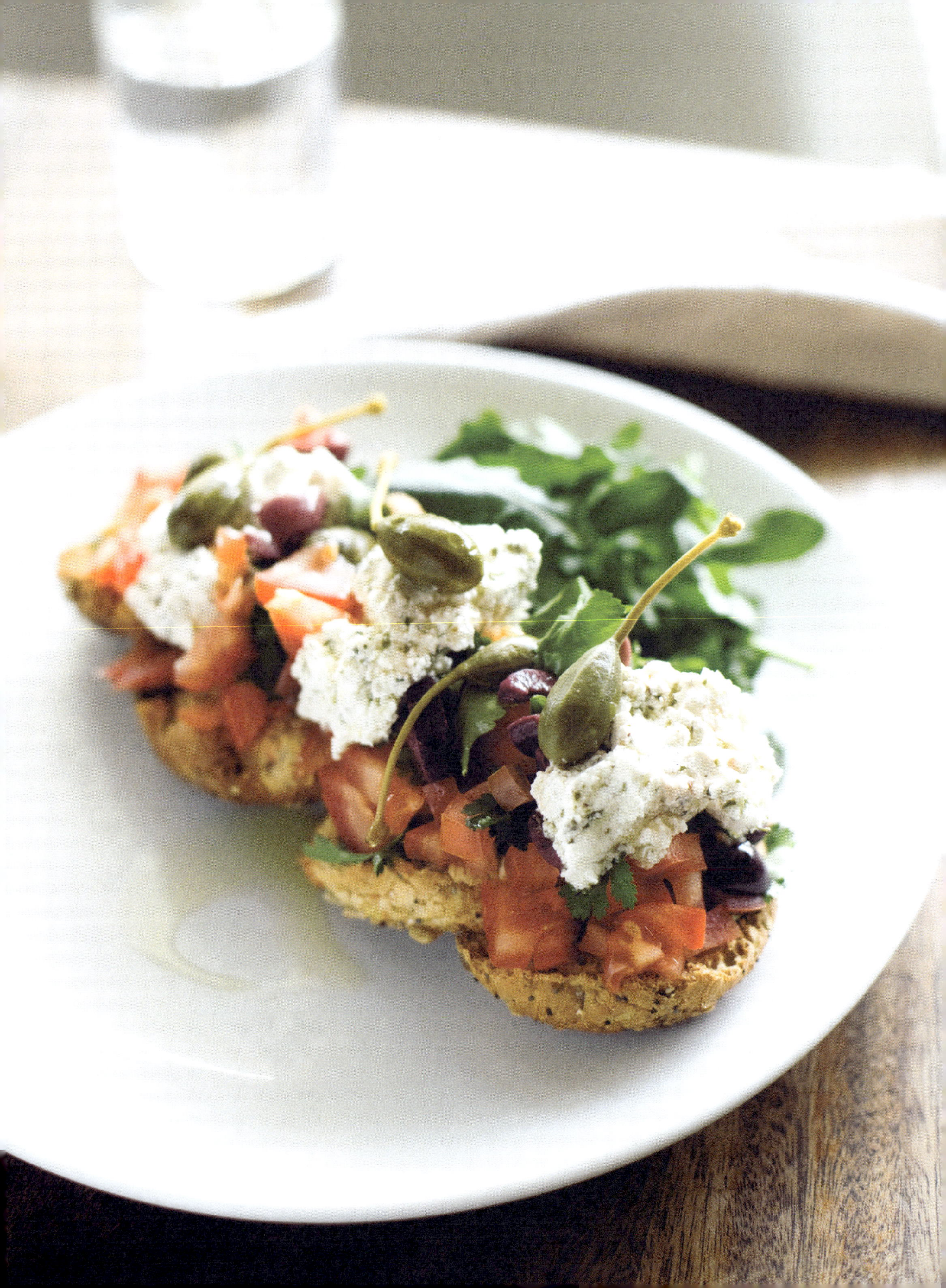

dakos salad

During wartime when food was scarce, Cretans dried their bread to make rusks. They ate them with tomatoes, cheese and generous glugs of olive oil. The rusks are made from barley, so they are quite sweet. You should find dakos at any good Greek deli but if you can't get any, make your own rusks with seeded, whole grain bread rolls.

FETA SPREAD
250 g Danish feta
5 tbsp olive oil
black pepper
pinch dried oregano

12 dakos bread rusks
or 6 whole grain bread rolls
4 tbsp olive oil
2 tbsp red wine vinegar
4 tomatoes, chopped
24 olives, roughly chopped
pinch coriander seeds, crushed

handful rocket
24 caper berries
freshly ground black pepper
olive oil

If you're using bread rolls instead of dakos, cut them in half and dry them out in the oven at 120 °C. After about an hour you should have hard, dry rusks.

To make the feta spread, mix all the ingredients into a smooth paste.

Use 3 rusks per person. Drizzle them with olive oil and red wine vinegar to soften them. Spoon on the chopped tomato, followed by the olives, coriander and feta spread on top of each rusk.

Garnish with rocket, caper berries and black pepper and a good glug of olive oil.

SERVES 4

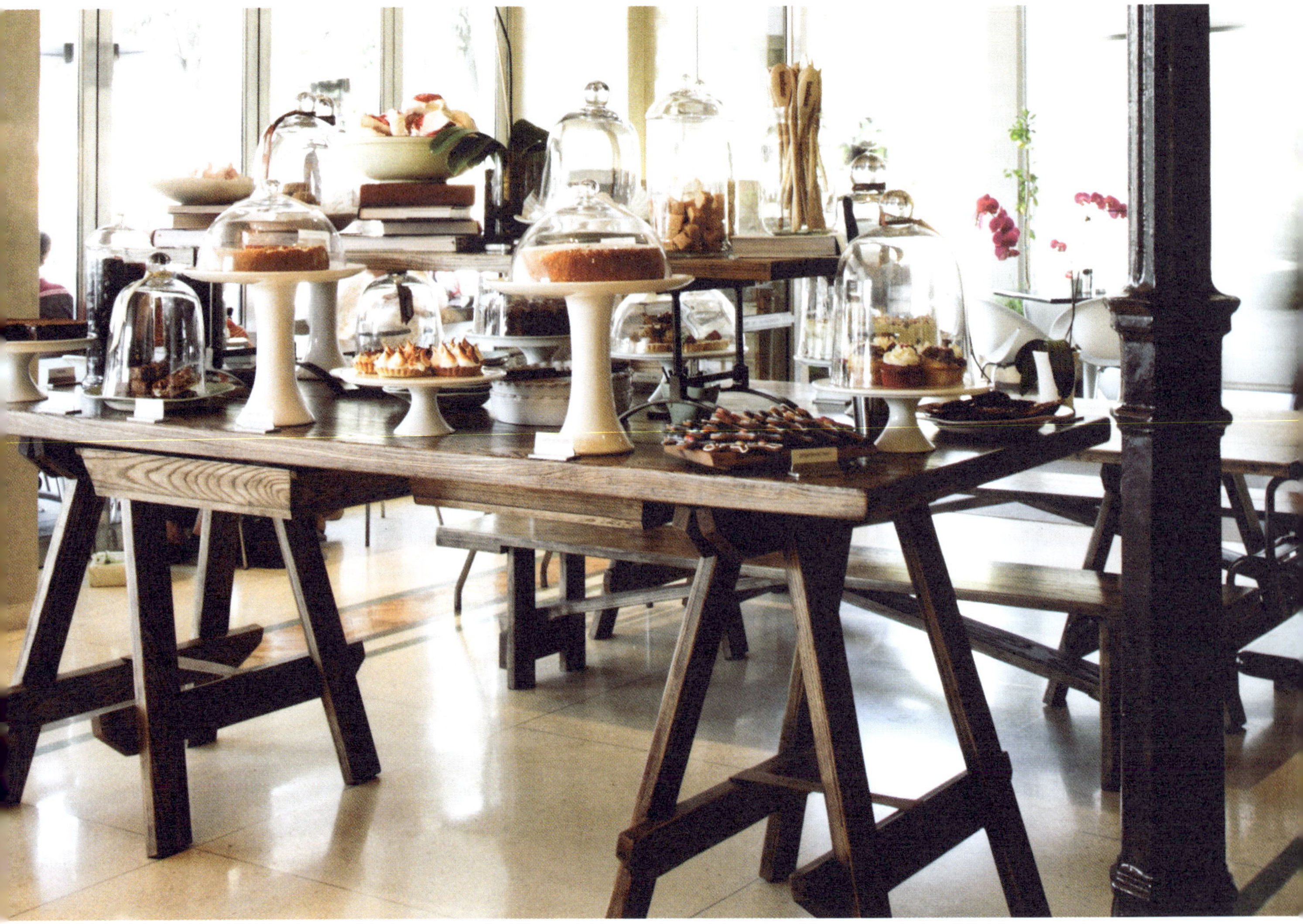

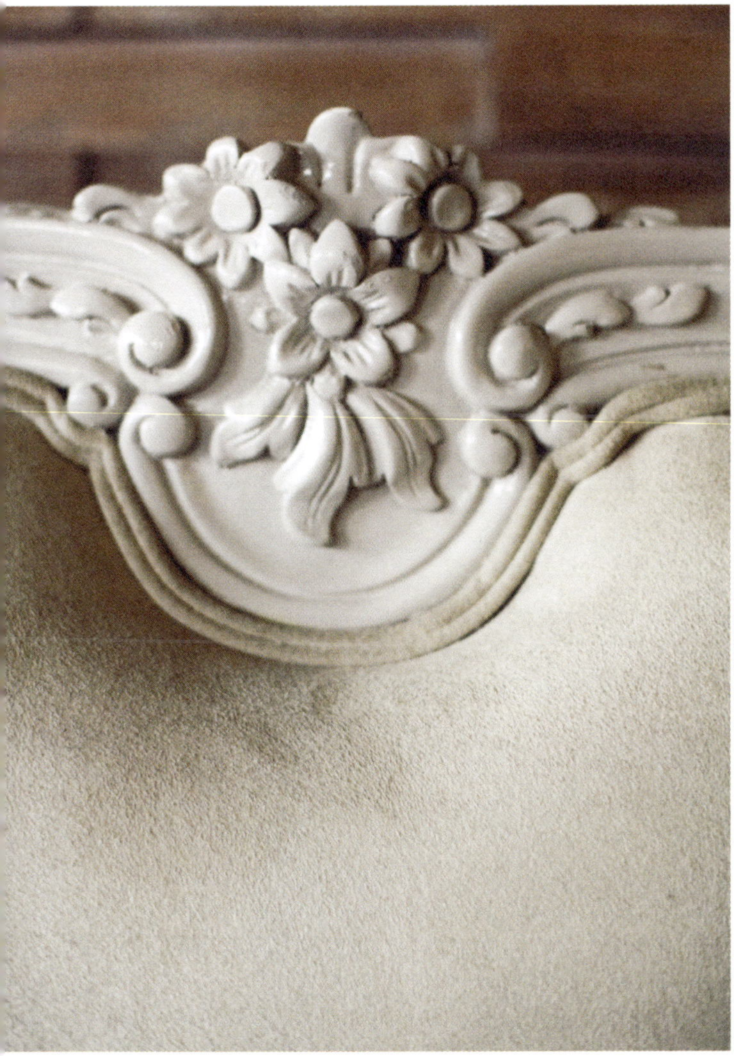

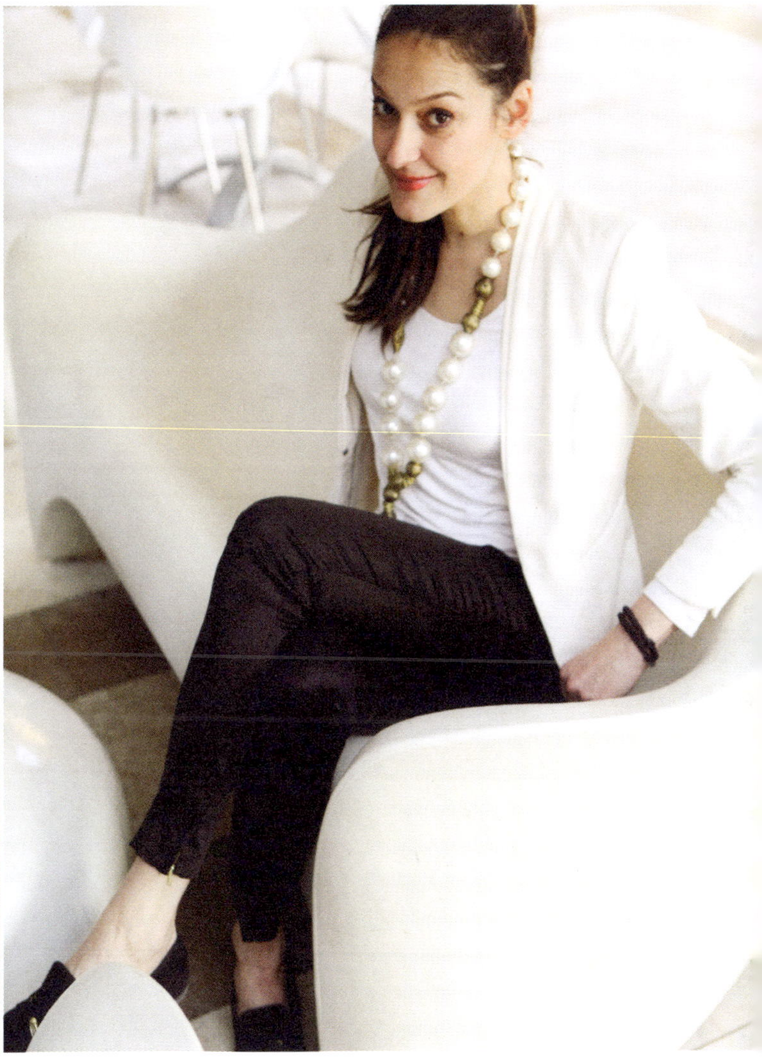

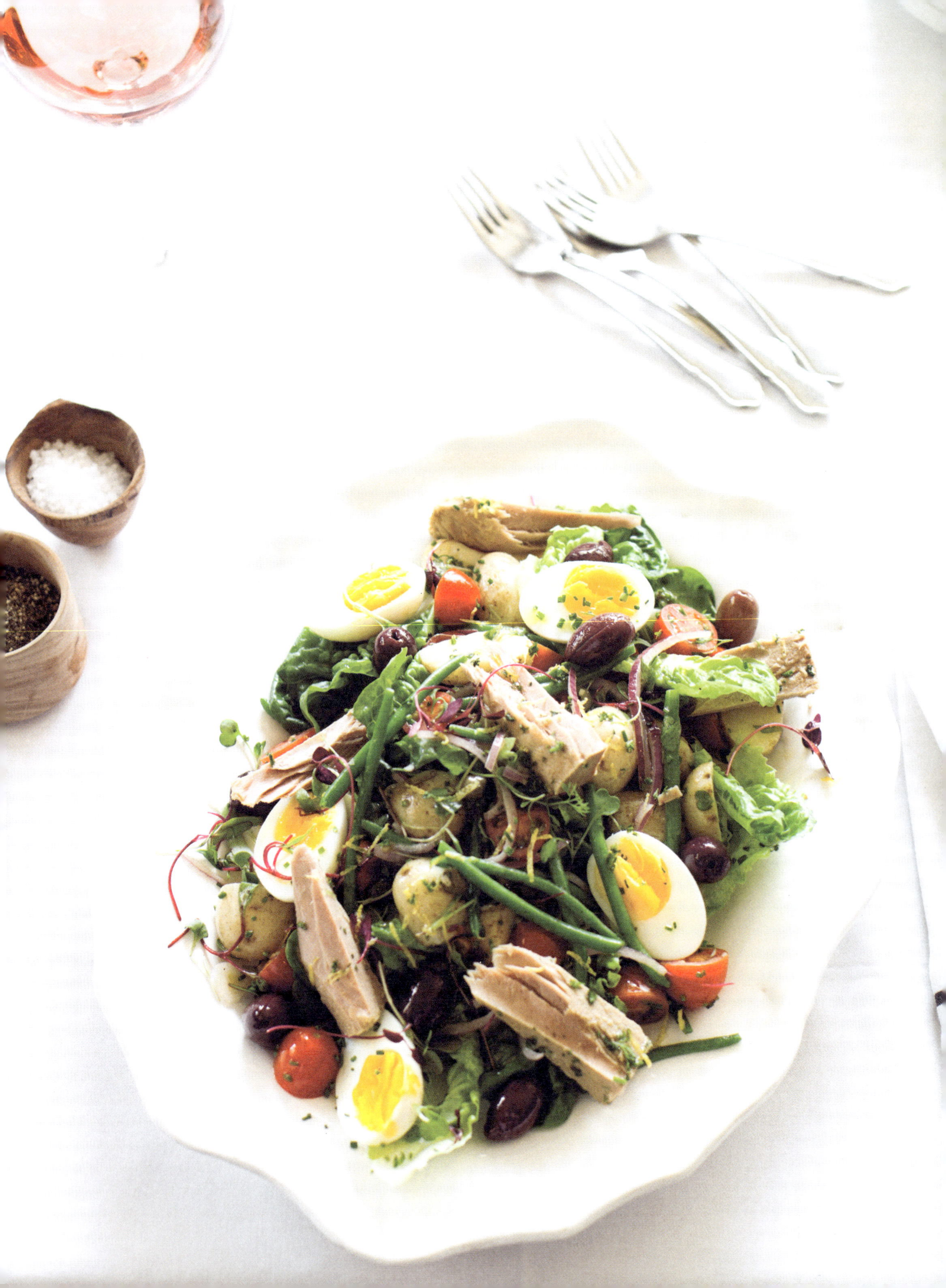

salad niçoise

There's a restaurant in the South of France that you can only get to by boat, with a booking made six months in advance. Salad Niçoise always reminds me of their white tablecloths, rosé wine and the azure sea. If you can't get fresh tuna, use tinned rather than frozen. Spanish and Italian tuna comes in a jar and is especially good. This is excellent as a late lunch or an early dinner, or as a late lunch that becomes an early dinner.

NIÇOISE DRESSING
100 ml olive oil
1 tbsp Dijon mustard
juice of 1 lemon
2 tbsp red wine vinegar
1 tsp sugar
salt and pepper
garlic clove

16 new potatoes, cooked
48 green beans, blanched
2 tbsp capers
24 pitted calamata olives
1 red onion, sliced
24 cherry tomatoes, halved
4 heads baby gem leaves
handful chives, chopped

4 x 120 g tuna fillets, fresh
salt and pepper
juice of 1 lemon
20 ml olive oil
4 eggs, hard boiled and halved

To make the dressing, blend the ingredients until smooth and creamy. Boil the new potatoes in their skins. When they're ready, drain and cut them in half. Allow to cool, then mix them in a large bowl with the beans, capers, olives, red onion and cherry tomatoes. Dress the salad. Gently toss with the gem lettuce and about half the chopped chives.

If you are using fresh tuna steaks, rub them with salt, pepper and olive oil. Sear them in a little olive oil on a very hot griddle pan. Once the tuna is cooked to your liking, cut it into bite-size chunks and mix with the lemon juice and olive oil in a separate bowl. You can use bottled Italian or Spanish tuna if you can't get fresh tuna.

Mix half the tuna through the salad and place it in a serving dish. Arrange the remaining tuna and the hard-boiled eggs on top of the salad. Garnish with the remaining chives.

SERVES 4

One of my favourite pasta memories is from a tour I did with some friends when I was eighteen.
We were at the Cathedral of St Francis of Assisi in Italy when we decided to have lunch.
We found a quaint little café and ordered pasta. It was served in the Italian buffet style where all the sauces are laid out in front of you but the waiter serves your pasta. You hold out your bowl and he starts serving and only stops once you take it away. It took us a moment to get that, so we all had a lot of pasta to eat. Not bad for teenagers on a budget.

pasta

napolitana sauce	106
pulled lamb pasta	111
spaghetti bolognaise	113
mascarpone & roast tomato penne	115
prawn & pea linguine	117
savva's seafood pasta	119
creamy chicken pesto	121
wild mushroom linguine	123
baked pasta	125

napolitana sauce

This classic sauce is so versatile and such an important staple in so many dishes. You can make it in bulk and freeze it for use in other recipes.

FOR 500 ml SAUCE
120 g butter
2 onions, chopped
2 pinches dried oregano
salt
2 kg tinned tomatoes, crushed
2 tsp white sugar

Melt 60 g of the butter and fry the onion, add the oregano and salt. Add the tomatoes and bring to the boil before adding the sugar. Stir well to dissolve the sugar. Add the rest of the butter and stir until it has melted. Turn down the heat and cook until reduced to half of the original quantity, for about 45 minutes.

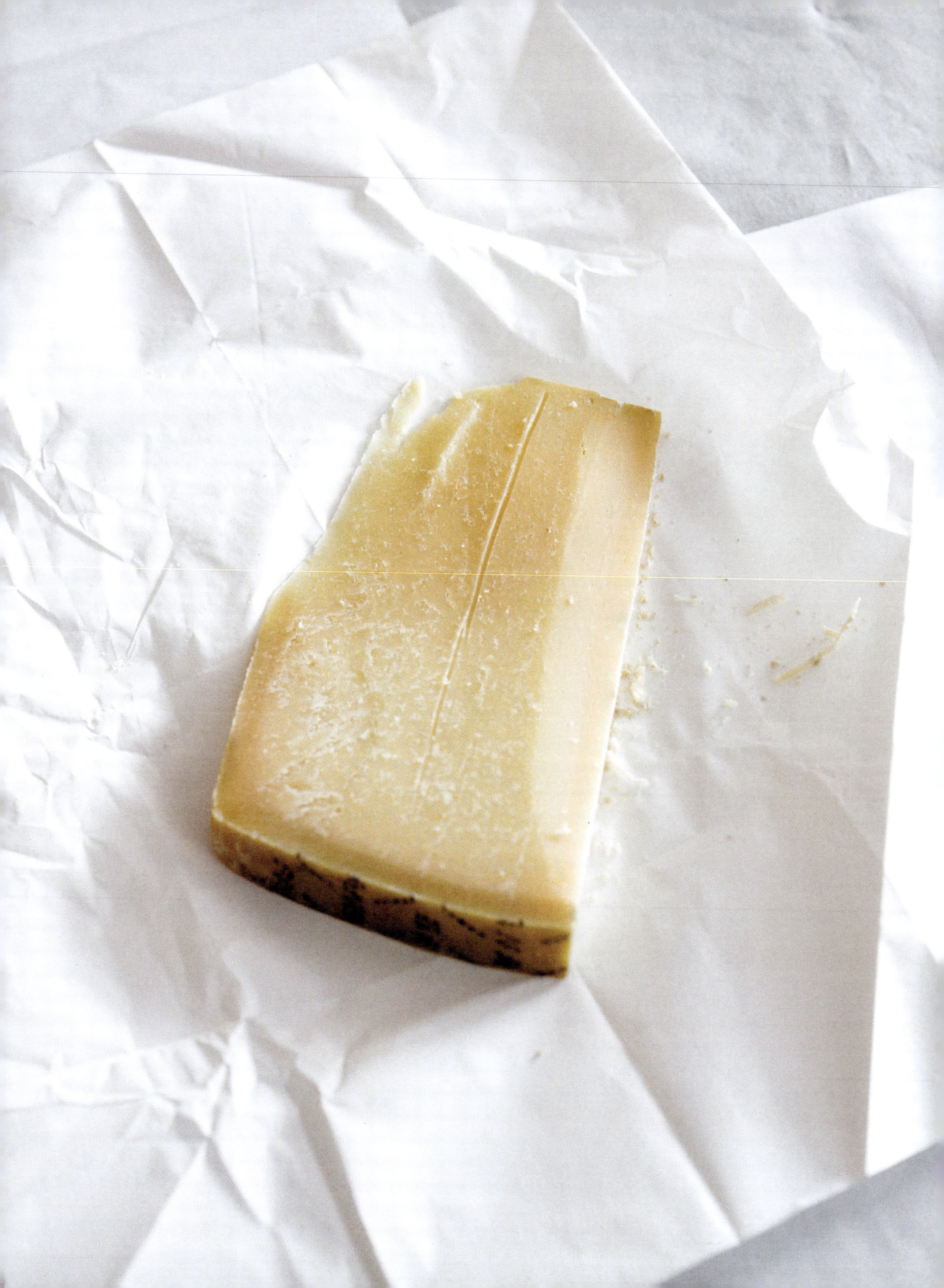

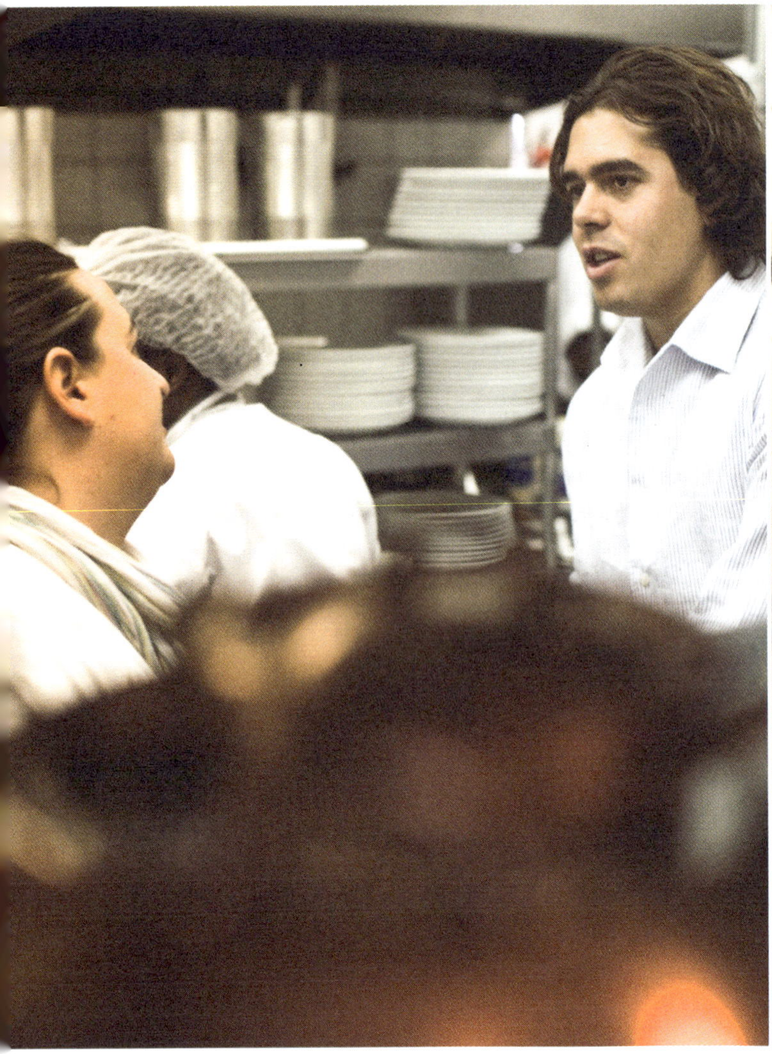
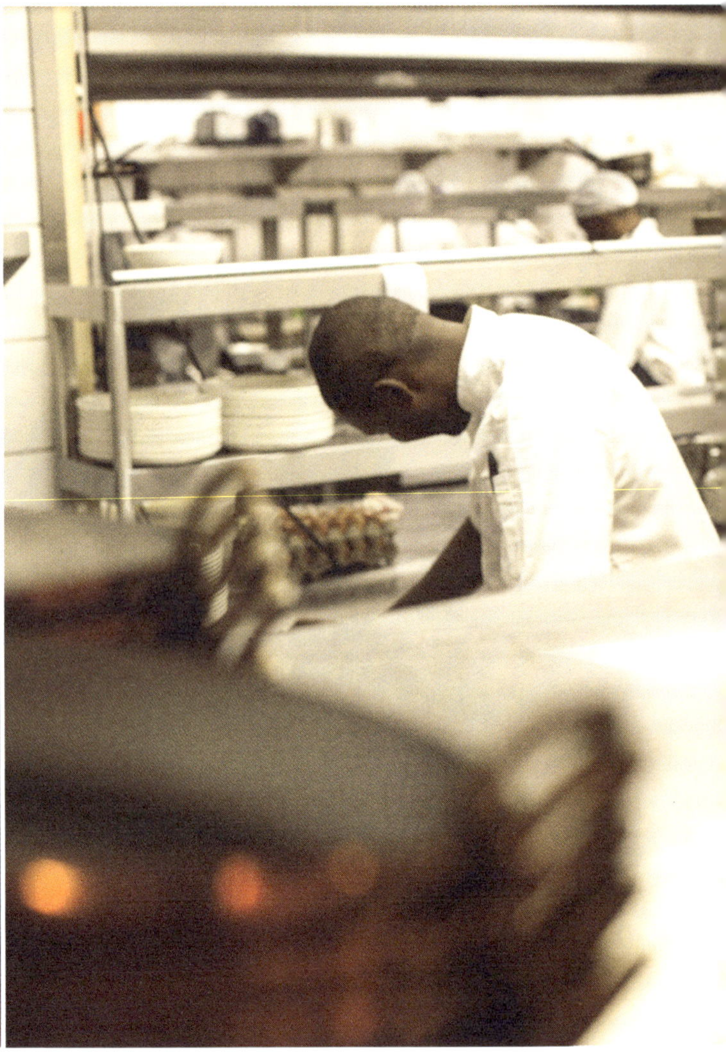

Soft Poach
Bacon
Single Egg
Soft Poach
White Bread
Med Poach
Normal Eggs
Bacon
NO Italian Sausage
NO Mushrooms
Royal Plain
Med Poach
Health Bread

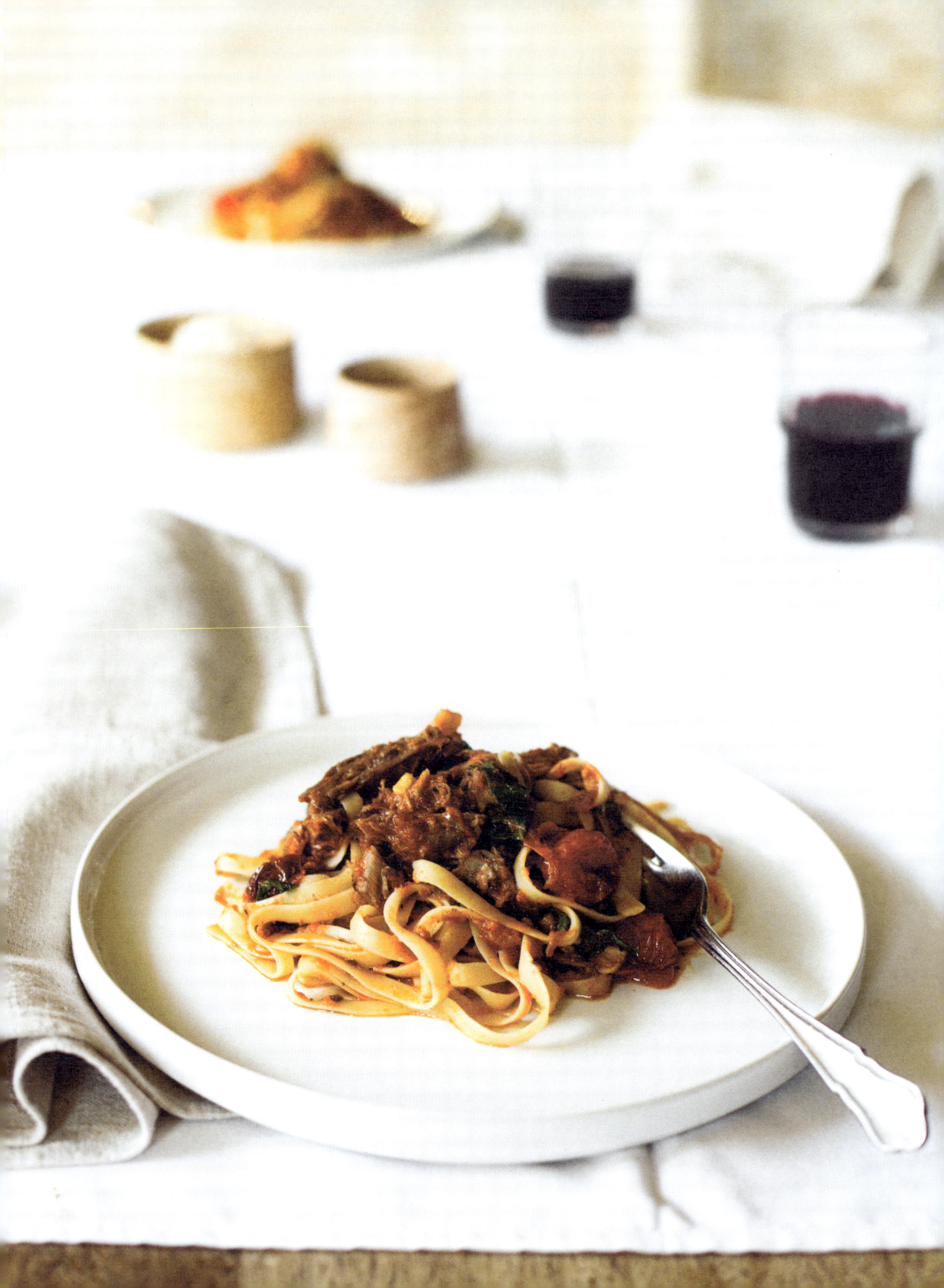

pulled lamb pasta

As pastas go, this one is fairly time-consuming because you have to roast the lamb first. You can save yourself the trouble if you have roast lamb leftovers. If you don't, it's well worth the extra effort of roasting the lamb from scratch.

roasted lamb (page 59)

OVEN-ROASTED TOMATOES
500 g cherry tomatoes
40 ml olive oil
salt and black pepper
1 sprig rosemary

SAUCE
1 red onion, sliced
10 ml olive oil
80 g butter
24 button mushrooms, quartered
160 g brinjal, cubed
2 tsp fresh chopped ginger
2 tsp cumin
2 tsp dried oregano
salt and pepper
30 ml lemon juice
250 ml Napolitana sauce (page 106)

500 g fettucine, cooked al dente
small handful fresh basil, chopped

Roast the lamb as per the recipe on page 59. Once it is cooked, pull the meat off the bone and stir it into the onions, garlic and meat juices in the roasting pan.

Place the tomatoes on a baking tray, drizzle with olive oil and sprinkle with salt and pepper. Scatter with rosemary and roast in the oven at 180 °C until wrinkled.

To make the sauce, sauté the sliced red onion in olive oil and butter. When the onion has softened, add the quartered mushrooms, brinjal cubes, ginger, cumin, oregano, salt and pepper. Add the roasted cherry tomatoes to this mixture, squashing the tomatoes to release the juice. Squeeze the lemon juice over the pan, add the pulled lamb, onions and garlic as well as the juices from the roasting pan. Stir in the the Napolitana sauce until it is heated through.

Serve the cooked pasta with a generous spoonful of the sauce and garnish with chopped basil.

SERVES 4

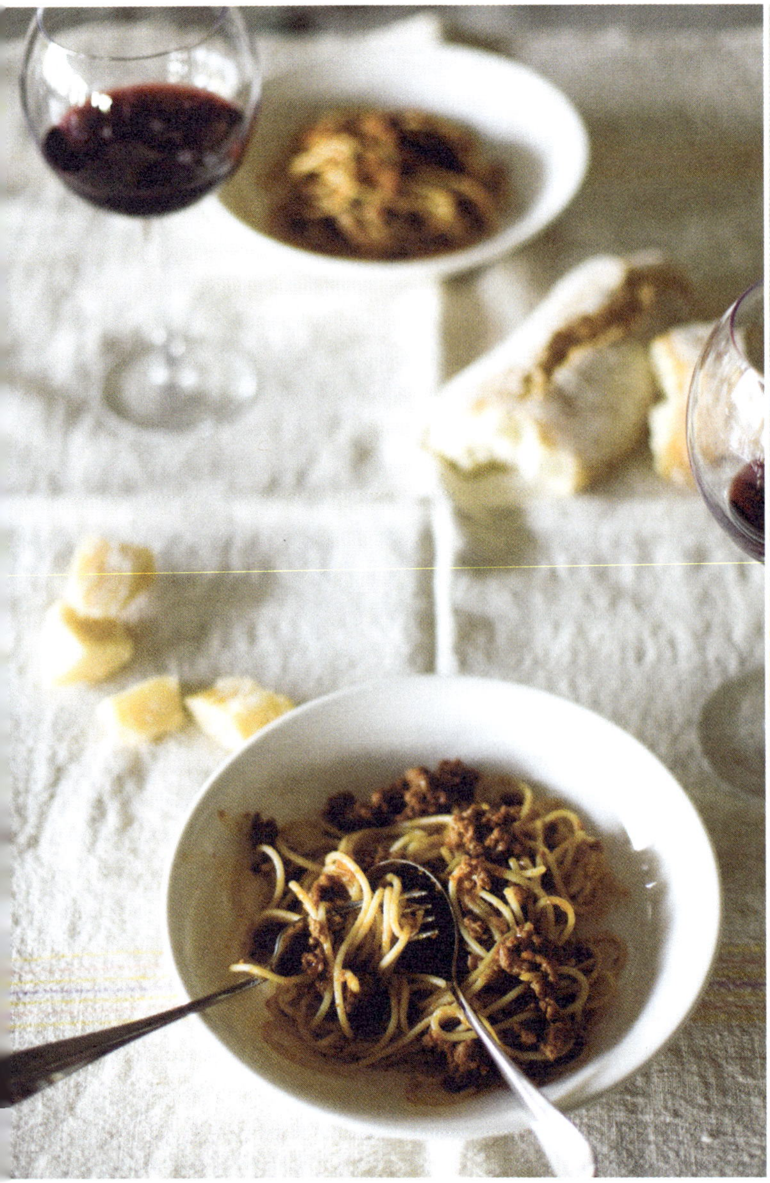
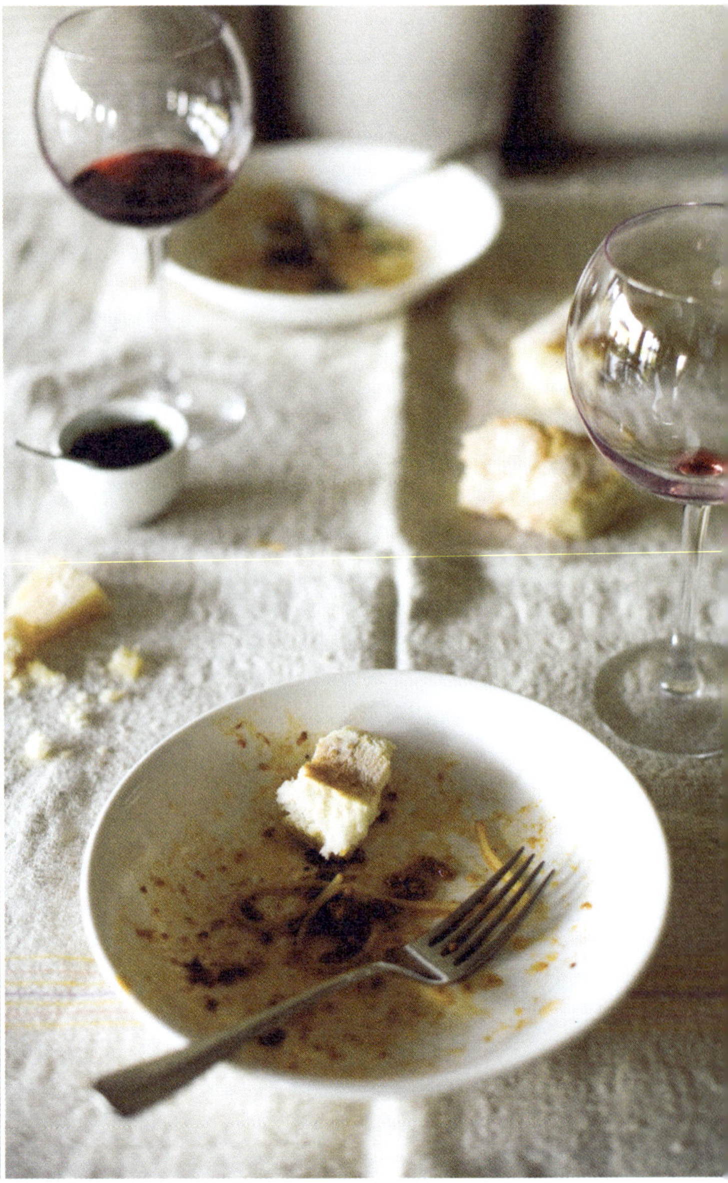

spaghetti bolognaise

Everyone says their mother makes the best spaghetti bolognaise, but really, my mother does. As a leftover enthusiast she often made it with pulled beef, but the mince has always been my favourite. Classic is an understatement when it comes to this pasta. Family dinner, dinner on your own, dinner for two or even breakfast, spaghetti bolognaise is the answer. We often had it before school and Savva still orders it when he is at a store for breakfast.

BOLOGNAISE
90 g onion, finely grated
2 tbsp olive oil
600 g mince
salt and pepper
80 g carrots, finely grated
60 g tomato paste
400 ml Napolitana sauce (page 106)

500 g spaghetti
30 g Parmesan cheese, grated

To make the bolognaise, sauté the onion in the olive oil until softened. Brown the mince in the saucepan with the onions and season with salt and pepper. Stir in the grated carrot and tomato paste. Lastly, add the Napolitana sauce and cook on medium heat for 15 minutes with the lid on.

Cook the pasta in plenty of boiling salted water until al dente. Drain and plate the pasta, top with bolognaise sauce and sprinkle with plenty of Parmesan cheese.

SERVES 4

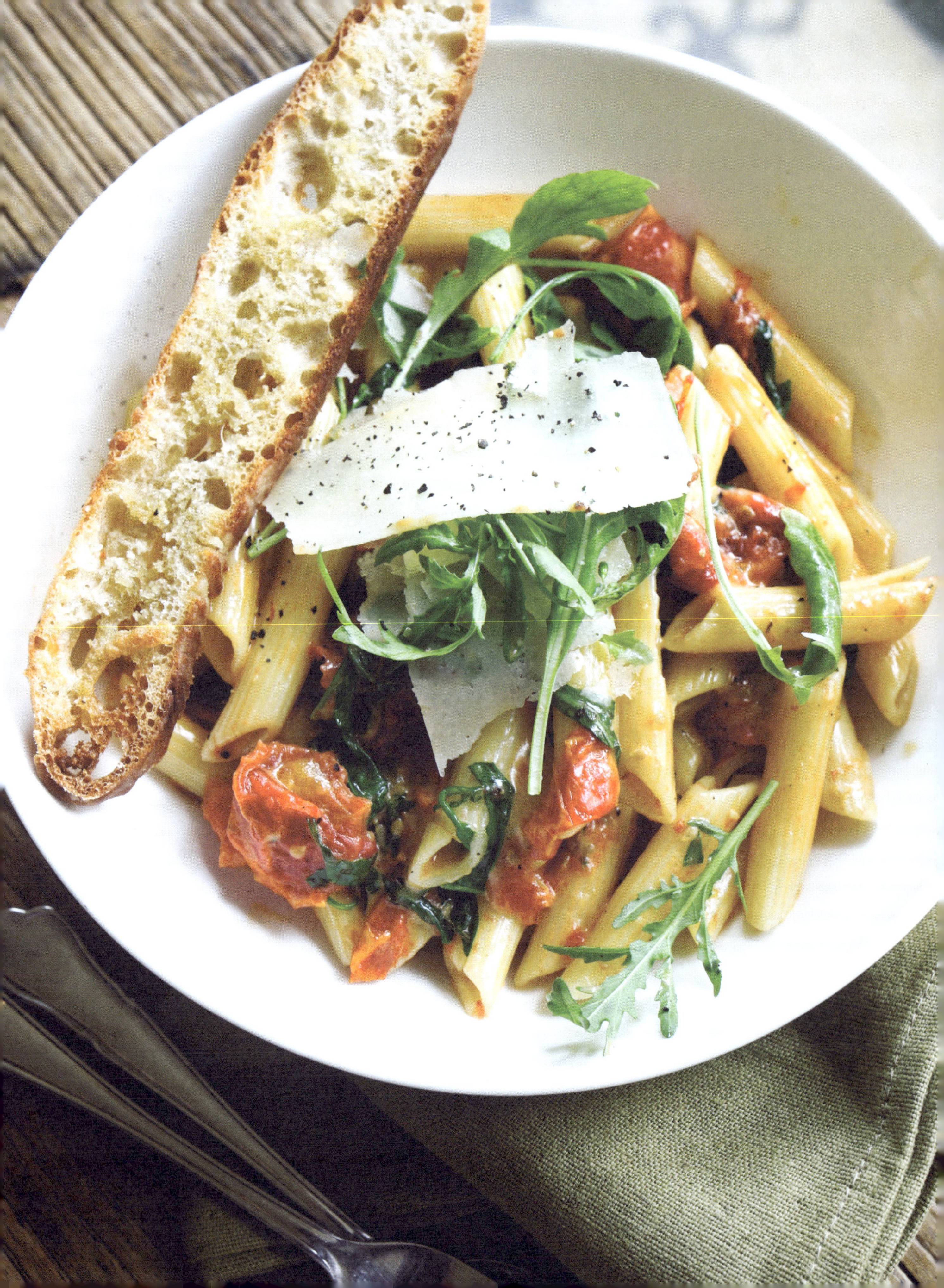

mascarpone & roast tomato penne

This is one of my favourite dishes. I love the combination of peppery rocket, salty Parmesan, creamy mascarpone and the smoky acidity of the roasted tomatoes, which cuts through the richness of it all. It is a bit decadent but somehow it's not heavy. It's the perfect pasta for a filling summer meal.

OVEN-ROASTED TOMATOES
1 kg cherry tomatoes
40 ml olive oil
salt and black
pinch rosemary

500 g pasta, uncooked
100 g butter
pinch fresh rosemary, chopped
320 g mascarpone cheese
salt and pepper
2 large handfuls rocket, chopped
40 g Parmesan shavings

Preheat the oven to 180 °C.

Place the tomatoes on a baking tray. Drizzle with olive oil, season with salt and pepper, scatter with rosemary and roast until wrinkled.

Cook the penne in a large pot of salted, boiling water until al dente.

While the pasta is cooking, melt the butter in a pan. Add the roasted cherry tomatoes and the remaining rosemary. Squash the tomatoes with the back of a spoon to release the juices. Add the mascarpone and allow it to melt slowly over a low heat. Then add one handful of the rocket and let it wilt. Season to taste.

Drain the cooked pasta and toss through the sauce.
Top with the remaining rocket and Parmesan shavings.

SERVES 4

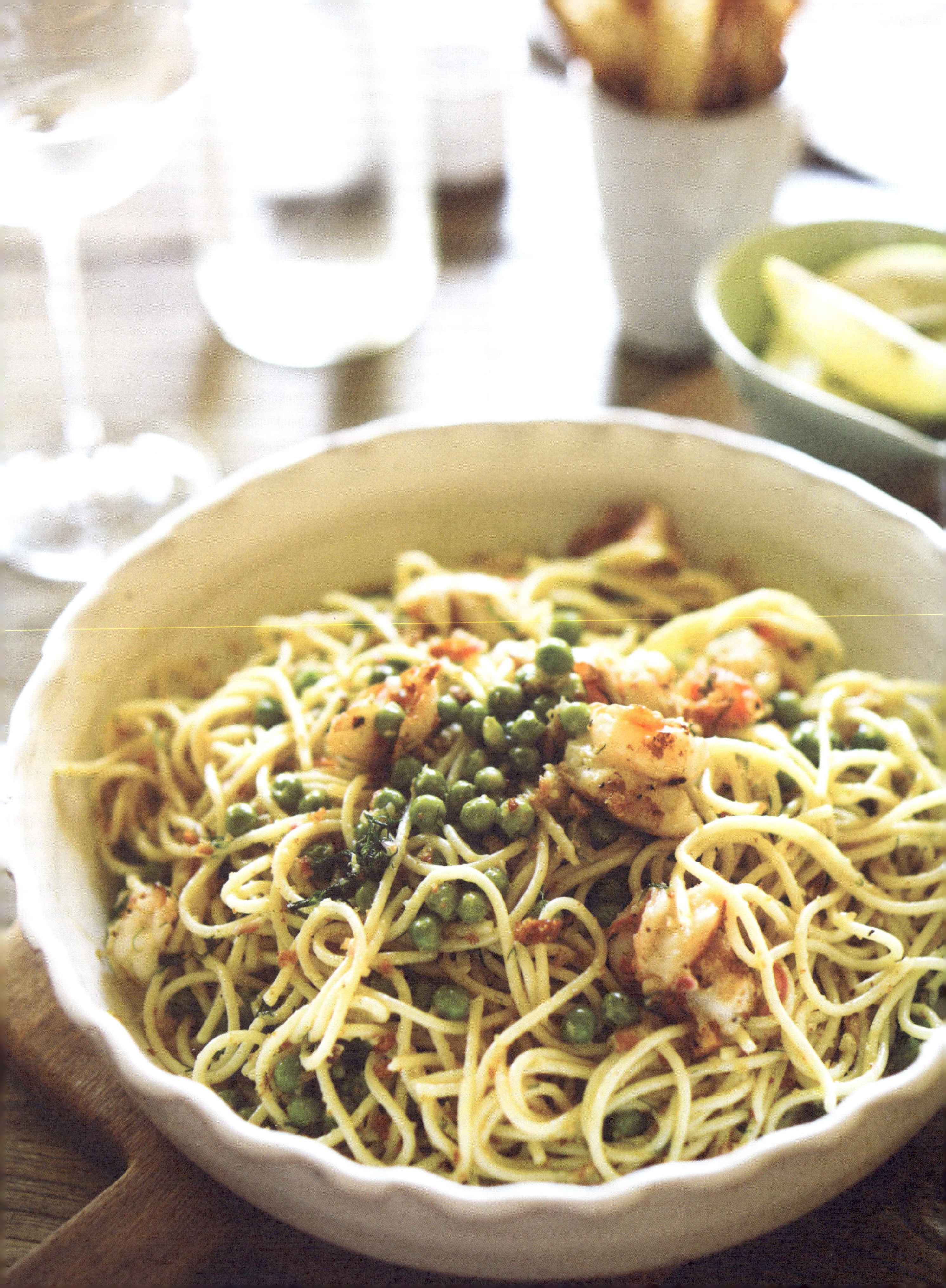

prawn & pea linguine

When we opened tashas Umhlanga one of our customers requested a light seafood pasta. As a rule, we try to accommodate our customers' needs as long as we have the ingredients in the kitchen. This is what I came up with. The ciabatta crumbs add a surprising crunch and if you have never had crispy crumb pasta I highly recommend that you try it.

4 slices ciabatta, dried and grated
400 g frozen peas
500 g pasta

SAUCE
21–25 prawns, shelled and deveined
salt and pepper
40 g butter
20 ml olive oil
1 red onion, sliced
5 ml chilli flakes
5 ml fish spice
juice of 1 lemon
300 g mascarpone cheese
handful dill, chopped

Preheat the oven to 200 °C.

Toast the ciabatta slices in the oven. When they are very dry and crispy, grate or crush them into fine crumbs.

Defrost the frozen peas.

Cook the pasta in a large pot of boiling, salted water, and start making the sauce.

To make the sauce, season the cleaned and shelled prawns with salt and pepper. Melt the butter in the pan with the olive oil and sauté the onions until soft and translucent. Add the prawns, chilli flakes, fish spice and pan-fry. You'll know they're cooked when they start to become opaque. Squeeze in the lemon juice and stir in the mascarpone. Bring the sauce to the boil and mix in the peas for just a few minutes. Don't overcook or the peas will lose their colour and begin to wrinkle.

Add the dill just before serving. Spoon the sauce over the cooked and drained pasta, sprinkle with the ciabatta crumbs and serve.

SERVES 4

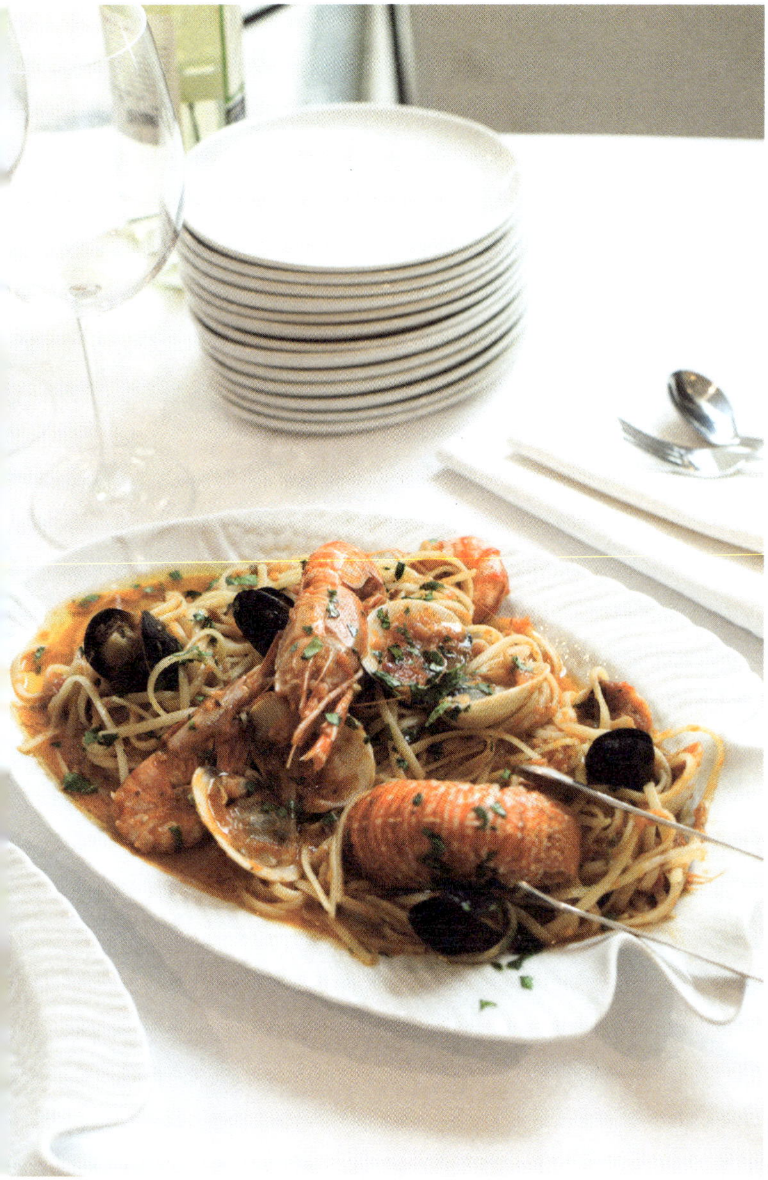

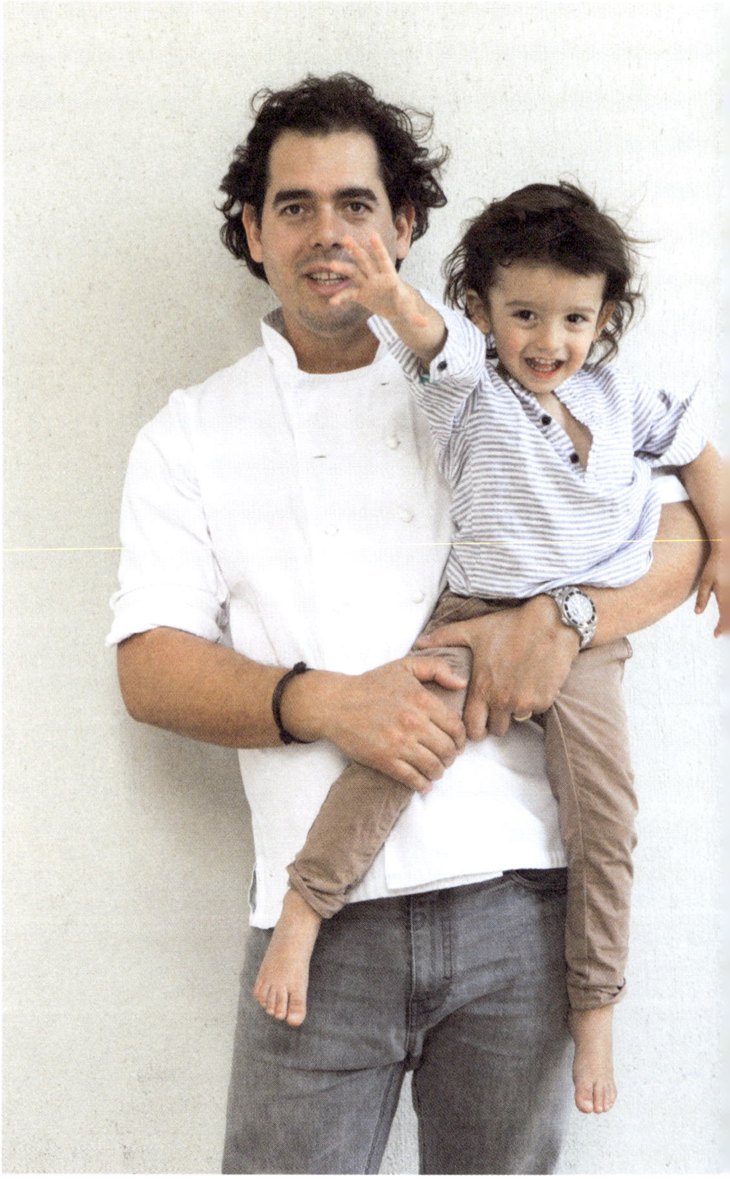

savva's seafood pasta

Every father leaves a legacy. Some fathers leave behind stamp collections, some leave behind vintage cars; some might even leave an old watch. In my family, fathers leave recipes. My great-grandfather was a fisherman, my grandfather was a baker and my father was a chef, but it was my brother, an interior designer, who perfected the recipe for our seafood pasta. We serve it at Le Parc with a bib, because it's a dig-in-and-get-dirty kind of dish.

OVEN-ROASTED TOMATOES
250 g cherry tomatoes
40 ml olive oil
salt and pepper
1 sprig rosemary

SEAFOOD SAUCE
40 ml olive oil
50 g butter
1 medium red onion, finely chopped
4 small garlic cloves, finely chopped
8 ripe tomatoes, grated
salt and pepper
400 ml Napolitana sauce (page 106)
24 black tiger prawns, butterflied and cleaned
4 langoustines
12 mussels, cleaned
16 clams, cleaned
250 ml white wine
large handful flat leaf parsley, chopped
500 g linguine, uncooked
60 g butter to burn
olive oil

Preheat the oven to 200 °C.

Roast the cherry tomatoes on a baking tray, drizzled with the olive oil and seasoned with salt, pepper and sprinkled with rosemary. Roast until the tomato skins are wrinkled.

Heat the olive oil and butter in a large pan and sauté the onion until golden brown. Add the roasted tomatoes, discarding the rosemary, and squash them gently to release the juices. Add the garlic and cook for 2-3 minutes. Stir in the freshly grated tomato and simmer for 5 minutes with the lid off. Taste and season with salt and pepper. Add the Napolitana sauce and bring to a boil. Carefully add the seafood, wine and half the chopped parsley. Make sure that the seafood is covered by the tomato sauce. Stir it gently and as little as possible or the seafood will disintegrate. Cover with a lid and cook on high heat for 5 minutes. Remove the lid, reduce the heat to medium and allow to simmer for another 20 minutes. The sauce should not be too thick or too runny. You will know it is ready when the mussels and clams open up. Meanwhile, cook the pasta in a large pot of boiling salted water until al dente.

In a separate pan, burn 60 g butter. The butter must melt at a high heat in the pan until it bubbles and turns golden. Drain the pasta, place it in a large bowl and pour the burnt butter over it. Then spoon the seafood sauce over the pasta. Garnish with the remaining parsley and a generous glug of olive oil.

SERVES 4

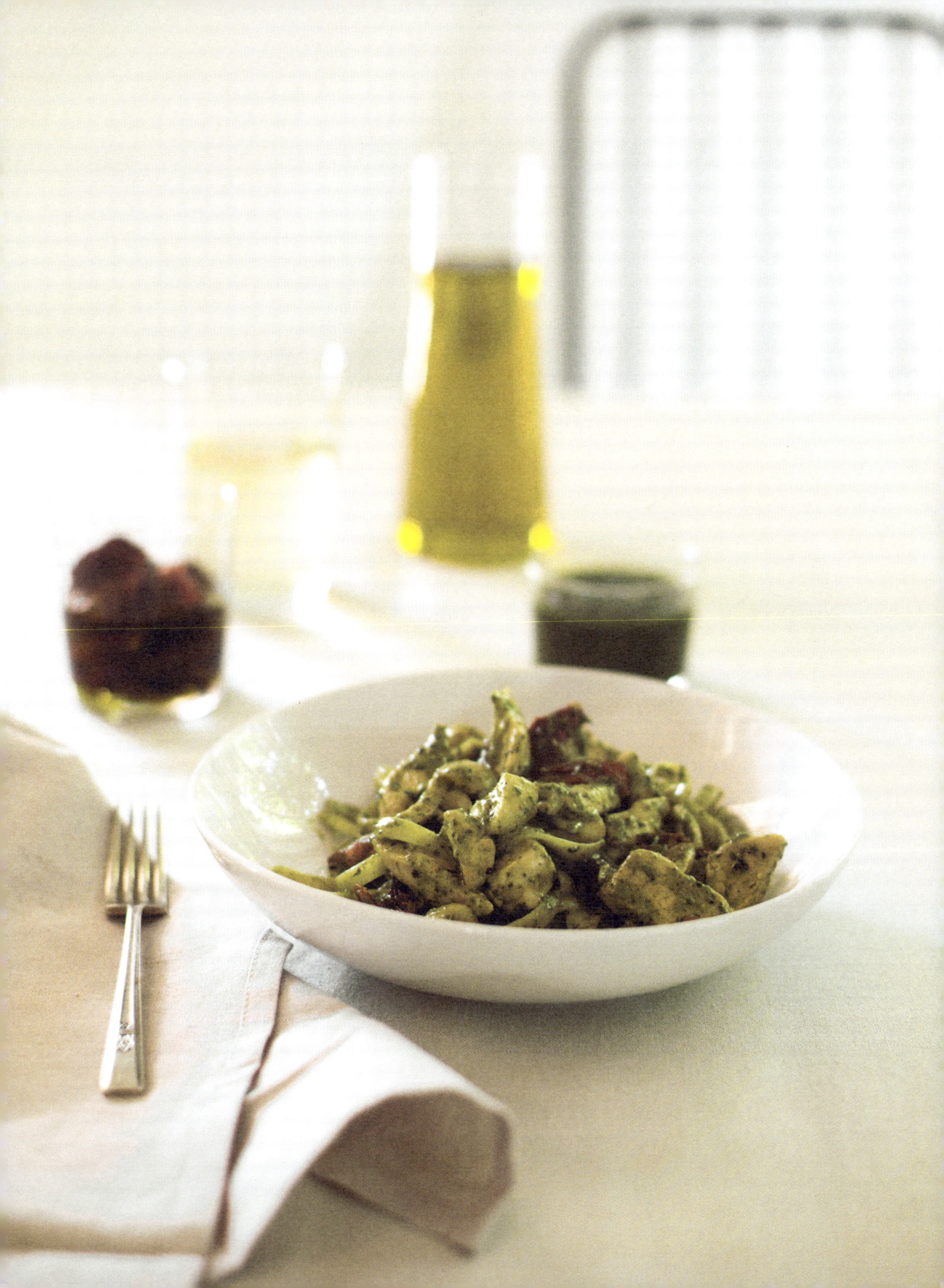

creamy chicken pesto

Pesto is one of my favourite sauces but, for many people, it's an acquired taste. The combination of chicken, cream and sundried tomatoes makes this a silky, rich and delicious pasta with only a hint of pesto running through it.

PESTO
15 g pine nuts, roasted
20 g Parmesan, grated
120 ml olive oil
60 g fresh basil
pinch salt and pepper
1 clove garlic

800 g chicken breasts
200 g butter
500 g fettucine
24 white button mushrooms, halved
250 ml white wine
500 ml cream
16 sundried tomatoes, halved
salt and pepper

handful basil leaves, chopped

To make the pesto, blend all the ingredients together in a blender. The pesto should not be too smooth but should have some texture.

Cut the chicken breasts into chunks. Melt half the butter in a pan and sauté the chicken until golden brown. While you are doing this, start to cook the pasta in plenty of salted, boiling water.

Remove the chicken from the pan, add the remaining butter and the mushrooms, keeping the chicken juices for flavour.
When the mushrooms are almost cooked through, add the wine and let it reduce for a few minutes. Add the cream and the sundried tomatoes. Slowly bring the cream to the boil, add the pesto, season to taste and stir well.

Add the chicken and the drained pasta to the creamy pesto sauce and serve.

Garnish with fresh, torn basil leaves.

SERVES 4

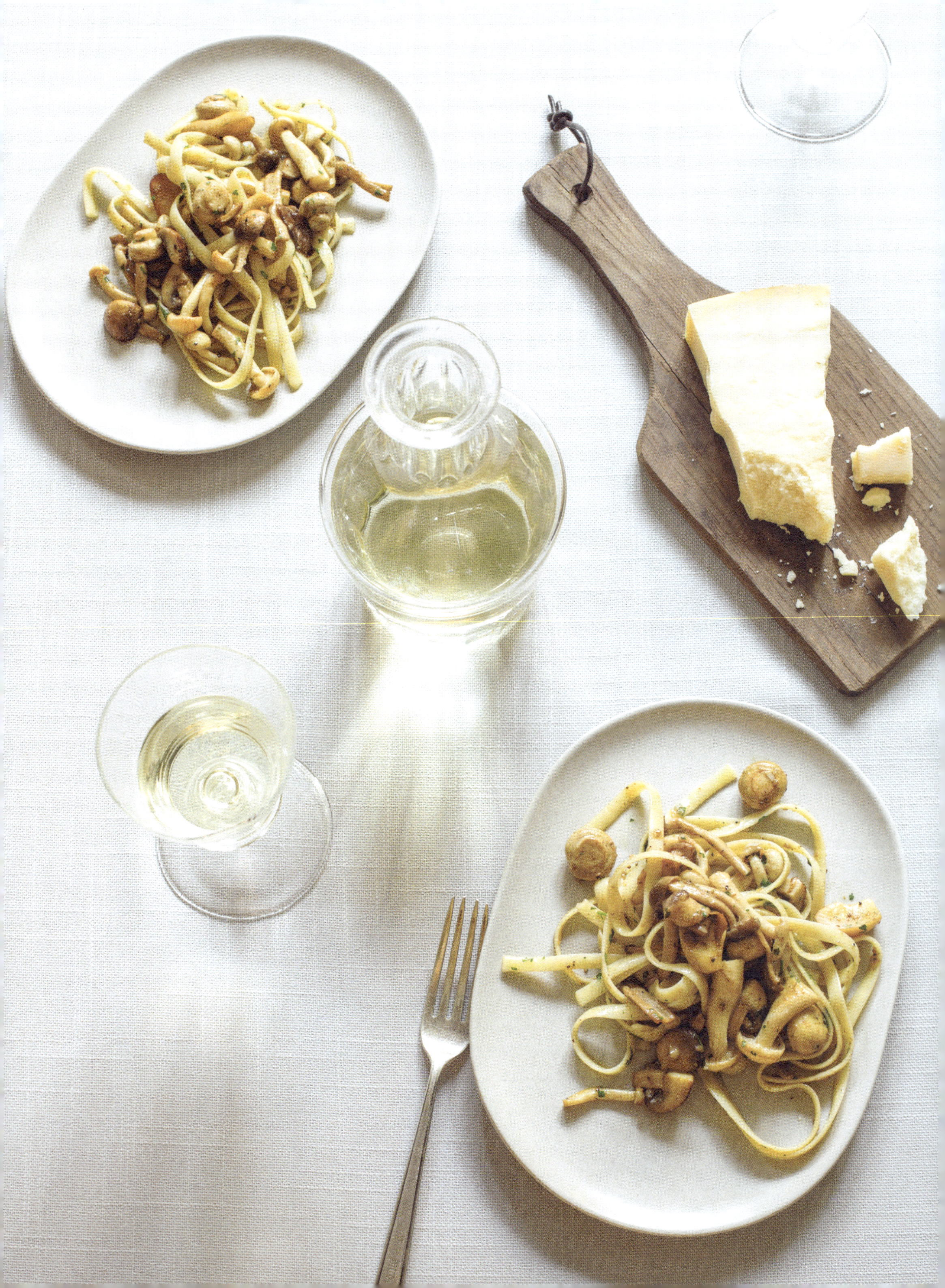

wild mushroom linguine

Find a variety of mushrooms to use in this dish. Delicate oyster mushrooms are often available at Chinese supermarkets and some green grocers. Try firm, brown chestnut mushrooms or tender white enoki mushrooms from Japan. Enoki are particularly pretty and take no time at all to cook, so leave them whole and add a splash of cream to make a richer sauce.

SAUCE
400 g wild mushrooms, sliced
200 g white button mushrooms
200 g black mushrooms
olive oil
60 g butter
2 cloves garlic, thinly sliced
2 sprigs fresh thyme
1 tsp dried oregano
salt and pepper
zest of 1 lemon
juice of half a lemon
1 tsp vegetable stock powder

500 g linguine
120 g Parmesan shavings
a little stock
OR 100 ml cream (optional)
handful of flat leaf parsley, chopped

Fry the mushrooms in olive oil and butter until golden brown. Add the garlic, thyme and oregano, season with salt and pepper. Stir in the lemon zest, lemon juice and vegetable stock powder.

Cook the pasta until al dente, toss with the sauce and half the Parmesan shavings.

Add a little stock to prevent the sauce from becoming too dry or if you would like a creamier version, add the cream now.

Serve in one big bowl or four separate bowls. Garnish with the remaining Parmesan shavings and chopped parsley.

SERVES 4

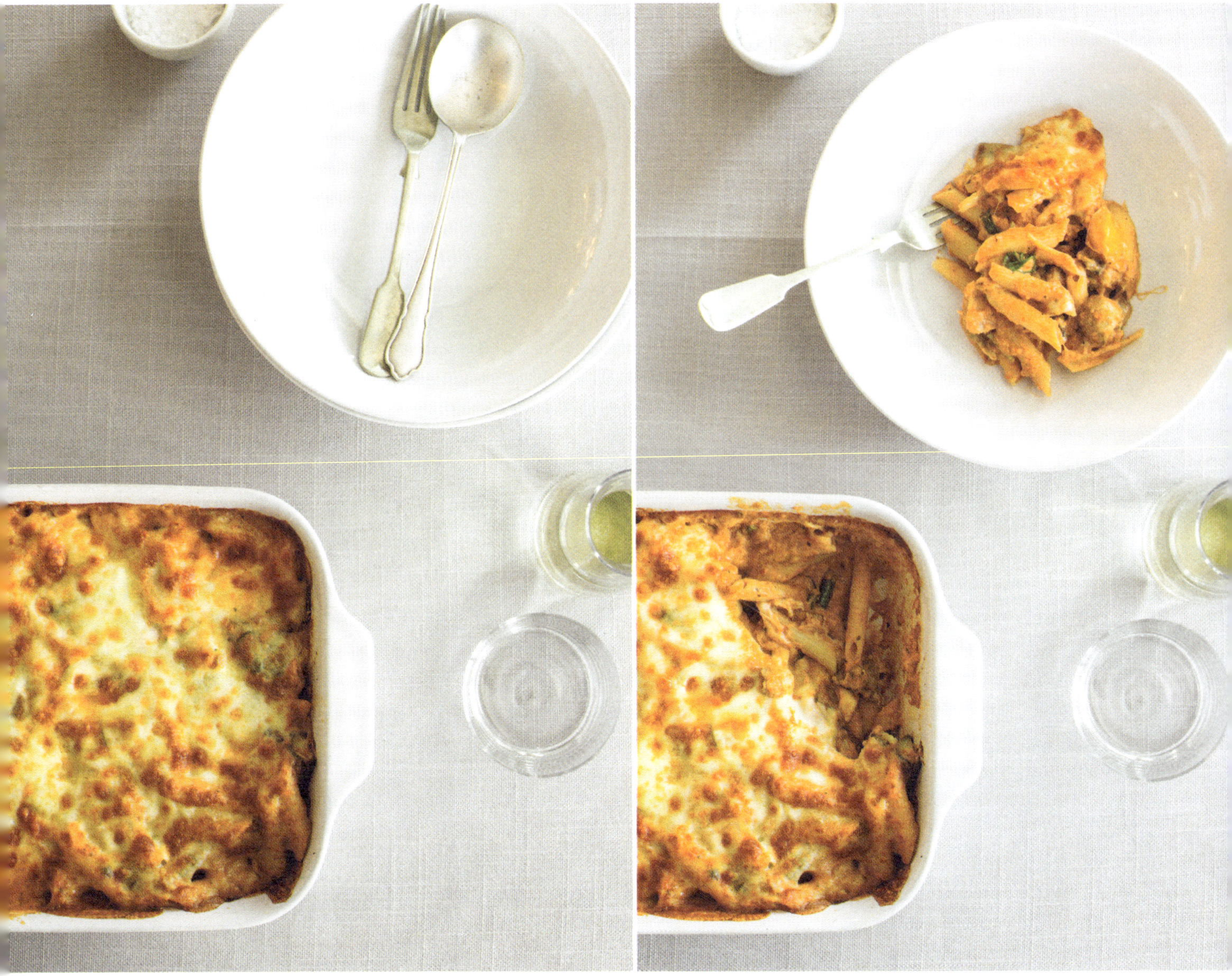

baked pasta

This pasta bake is my mother's recipe. What makes it special is its luxurious creaminess and the fact that it's so versatile. It works with most leftovers you may have in your fridge – roasted vegetables, bolognaise sauce, chicken, spinach – as long as you don't skimp on the cream or the cheese. It's great both as a meat or a meat-free meal and served with crusty bread and a fresh salad.

BOLOGNAISE SAUCE
90 g onion, finely grated
30 ml olive oil
600 g mince
salt and pepper
80 g carrots, finely grated
60 g tomato paste
500 ml Napolitana sauce (page 106)

500 g penne
16 rashers back bacon
250 ml cream
120 g Parmesan, finely grated
20 slices mozzarella

Preheat the oven to 200 °C.

To make the bolognaise, sauté the onion in olive oil in a large pan. When they are translucent, add the mince and brown it. Season with salt and pepper. Stir in the carrots and tomato paste, then add the Napolitana sauce. Cover and cook on medium heat for 15 minutes.

Bring a pot of salted water to boil. Add the pasta and cook until al dente. While the pasta is cooking, chop and fry the bacon. Add the bacon and cream to the bolognaise and stir through. Drain the penne and add it to the sauce with half of the Parmesan. Pour into an ovenproof dish and sprinkle with the remaining grated Parmesan. Finish with sliced mozzarella.

Bake at 200 °C for 15–20 minutes until the cheese has melted.

SERVES 4

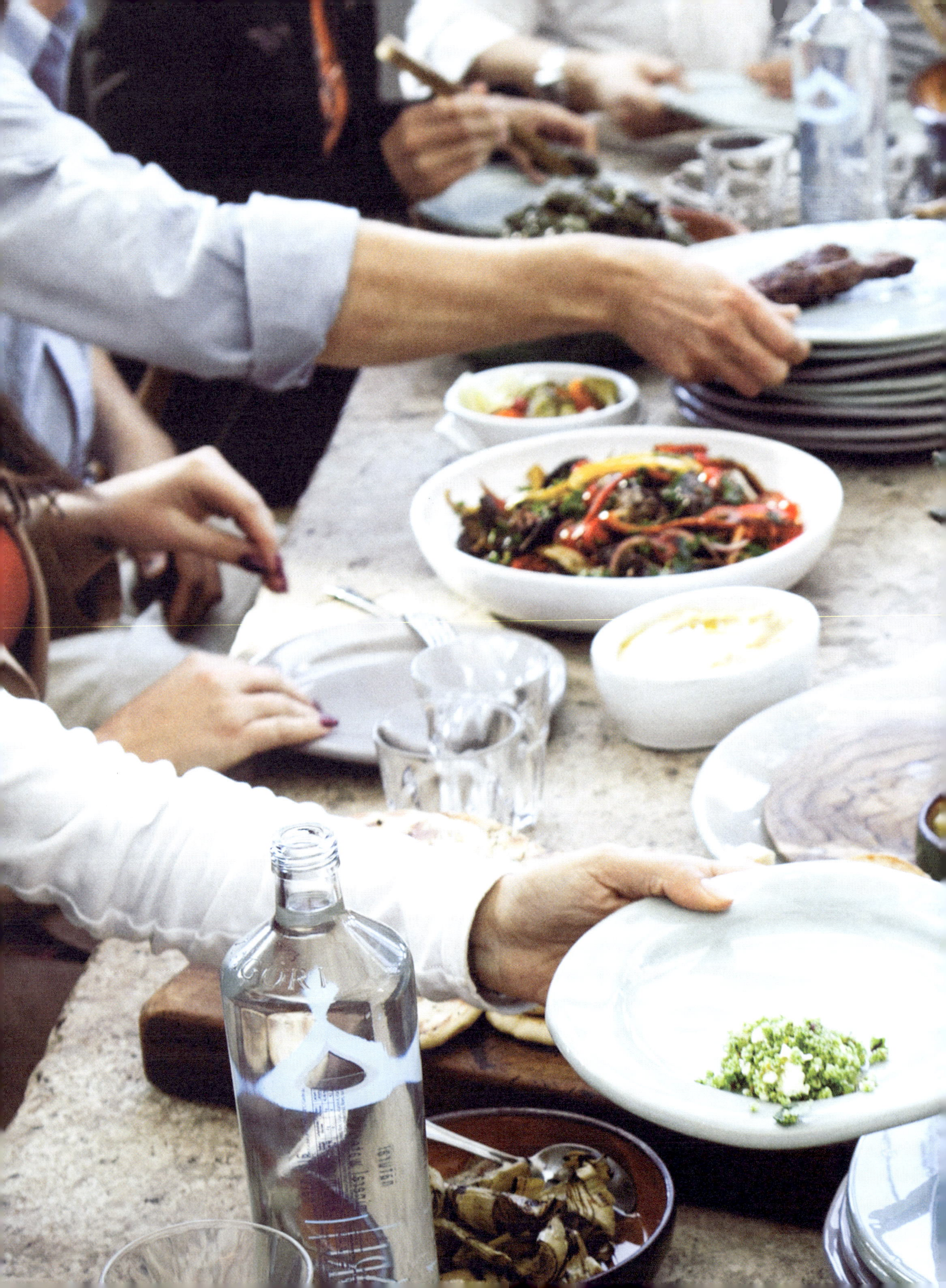

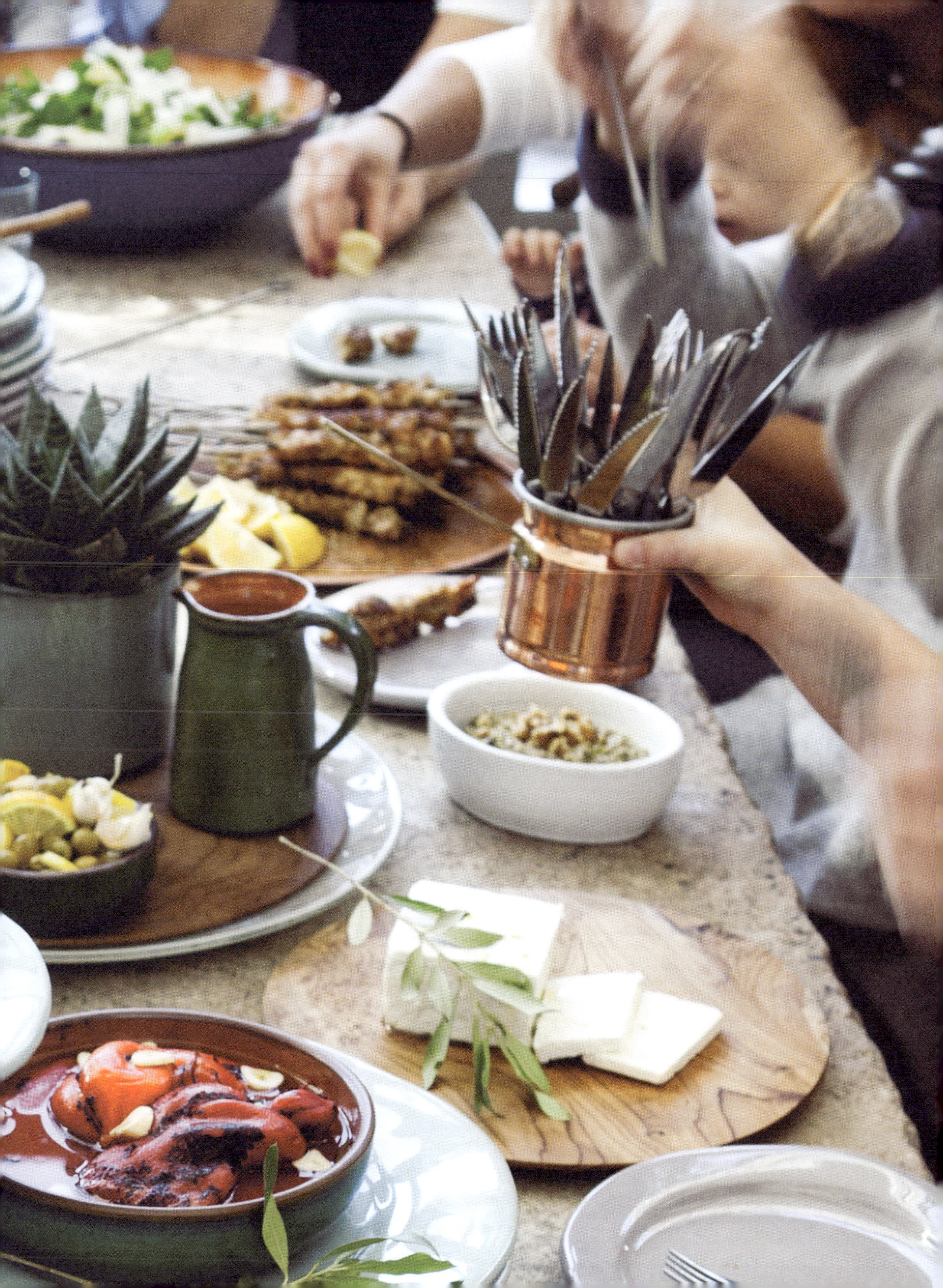

The best way to explain easy eating is to describe a little café I know in Mykonos.
It clings to a hillside overlooking the sea, completely hidden from the road. The only way to find it is to follow the smoke curling up from the chimney. The restaurant is built around a tree, it is white-washed and thatched, as it should be, and has no electricity. The owner grills lamb chops and squid and his wife makes the salads. The tomatoes are the freshest, the chops are the best and if they don't get good tomatoes they don't serve tomatoes. They do as little as possible to the ingredients. The tomatoes are drizzled with olive oil and sprinkled with oregano and salt at most. That's it. The ingredients are the heroes.

easy eats

salmon fish cakes	133
fish goujons	135
beer batter fish & chips	137
linefish with sauce vierge	139
a box of prawns	141
parmesan chicken couscous	143
easy tart	145
minestrone	147
chicken pot pie	149
greek lamb cutlets	151
steak tagliata	153
sticky apricot ribs	155
steak tartare	159

tashas
morningside

tashas

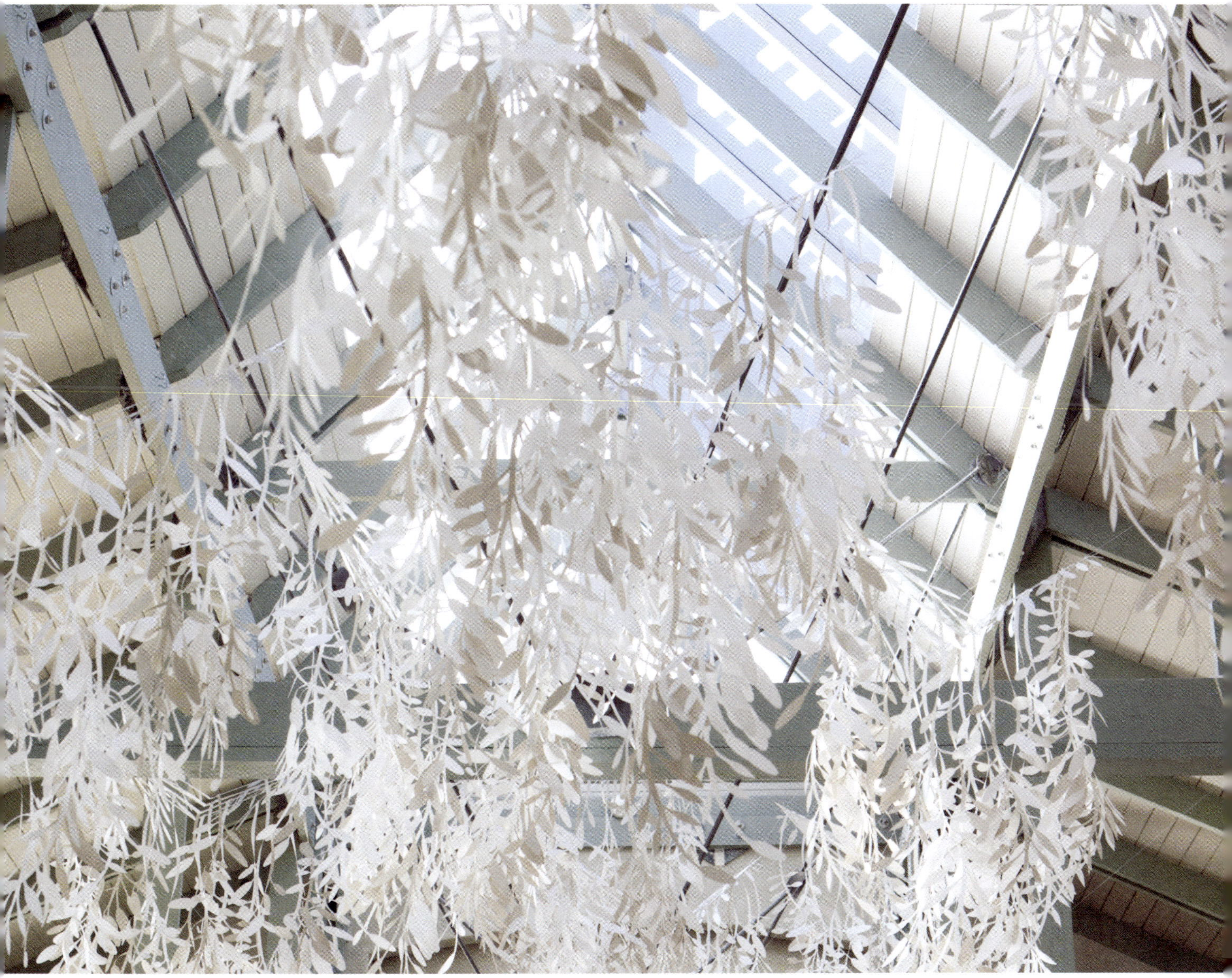

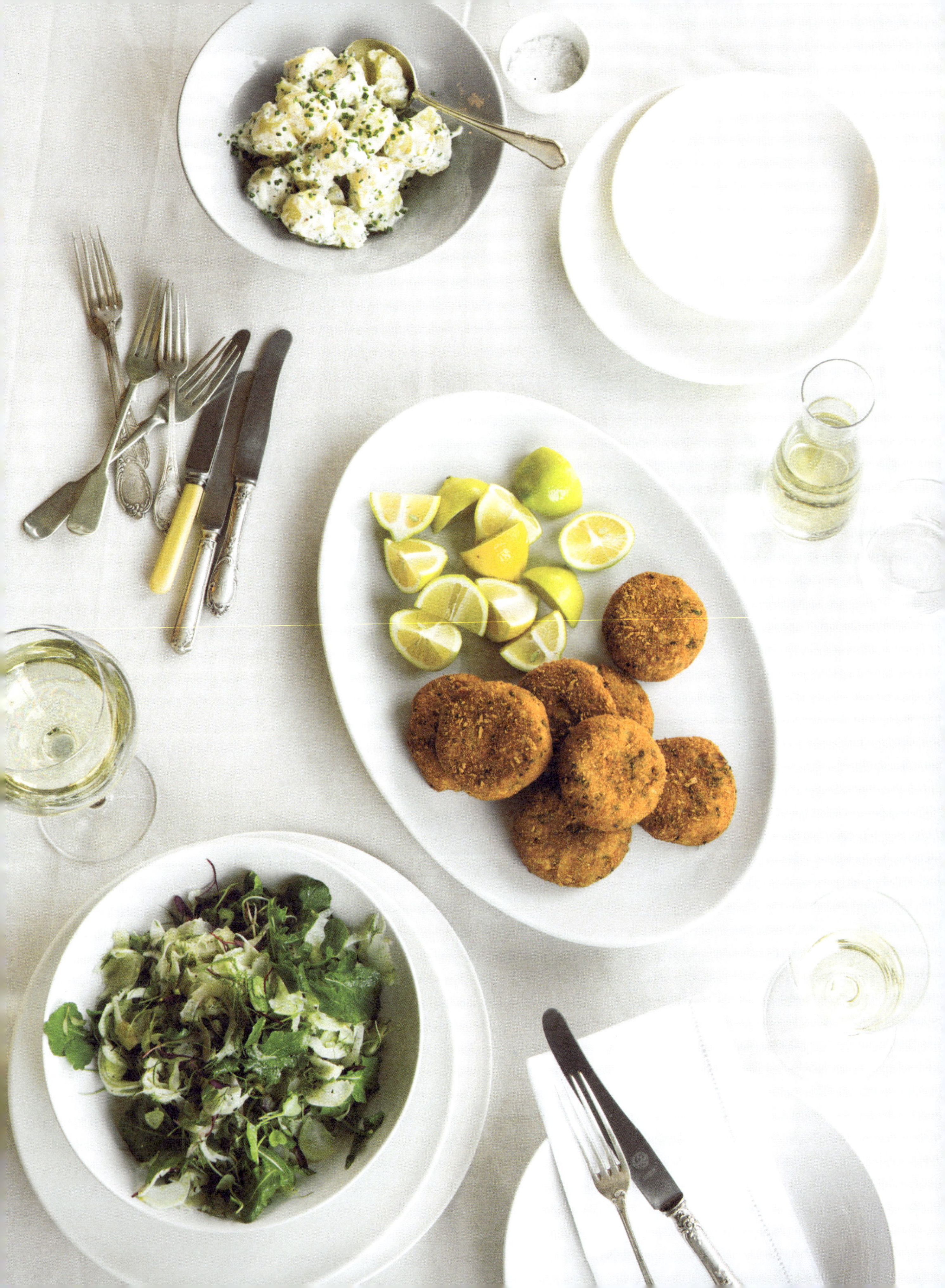

salmon fish cakes

These fish cakes are an iconic tashas menu item. They're so popular that people have been begging for the recipe since we first opened. This was the one recipe we knew for certain we had to include in the book. We use tinned salmon instead of tuna and more fish than potato for our fish cakes. They are lovely served plated or as part of a summer salad buffet.

FISH CAKES
250 g baby potatoes
5 small tins salmon
5 eggs
60 ml lemon juice
15 ml lemon zest
300 ml mayonnaise
1 small red onion, chopped
small handful dill, chopped
small bunch chives, chopped
salt and pepper
150 g breadcrumbs
oil for deep-frying

POTATO SALAD
24 baby potatoes
60 g mayonnaise
120 ml yoghurt
20 ml red wine vinegar
pinch chives, chopped
salt and pepper
olive oil

ROCKET, FENNEL & HERB SALAD
handful rocket
1 fennel bulb, finely sliced
handful micro greens
lemon juice
olive oil
salt and pepper
1 lemon, cut in wedges

Start with the fish cakes. Cook the baby potatoes in boiling, salted water. When they are done, peel them and roughly chop into small pieces. Don't mash them or you'll end up with a mushy fish cake. Drain the tinned salmon and remove the skin and bones. Mix the potatoes and salmon with the remaining fish cake ingredients (except the breadcrumbs) in a mixing bowl. Roll into 6 cm balls. Flatten them a bit and cover lightly with breadcrumbs. Deep-fry the fish cakes until they are golden brown.

To make the potato salad, cook the potatoes in boiling, salted water. When they are cooked, peel and cut them in half. Mix the mayonnaise, yoghurt, red wine vinegar, chives, salt and pepper and a drizzle of olive oil, and dress the potatoes. Garnish with a sprinkle of chives.

Mix together the rocket, finely sliced fennel and micro greens. Dress with a squeeze of lemon and olive oil, season with salt and pepper. Serve on the side of the fish cakes with a few lemon wedges.

SERVES 4

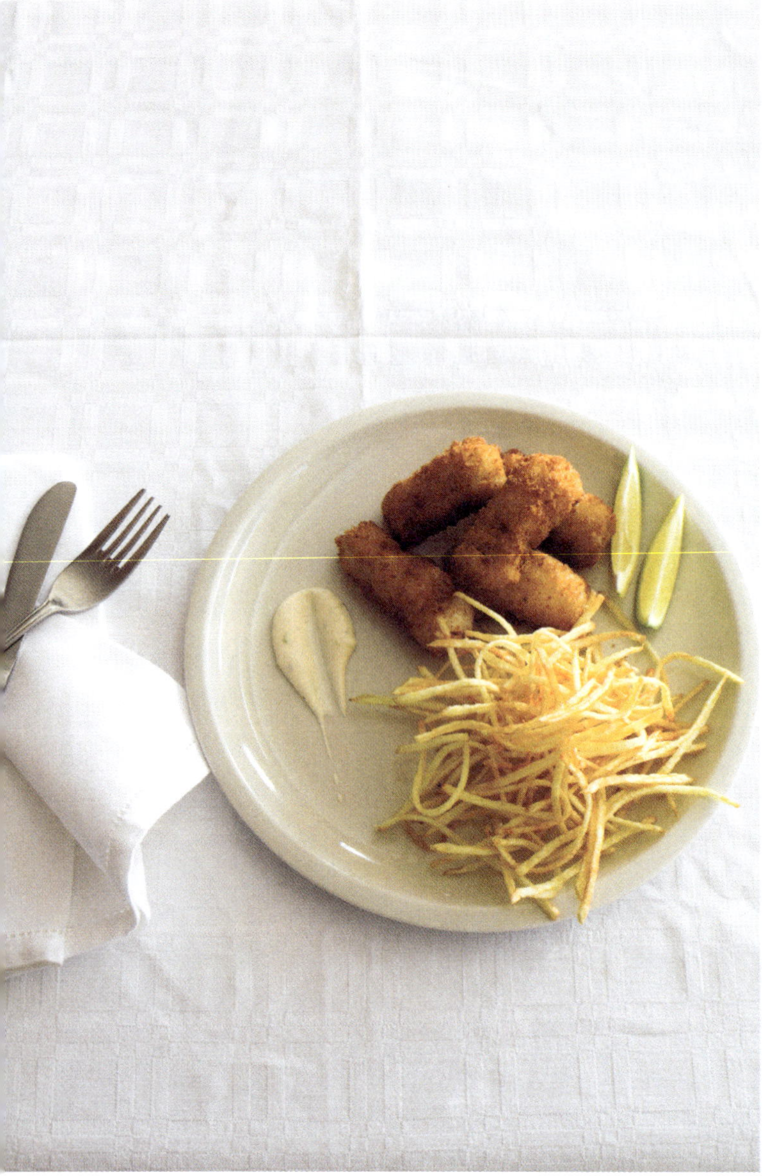

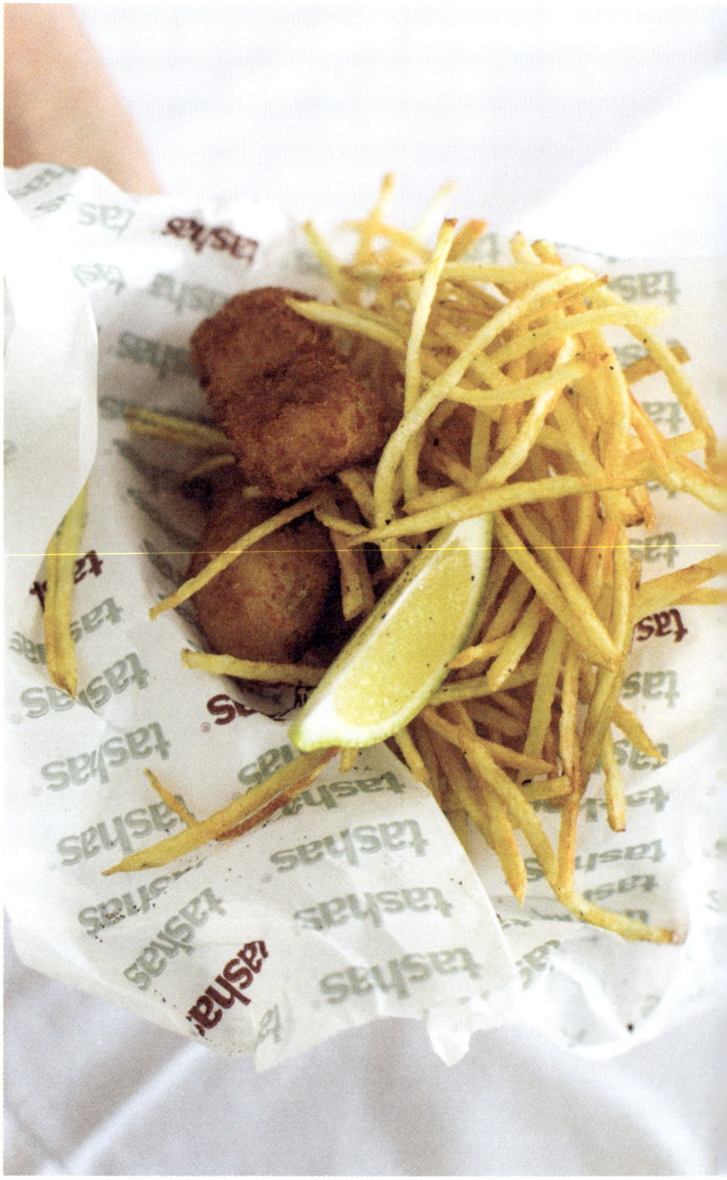
tashas

fish goujons

Fish fingers are not exactly the epitome of culinary sophistication but call them goujons and suddenly everyone's impressed. You can find Japanese panko breadcrumbs at Chinese supermarkets. Panko breadcrumbs are very flaky and make a lovely, light batter.

300 g flour
600 ml soda water
salt and pepper
4 x 180 g hake fillets, cut into strips
400 g panko breadcrumbs
oil for deep-frying

SAUCE
120 g French-style mayonnaise
juice of 2 lemons
zest of 1 lemon
salt and pepper

4 medium potatoes
oil for deep-frying

4 lemon wedges

To make the batter, whisk together the flour and soda water and season with salt and pepper. Dip the fish into the batter and then coat with the panko crumbs. the best way to do this is to spread the breadcrumbs over a large plate and then turn the battered fish in them. Deep-fry the fish until golden brown and crispy.

To make the sauce, combine the mayonnaise, lemon juice, lemon zest and season with salt and pepper. Pour into a small bowl and set aside.

Serve the goujons with matchstick fries and lemon wedges. You can make the fries using a mandolin slicer. Fry like regular chips in very hot oil.

These goujons make an elegant dinner served on a plate with an accompanying salad, or a great informal meal served in paper.

SERVES 4

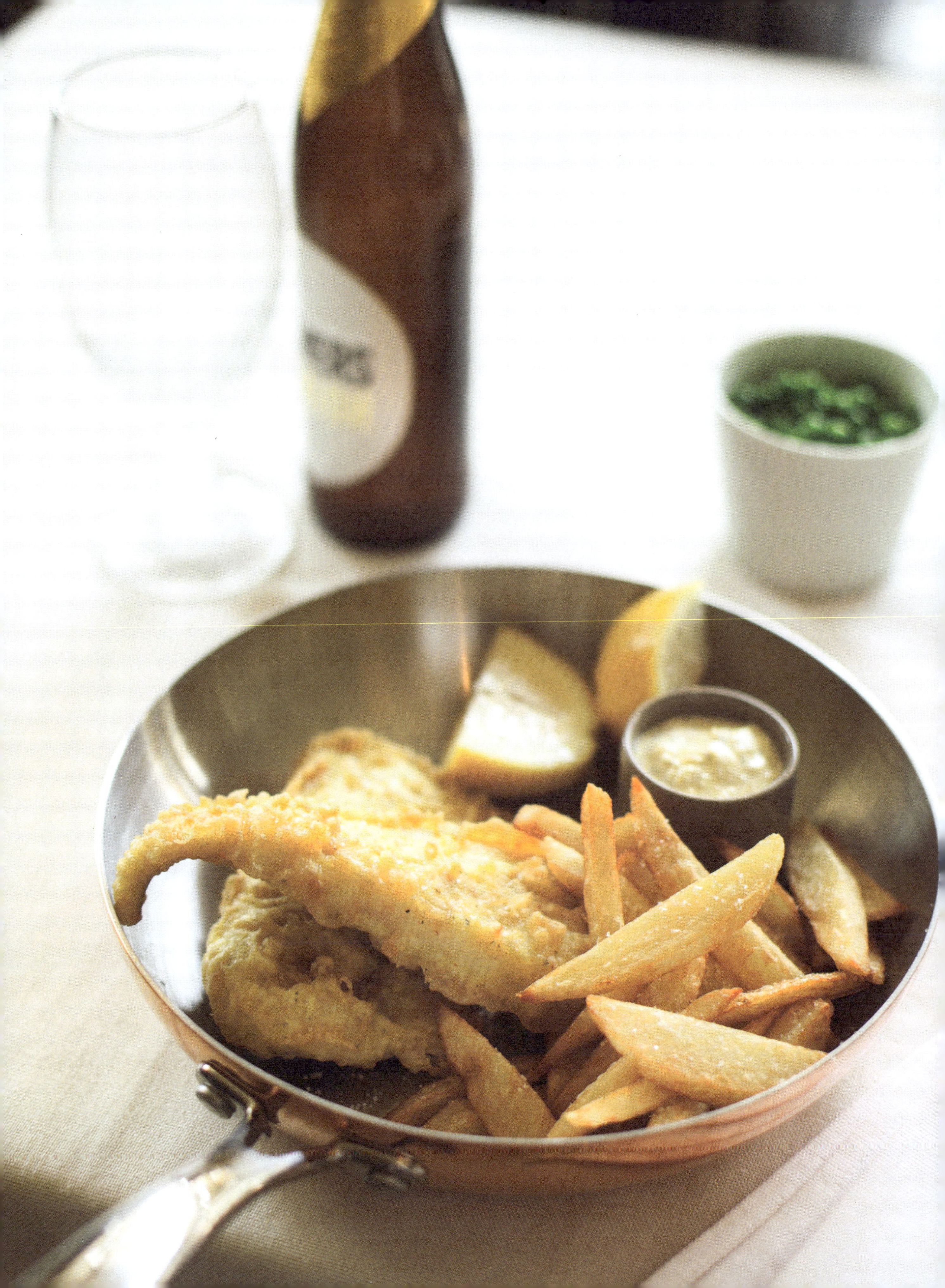

beer batter fish & chips

This is our South African version of the traditional British fish and chips with mushy peas. The batter is light and crispy and, for best results, should be made with a Black Label beer. Dress the chips with white spirit vinegar and wrap in newsprint for a real street food experience.

TARTAR SAUCE
3 hard-boiled eggs, finely chopped
60 g gherkins, finely chopped
10 g capers in brine, finely chopped
20 g red onion, finely chopped
100 g mayonnaise
salt and pepper

BEER BATTER
330 ml beer
75 g cornflour
200 g plain flour
5 ml fine sea salt
black pepper
2 tbsp white wine vinegar
pinch turmeric

salt and pepper
4 hake fillets, skinned
flour for dusting
oil for deep-frying

Finely chop the ingredients for the tartar sauce and mix with the mayonnaise in a bowl. Season to taste with salt and pepper.

To make the batter, whisk the beer, cornflour and flour together. Add the sea salt, pepper, vinegar, turmeric, and mix well. Season each piece of fish and dust with a little flour before dipping it into the beer batter. Place the fish gently in the deep-fryer and fry at 180 °C until the batter is golden brown and crispy and the fish is cooked. Serve with peas and chips.

SERVES 4

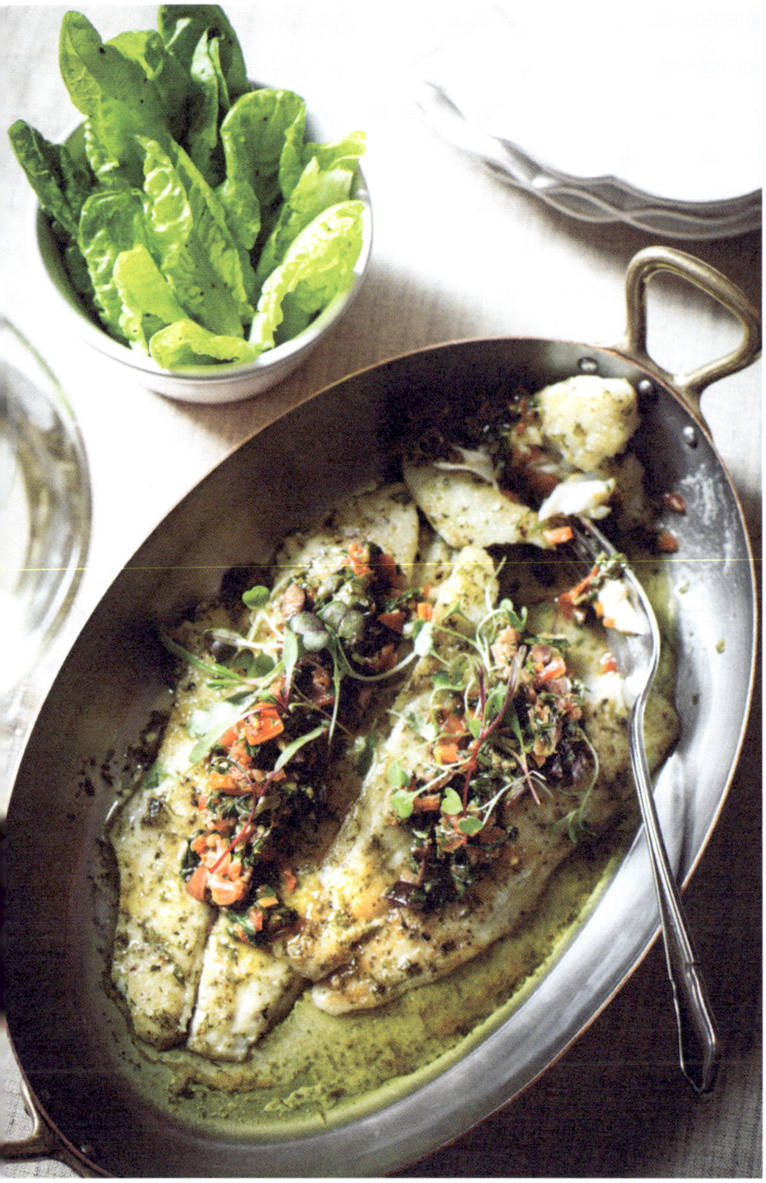

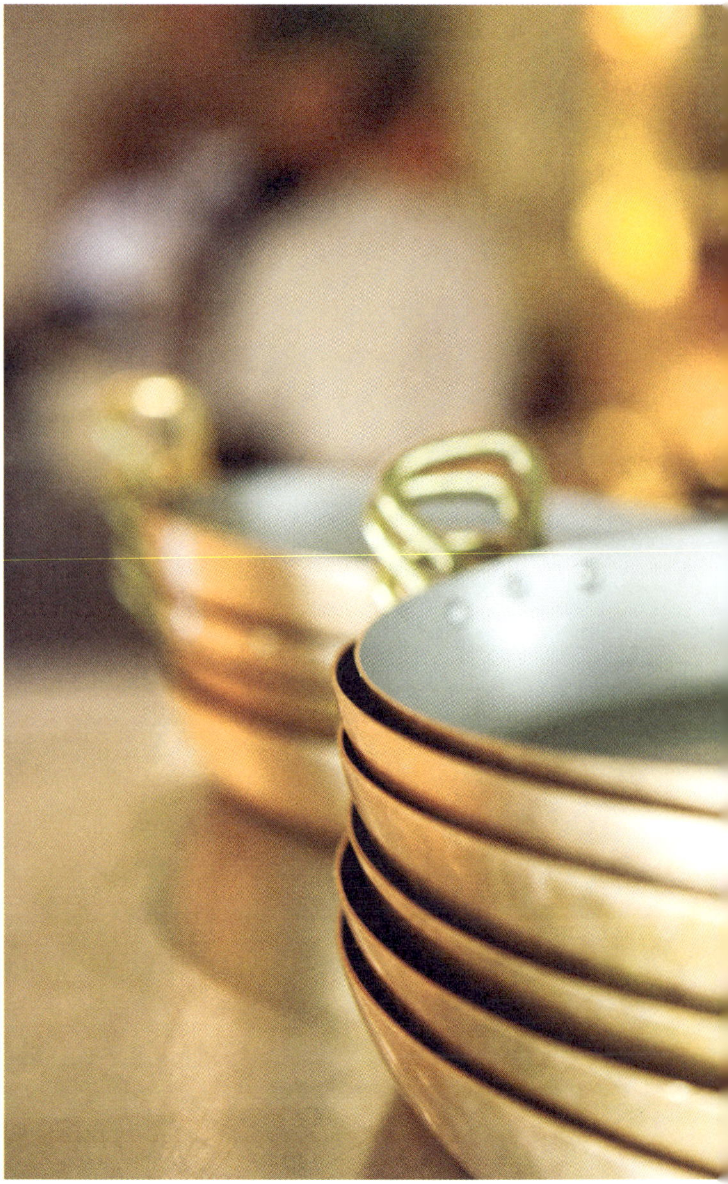

linefish with sauce vierge

It makes all the difference if you use fresh fish for this recipe. Choose a firm, flaky white fish and ask your fishmonger to fillet it but leave the skin on. The caper tomato sauce served on top of the fish cuts through the richness of the lemon butter. It's very French and very good.

4 x 280 g fresh fish fillets, skin on
30 g butter plus extra
30 ml olive oil
salt and pepper
squeeze lemon juice

SAUCE VIERGE
juice of half a lemon
60 ml olive oil
60 g butter
small handful dill, chopped
small handful chives, chopped
small handful basil, chopped
4 tbsp capers, finely chopped
200 g cherry tomatoes, diced
200 g calamata olives, pitted and finely chopped
half a tsp lemon zest

2 lemons, cut into wedges

Preheat the oven to 180 °C.

Pat the fish dry and fry it in a pan that you can transfer to the oven. Fry it skin-side down first, with 30 g butter, olive oil, salt and pepper. Then turn it over and cook for just a minute more. Add a squeeze of lemon and some more butter.

To make the sauce vierge, heat the lemon juice in a pan and then add a small amount of the olive oil and butter. Add the dill, chives, basil, capers, tomatoes, olives and lemon zest. The sauce should be heated through but shouldn't boil, so remove it from the heat before it begins to bubble.

To serve, dress the fish with the sauce and garnish with lemon wedges on the side.

SERVES 4

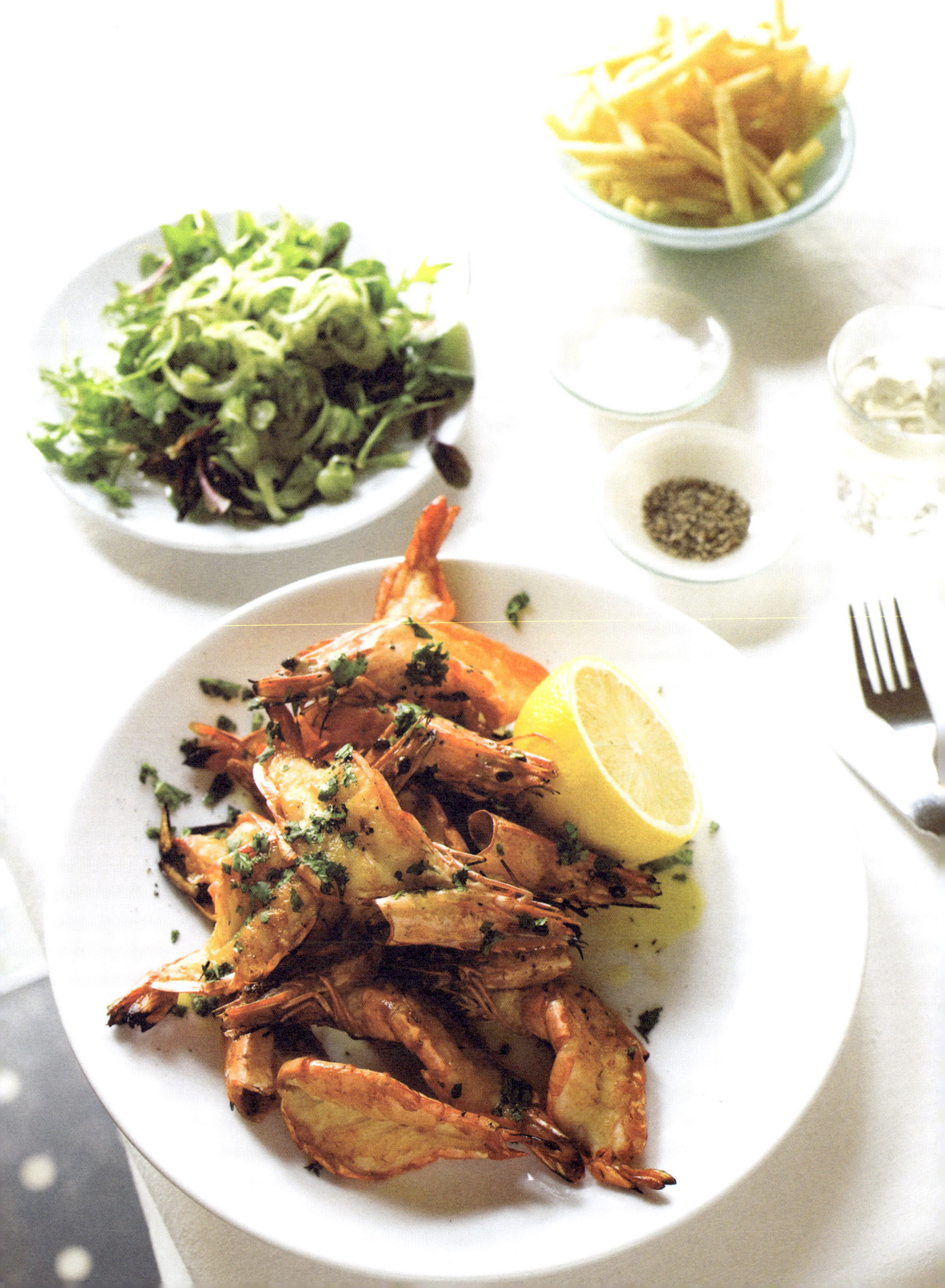

a box of prawns

My great grandfather, Kosta Livanos, was a fisherman from the small coastal village of Agios Nikolas in the Peleponise region. He emigrated to Lorenço Marques in Moçambique to find his fortune where he came to be known as 'The King of Prawns'. He had a fleet of eight fishing trawlers that caught prawns in traps called *gamboas* and he pioneered the prawn export trade by rail from LM to Johannesburg. He was also the first to start laying them out lengthways between layers of crushed ice in paraffin tins – like crayons in a box. My dad was born in LM and, like his grandfather, he knew his prawns. He always said that the only way to cook them is on an open charcoal grill. To this day, prawns are still packed the way my great grandfather did and we still cook them the way my dad did.

LEMON BUTTER SAUCE
120 ml lemon juice
700 g salted butter
half a tsp salt
half a tsp black pepper
pinch paprika

2,5 kg prawns
salt
pinch flat leaf parsley, chopped
pinch coriander, chopped

FENNEL SALAD
2 fennel bulbs, stalks and leaves
2 handfuls rocket
60 ml olive oil
30 ml lemon juice
salt and pepper

Make the lemon butter sauce in a pan. Bring the lemon juice to the boil and then add the butter. If you heat the lemon juice first, the sauce won't separate. Add salt, pepper and paprika and stir well.

Butterfly the prawns and devein them if needed. Season with salt. You can cook them on the grill or in a pan but they're best on an open fire. If you are cooking them on the grill, put them shell-side down first. If you are pan-frying them, cook them flesh-side down first. When the prawns start curling and the flesh turns white and the shells pink, they are cooked. Drizzle the lemon butter sauce over them and garnish with the chopped parsley and coriander.

To make the salad, finely slice the fennel bulbs, stalks and leaves. Mix with the rocket and dress with olive oil and lemon juice. Season with salt and pepper.

Serve the prawns with salad and chips or rice.

SERVES 4

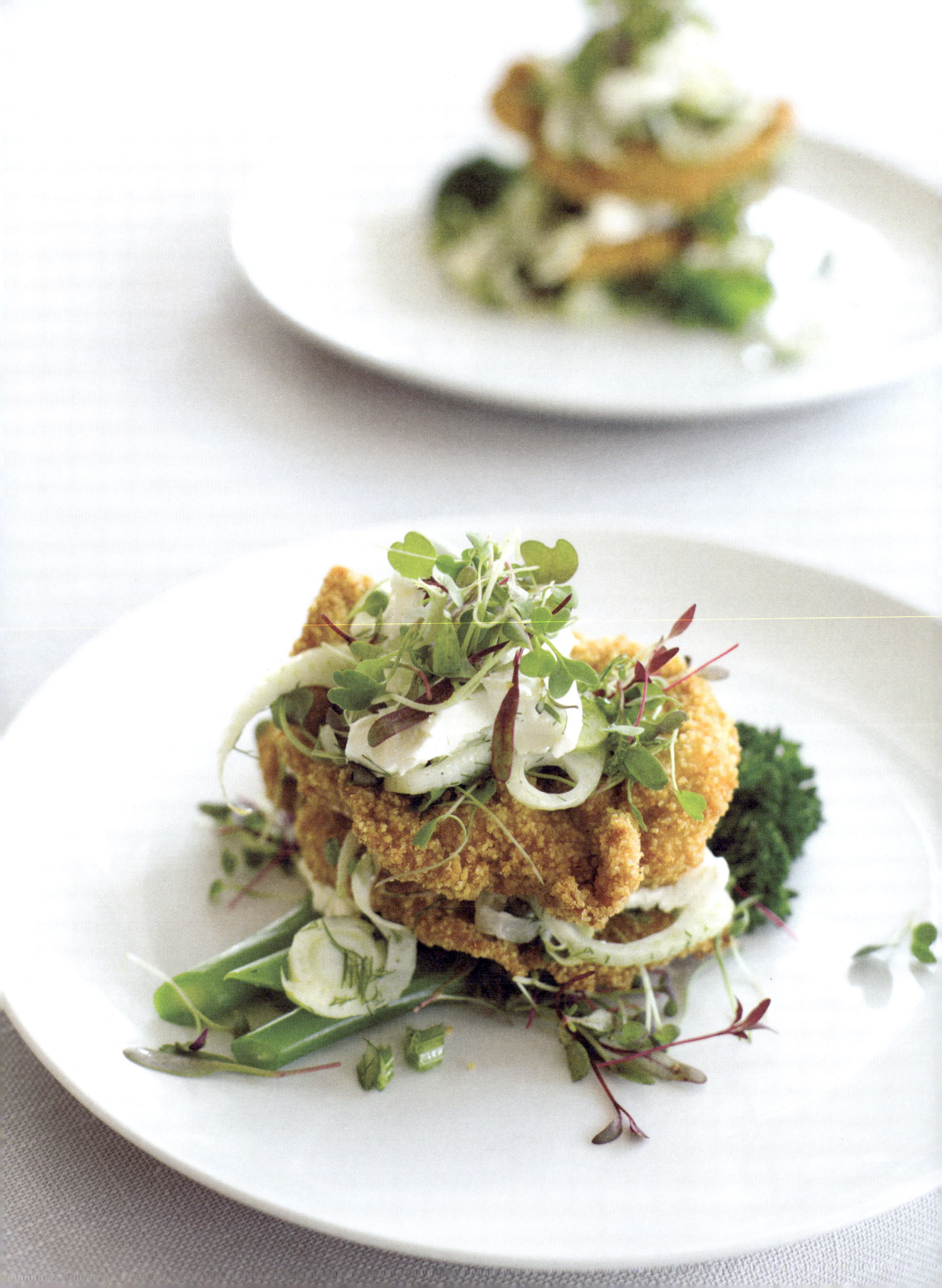

parmesan chicken couscous

This is a lighter version of chicken schnitzel. Donna Hay created something similar and I fell in love with it. It's a summery dish complemented with sliced fennel, lots of lemon and creamy chevin. We crumb it with raw couscous and deep-fry it. You can shallow-fry it, but the crumbs tend to fall off and it ends up either over- or underdone. Surprisingly, deep-frying the chicken doesn't make it oily, just perfectly crispy.

16 pieces tender stem broccoli
ice water

8 chicken breasts
3 eggs, beaten
salt and pepper

800 g COUSCOUS BREADCRUMB
100 g Parmesan cheese
200 g breadcrumbs
500 g couscous

oil for deep-frying

1 fennel bulb, thinly sliced
60 ml olive oil
juice of 1 lemon

200 g goat's cheese chevin
large handful micro greens
2 lemons cut into wedges

Blanch the broccoli stems in boiling water for about 2 minutes. Take them out and shock them in a bowl of ice water to stop the cooking and retain their colour. Drain and set aside until needed.

Flatten the chicken breasts with a meat mallet. Beat the eggs in a bowl and season with salt and pepper.

Shave the Parmesan cheese and then break the shavings into small pieces. Mix them with all the other ingredients for the couscous breadcrumb mixture and spread it out on a plate. Dip each chicken breast into the beaten egg and then into the couscous breadcrumbs. Coat each one evenly. Deep-fry the chicken. It should be well cooked and the crumbs golden brown.

While the chicken is cooking, slice the fennel thinly into slivers and marinate in olive oil and lemon juice.

Plate the broccoli, then the chicken, fennel, chevin and micro greens. Garnish with lemon wedges.

SERVES 4

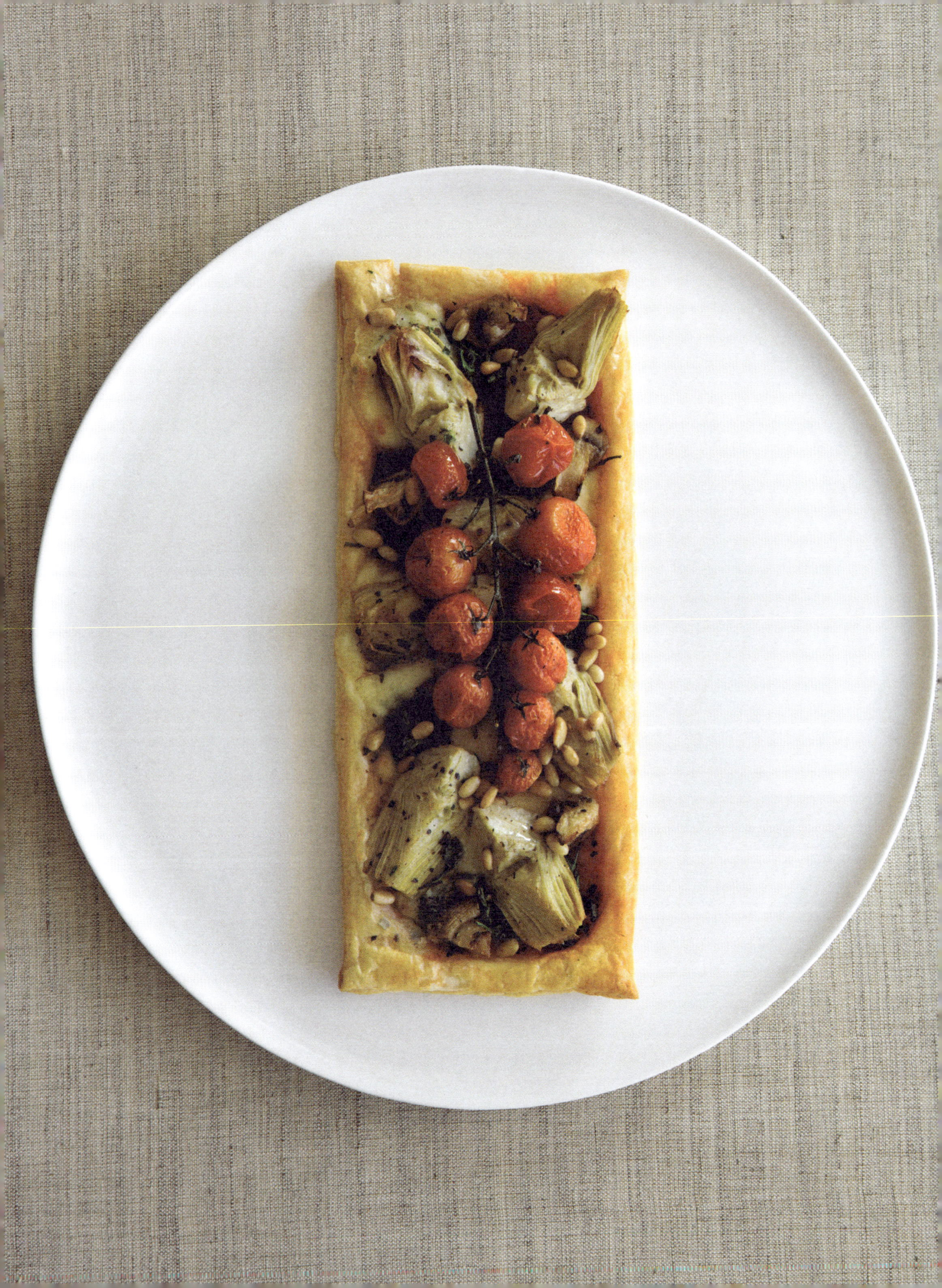

easy tart

Apart from a baked potato, this has to be one of the easiest oven recipes to impress your friends with, and it will. It's basically a baked open sandwich but it has the extra appeal of the golden, puff pastry. It's beautiful, it's versatile and it's quick to make. If you're too time-pressed to make the Napolitana sauce for the base, you can substitute with a shop-bought sauce, a spoon of pesto or spread it with a thick layer of creamy goat's cheese.

120 ml Napolitana sauce (page 106)
24 button mushrooms, sliced
butter
80 g baby spinach
2 sheets puff pastry, each cut in half
1 egg, beaten
120 g mozzarella, grated
12 marinated artichokes, quartered
40 g pine nuts, toasted
1 tsp dried oregano
4 vines cherry tomatoes
5 ml olive oil
salt and pepper

Preheat the oven to 200 °C.

Make the Napolitana sauce as per the recipe on page 106.
Sauté the sliced mushrooms in a little butter and remove from the pan. Wilt the spinach in the same pan with a little more butter and salt and set aside.

Using the tip of a sharp knife, score a 1 cm frame along the edge of each pastry half. Brush the frames with beaten egg. This will make the edges nice and golden.

Spread about a tablespoon of the Napolitana sauce onto each of the pastry halves (but not the edges). Sprinkle some grated mozarella over the sauce and then layer with small amounts of wilted spinach, mushrooms and artichoke quarters.
Less is more here: if you overburden the pastry with toppings it will end up heavy and soggy. You want a light, flaky tart.
To finish, sprinkle with a few toasted pine nuts, a pinch of dried oregano and top with a vine of cherry tomatoes. Drizzle with olive oil, season with the remaining oregano and salt and pepper.

Bake for 15–20 minutes or until golden brown.
Serve with a fresh herb salad.

SERVES 4

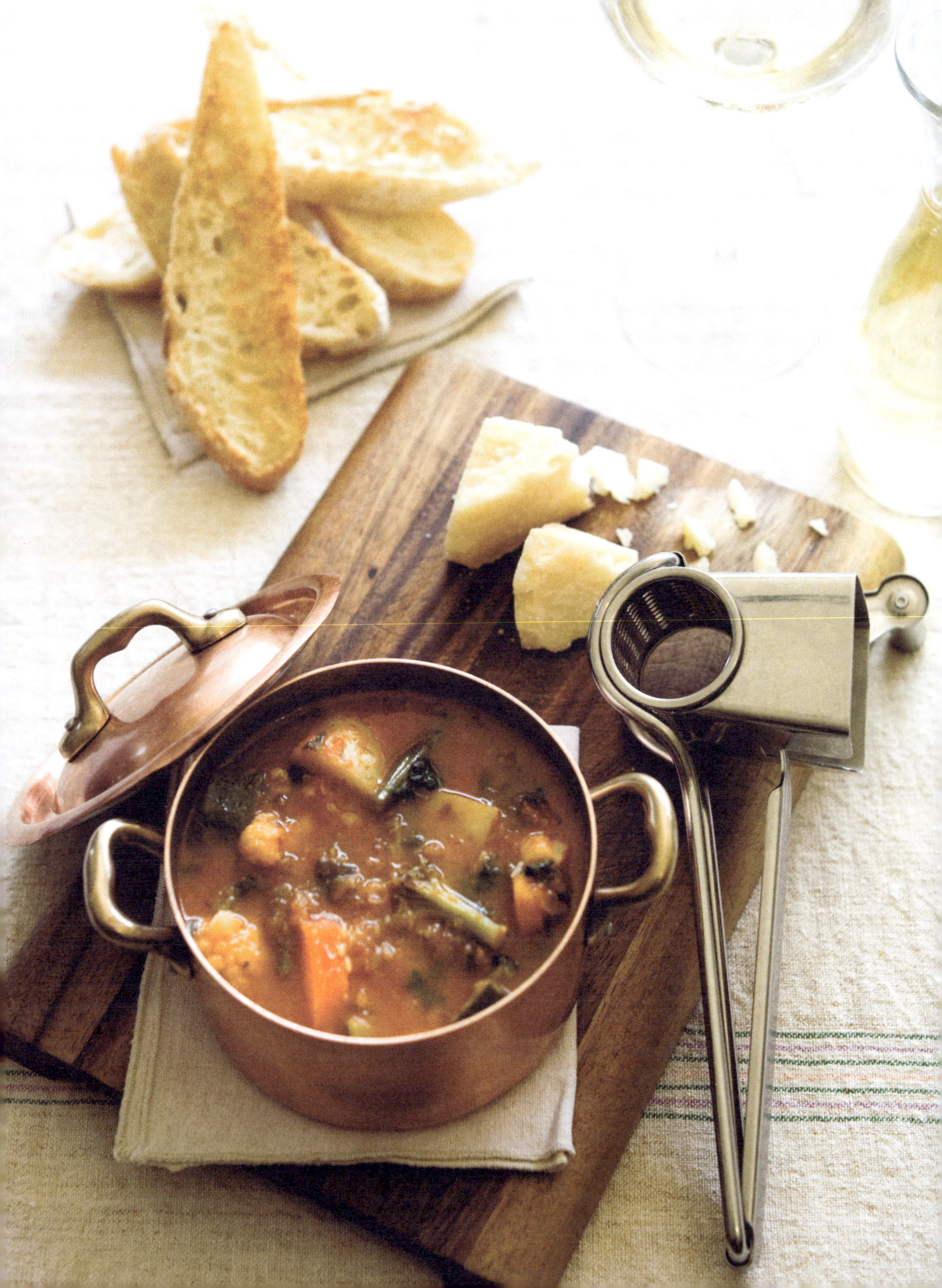

minestrone

For me, winter hasn't begun until I've made this soup. It's a hearty, meat-free meal. Bring it to the table in a big, beautiful pot and ladle into individual bowls. Have plenty of Parmesan and hot, crispy ciabatta toast ready. You can make it a *verdi* (green) minestrone by leaving out the Napolitana sauce.

700 ml Napolitana sauce (page 106)

3 tomatoes, peeled and deseeded
boiling water

half an onion, finely chopped
half a bunch celery, roughly chopped
10 ml olive oil
60 g butter
4 medium carrots, peeled and sliced
2 large potatoes, peeled and roughly diced
salt and pepper
2 tsp chicken stock powder
2 litres water
4 baby marrows, sliced
half a head broccoli florettes
half a head cauliflower florettes
50 g green beans
1 handful spinach, roughly chopped

Parmesan cheese
ciabatta toast

Make the Napolitana sauce as per the recipe on page 106.

Peel the tomatoes, by piercing them a few times with a sharp knife and pouring boiling water over them in a large bowl. Leave them until their skins begin to pull away from the flesh, then remove them to a bowl of cold water and peel.

In a large pot, sweat the onion and the celery in a little olive oil and half the butter. When they are soft, add the chopped carrots and potatoes, season with salt, pepper and the chicken stock powder and cook for another 10 minutes. Roughly chop the peeled tomatoes and add to the pot. Cook them for about 5 minutes before adding the 2 litres of water, the Napolitana sauce. Bring the soup to the boil, and when the potatoes are soft, add the rest of the vegetables except the spinach. Cook the soup on a slow boil for about another 15 minutes or until the vegetables are cooked to your preference. Just before serving, add the spinach add the remaining butter. The soup is ready when the spinach has wilted.

Serve with Parmesan cheese and ciabatta toast.

SERVES 4

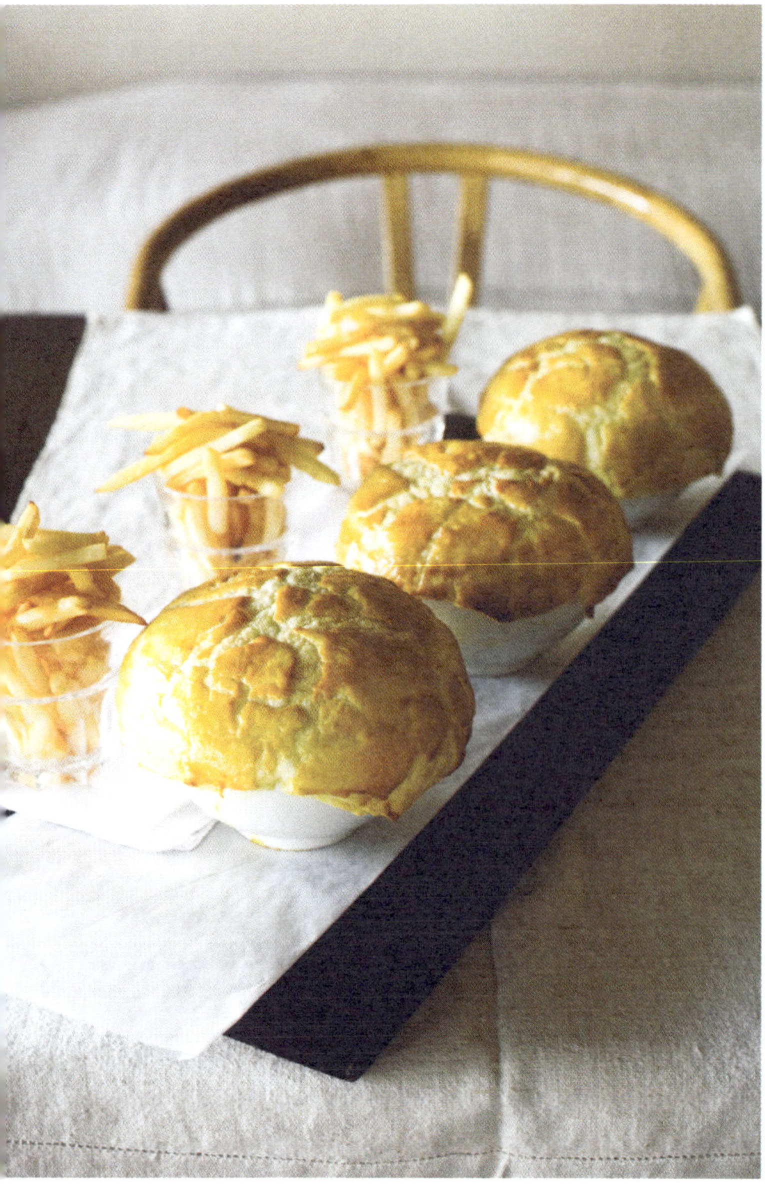

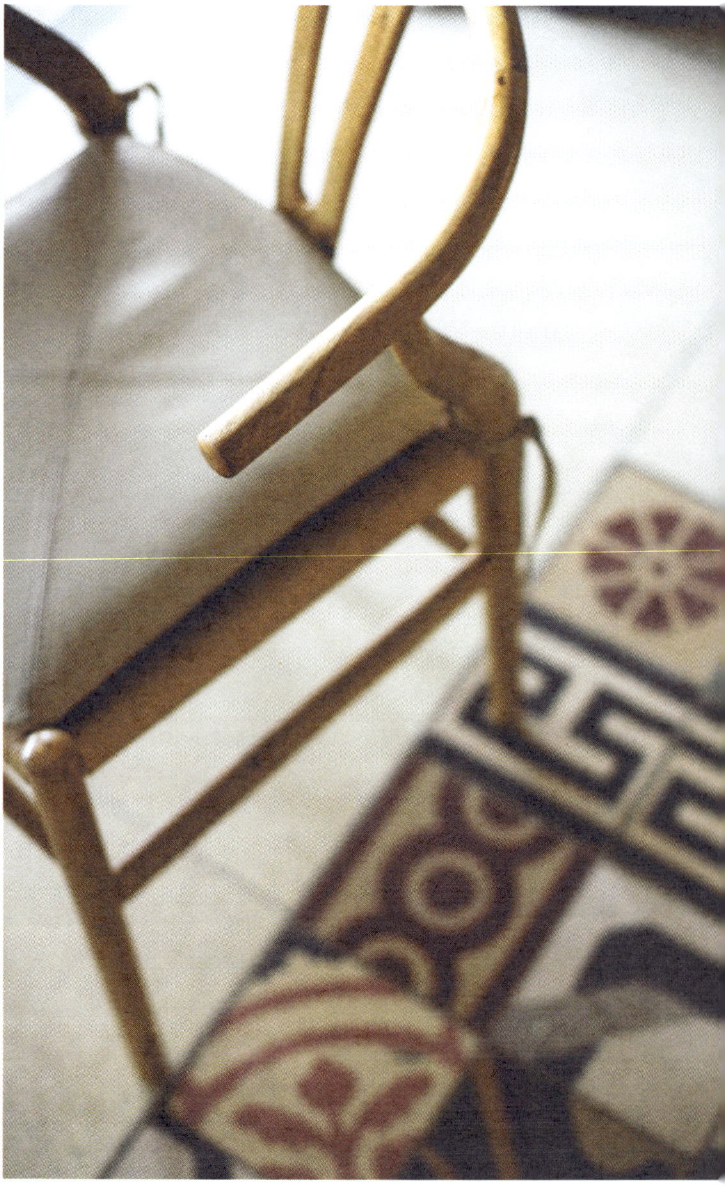

chicken pot pie

There are some days that just call for chicken pot pie. Some of my best memories are of my mother making this for me after I'd had a rough day. This pot pie is the ultimate winter comfort food but when we took it off our summer menu it almost caused a riot. So it's back, but only on the signature menus at Nicolway and Constantia. Ideally, it should be made from scratch, so be prepared to wait about 30 minutes.

8 chicken breasts, about 1 kg
24 button mushrooms, about 340 g
4 spring onions, sliced finely
4 tbsp chives, finely chopped
4 tbs olive oil
salt and pepper
1 tsp fresh thyme
125 ml white wine
2 tsp chicken stock powder
375 ml cream
40g butter, cut into 4 cubes
1 tsp flour
1 egg, beaten
2 sheets puff pastry

Preheat the oven to 180 °C.

Cut the chicken breasts into bite size cubes and the mushrooms into quarters. Slice the spring onion finely and chop the chives.

In a large saucepan, heat half the olive oil to smoking hot and quickly sauté the chicken. Season with salt and pepper and the thyme. When the chicken is sealed all over and begins to colour, remove from the pan and set aside. Add a little more olive oil to the pan and sauté the mushrooms and spring onions until the mushrooms are nicely browned. Return the chicken to the pan with the wine and stock powder. Boil until the wine has reduced by half, then add the cream.

Toss the cubes of butter in a little flour and stir them into the cream sauce. Cook the sauce on a high heat for about 5 minutes or until it has thickened. The sauce should coat the back of a spoon. Take care not to thicken it too much or your pie will be dry.

Add the chives and season to taste. Pour the mixture into a large pie dish or 4 small dishes. Beat the egg for the egg wash. Cut the pastry and cover the pies, pressing down the edges with a fork. Egg wash the pastry and bake until the pastry has puffed and turned golden brown. Smaller pies will take about 20 minutes, the larger pie should bake for about 30 minutes.

SERVES 4

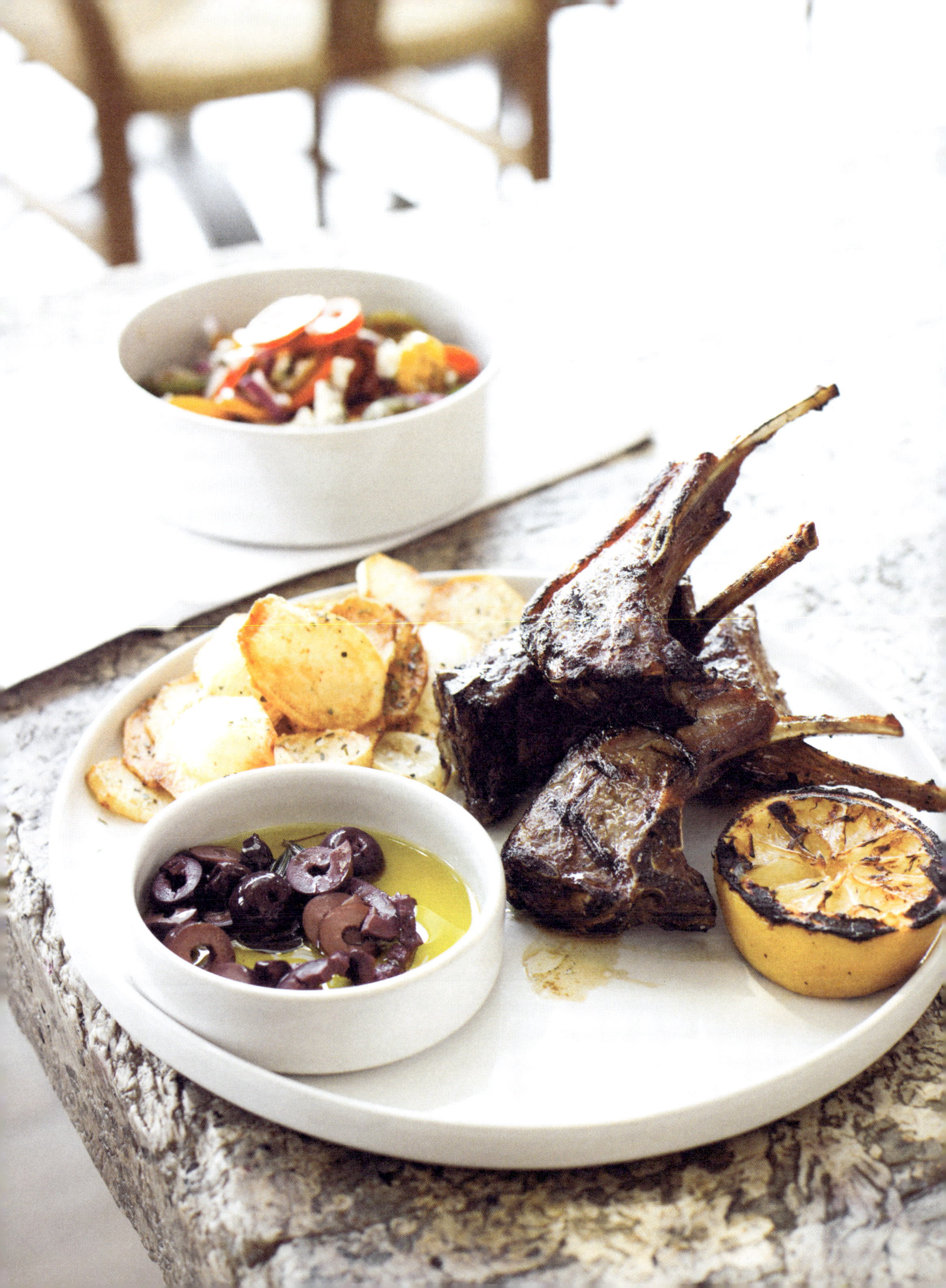

greek lamb cutlets

There isn't a taverna in Greece that doesn't serve lamb chops. One of my favourites uses brown paper 'tablecloths' and tips the grilled chops directly onto them. You tuck into them just as you were meant to, with your hands. It's genius – no laundry, no washing up. No fuss, no mess. Use good-quality lamb and ask your butcher to French-trim it. The meat is best cooked on an open fire but you can also do it in a griddle pan.

16 lamb cutlets about 100 g each
salt and pepper

BASTING SAUCE
240 ml olive oil
120 ml lemon juice
2 sprigs rosemary, stalks removed
salt and pepper
pinch dried oregano

TOMATO SALAD
2 large salad tomatoes, sliced
20 baby heirloom tomatoes, sliced
half a red onion, sliced
200 g feta, crumbled

TOMATO SALAD VINAIGRETTE
80 ml olive oil
15 ml red wine vinegar
salt and pepper
pinch dried oregano

4 lemons, ends cut off
4 medium potatoes, 5 mm slices
oil for deep-frying
20 calamata olives, pitted and sliced across the width

Season the lamb chops and set aside.
Combine the basting sauce ingredients.

Prepare the tomato salad by mixing all the salad ingredients together in a bowl. Whisk the vinaigrette ingredients and drizzle over the salad.

Grill the lamb cutlets on an open flame, basting them with the sauce as they cook. Grill for about 3 minutes on each side. Place the lemons on the grill flat-side down until they are just brown.

While the cutlets are on the grill, deep-fry the potato slices until golden brown. Dip the lamb chops in the basting sauce once more before serving.

Serve on individual plates or on large serving platters in the centre of the table so people can help themselves.
Serve with the tomato salad and small bowls of olives on the side.

SERVES 4

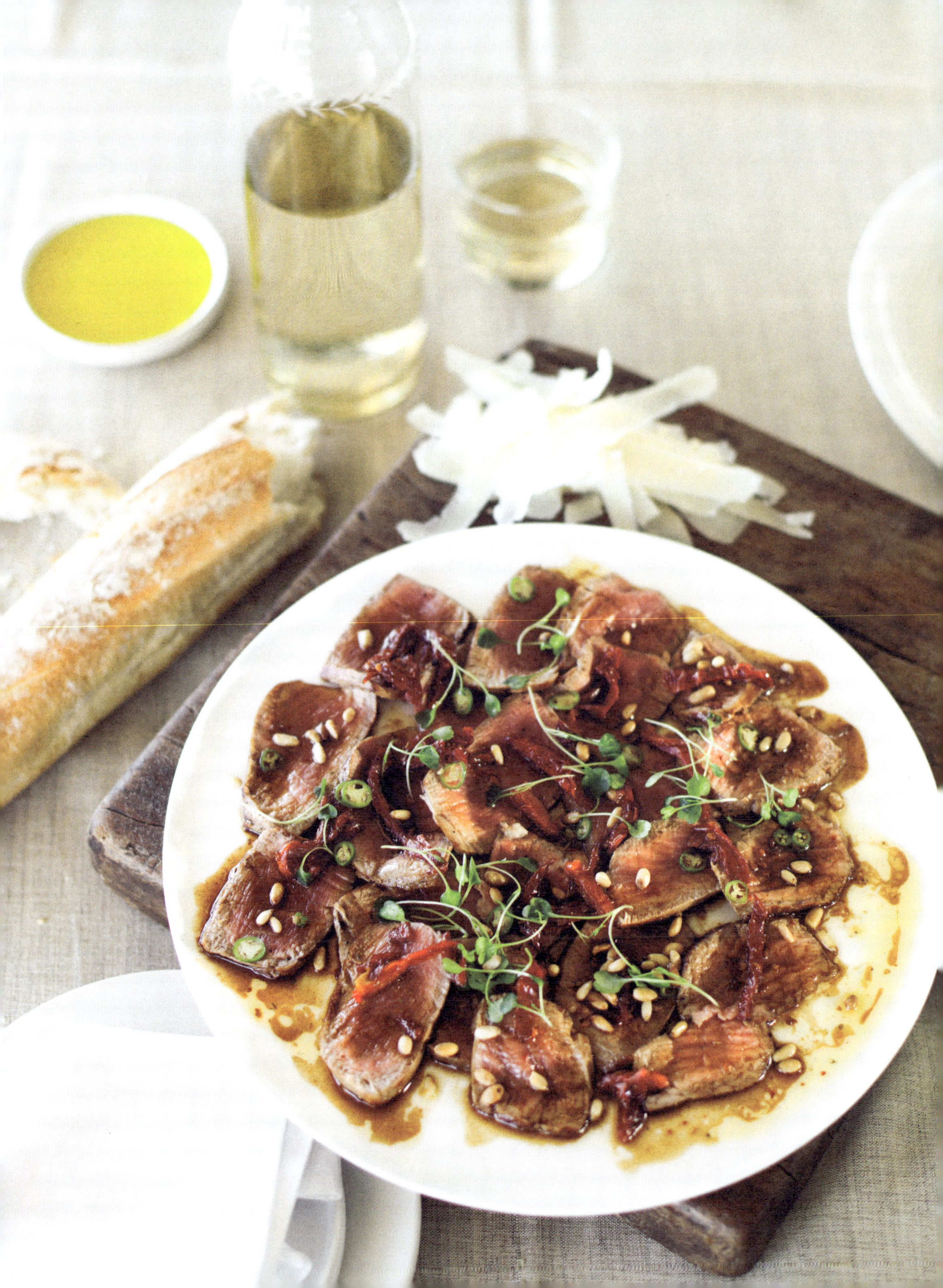

steak tagliata

I'll never forget the first time I had tagliata. A large group of my friends and I sat under a huge tree that creaked overhead. Gravel crunched under our shoes. Chairs and elbows rubbed against each other. The waiter arrived with a series of small silver stands which he placed down the centre of the table. We were intrigued. Our Italian was dodgy so we weren't entirely sure what we had ordered. Then platters of slivered steak, fat tomatoes drenched in olive oil, pickled peppers and marinated zucchini arrived with a flourish. This is the recipe for the slivers of steak.

1 kg beef fillet
10 ml olive oil

SAUCE

1 medium red chilli, deseeded, sliced
5 ml fresh ginger root
2 small garlic cloves, minced
80 ml soya sauce
100 ml olive oil
8 sundried tomatoes, not marinated
20 g pine nuts, toasted
pinch ground black pepper

handful rocket or micro greens
40 g Parmesan shavings

toasted ciabatta
linguine or chips

Rub the meat with olive oil and sear in a griddle pan. Medium rare is best for this recipe. Allow the meat to rest for 2–3 minutes before slicing it across the width to create thin slices. Place on a large serving plate.

To make the sauce, deseed and slice the chilli paper thin. Peel the ginger and cut it into very thin matchsticks and mince the garlic. Stir all of the sauce ingredients together with the chilli, ginger and garlic in a bowl and dress the warm fillet slices.

Garnish with rocket or micro greens and the Parmesan shavings. Serve with toasted ciabatta, linguine or chips.

SERVES 4

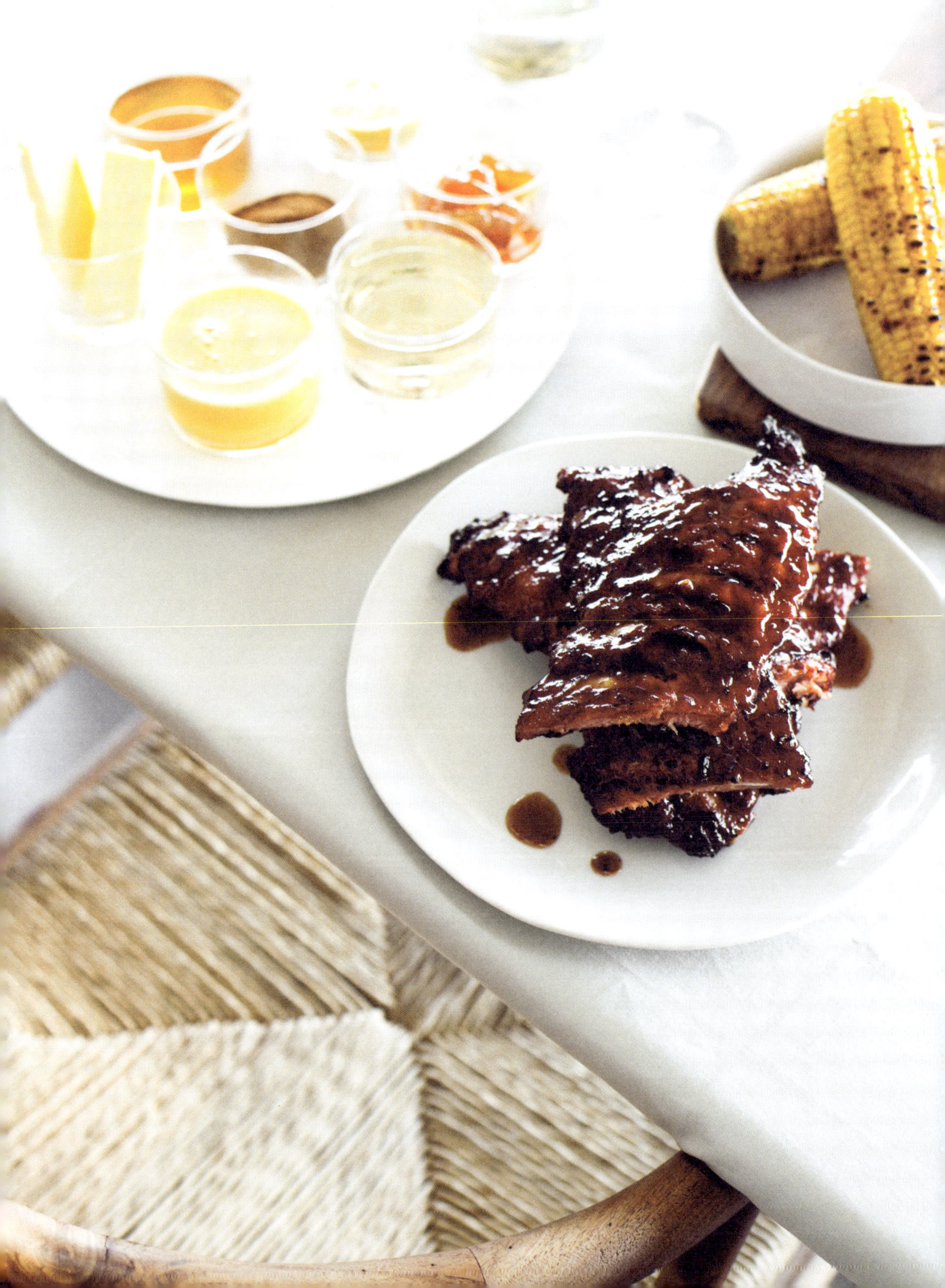

sticky apricot ribs

The basting recipe for these ribs comes from Savva's father-in-law, Athos Kolokotronis. He's been making it for almost 30 years. He's an enthusiastic cook and an experienced restaurateur who used to feed around 12 000 workers daily. At 68, he still runs on the beach every morning. He has a black belt in karate, makes his own cheese, dries olives and cures meat and sausages on his patio, which usually sports a hanging octopus he has caught himself. Like the man, this recipe is pretty impressive.

FOR 400 ml RIB BASTING SAUCE
60 g butter
1 tsp ground cinnamon
50 g honey
300 g apricot jam
100 ml orange juice
100 ml white wine
juice of half a lemon
pinch salt

1,4 kg spare ribs (precooked)
8 sweetcorn cobs, cut in half

To make the basting sauce, combine the ingredients in a pot and mix well. Bring to a boil and cook until the sauce has reduced and become sticky, like syrup. Set aside to cool.

Grill the spare ribs bone down on an open flame. Once they are char-grilled, take them off the fire and baste with the sauce. Return them to the grill. Repeat three times and then baste them again just before serving. Parboil the sweetcorn for 3 minutes in boiling water and then grill them on the open flame.

Serve with plenty of paper napkins or big linen bibs.

SERVES 4

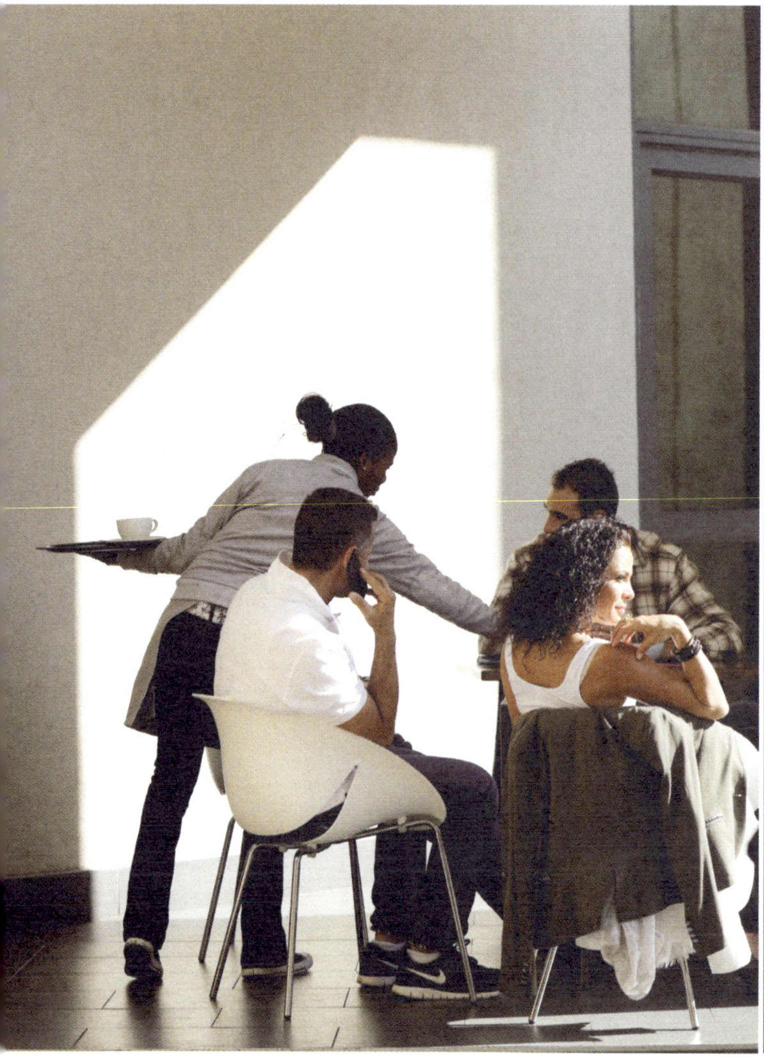

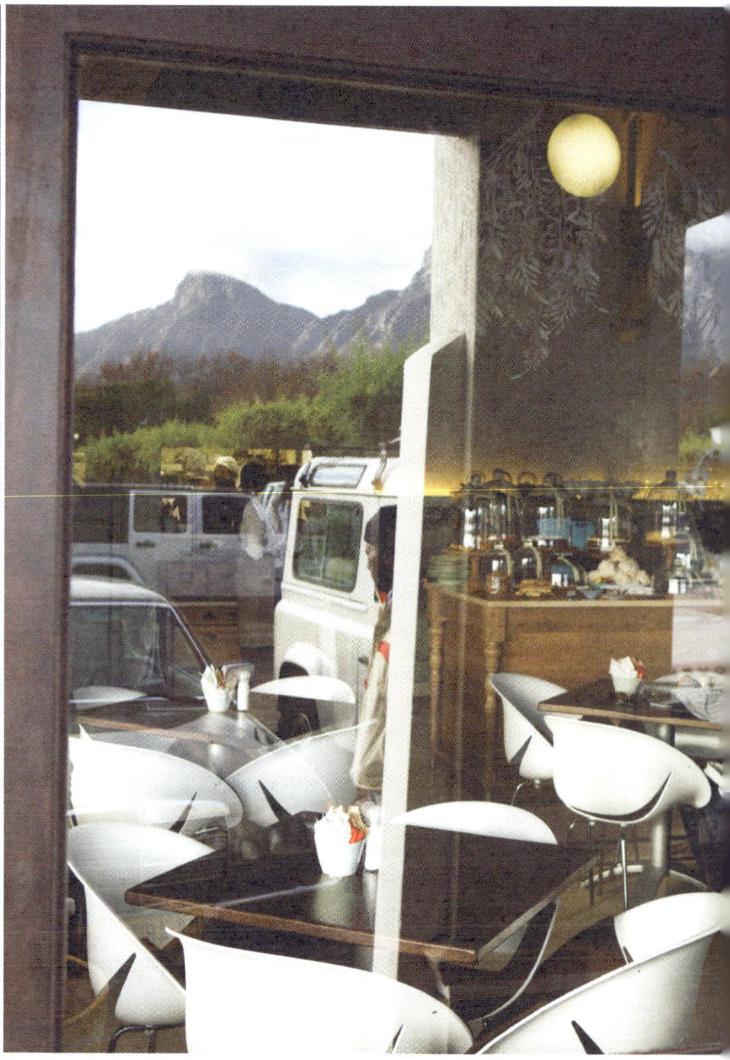

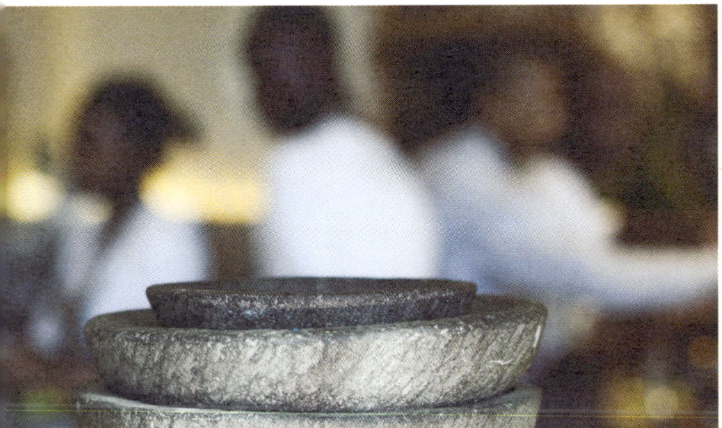

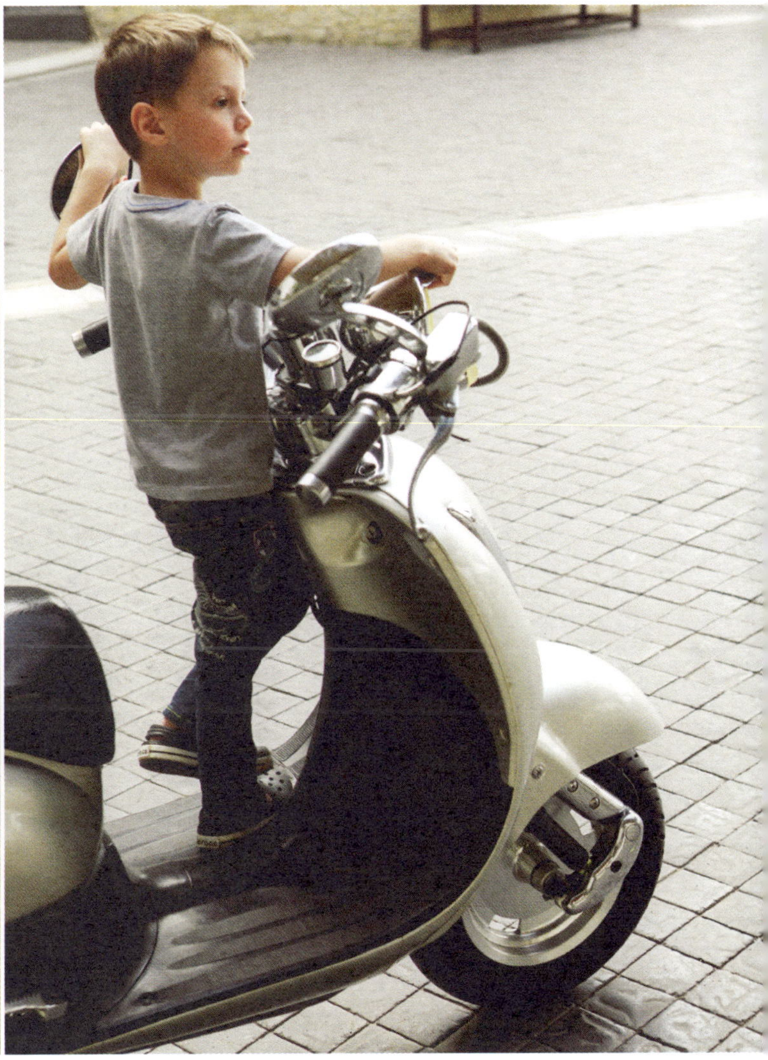

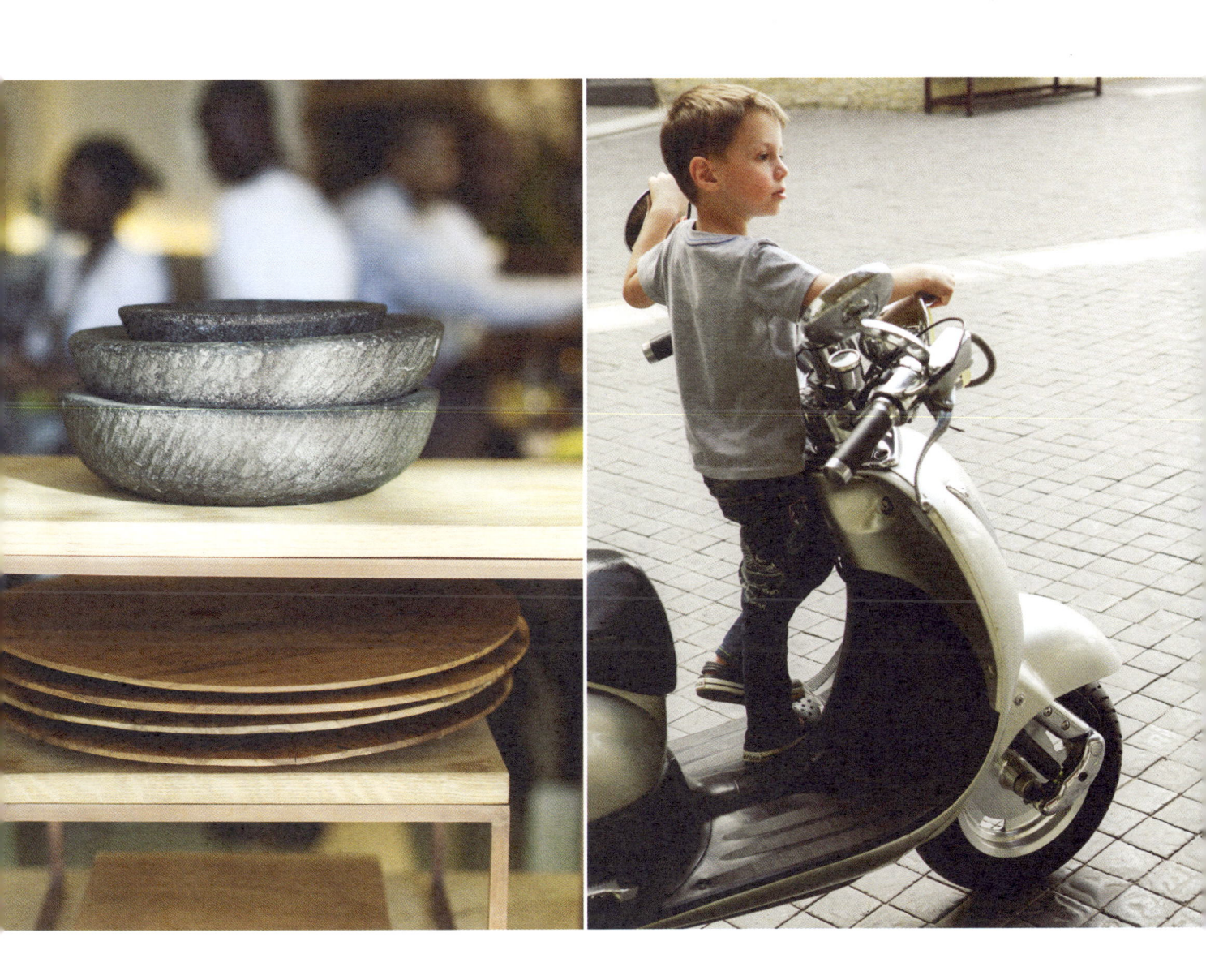

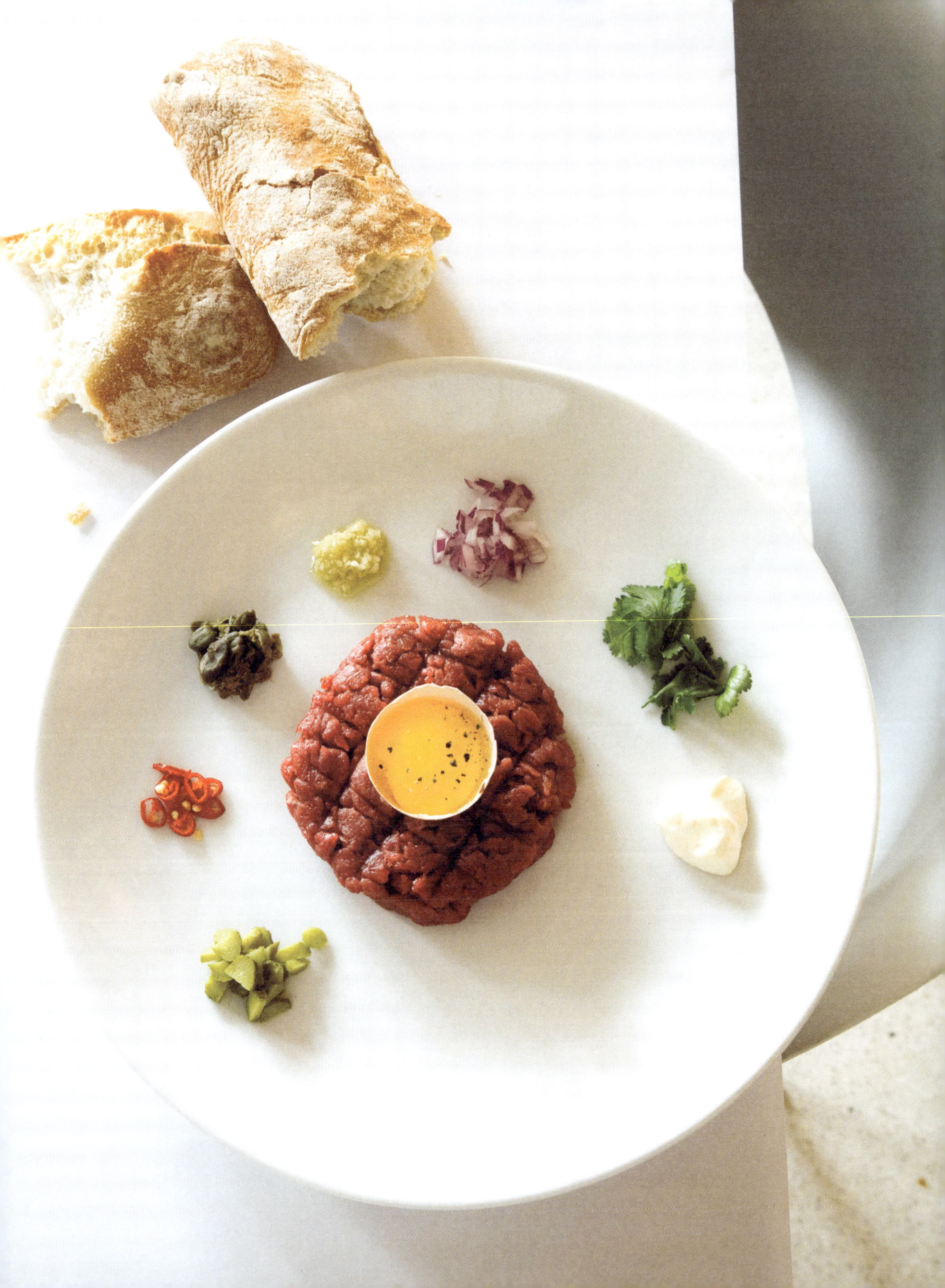

steak tartare

Most parents hide the cookie jar from their kids, mine had to hide the steak tartare. I still have the little white scar from the time I tried to steal a bite while my mother was cutting the fillet. It's a reminder that tartare should absolutely always be hand cut, and also that you should never get caught with your hand in the tartare.

1 kg beef fillet, finely chopped
salt and pepper
8 drops Tabasco sauce
40 ml Worcestershire sauce
1 red onion, chopped

4 egg yolks
40 ml garlic, crushed
40 ml gherkins, chopped
40 ml parsley, chopped
40 ml capers, chopped
40 ml mayonnaise
100 ml olive oil
2 red chillies, deseeded, sliced

chips or bread

Finely mince the fillet by hand using a very sharp knife. Season with salt and pepper, the Tabasco and Worcestershire sauces and half the finely chopped red onion.

Plate each portion individually. Make a mound of the fillet in the middle of the plate and score it as pictured. Separate the egg yolks from the whites, discard the whites and keep half of each egg shell.

Top each mound of fillet with an egg yolk in a half shell and arrange a small portion of each of the other ingredients around the steak tartare.

Serve with chips or bread on the side

SERVES 4

I want you to walk into tashas, any tashas, and feel welcome.
I always wanted to create a place you'd want to come back to, a place that feels a bit like home. A big part of this experience has to do with the interior design. I've always loved good architecture, well-made objects and beautiful interiors. Design inspires me.
My interior architect and designer, Neydine Bak and I work with carefully choosen materials that will last but also age gracefully; marble counters that wear naturally on the corners and still look good, wood that acquires a lived-in patina over the years, contemporary moulded plastic chairs or patterned terrazzo floors that can handle foot traffic.

Once I'd conceived the idea of the tashas 'inspired by...', I realised that design would play a significant role in maintaining the separate identities of each store. Good design is not formulaic, so although there is a common design thread, there are no replicas. The tashas restaurants are like a group of best friends – they're all different but they hang together beautifully. Atholl was my first store and so that design became the footprint for the others that followed. In every tashas you'll find the graceful curve where the wall meets the ceiling, the elegant horizontal axis of the interior layout and the terrazzo tiles, and yet each has its own personality. I would like to think that our interiors glow with the warmth of wood, the polished sheen of copper, brass and marble but more importantly, I hope that they glow with the warmth of people having a good time.

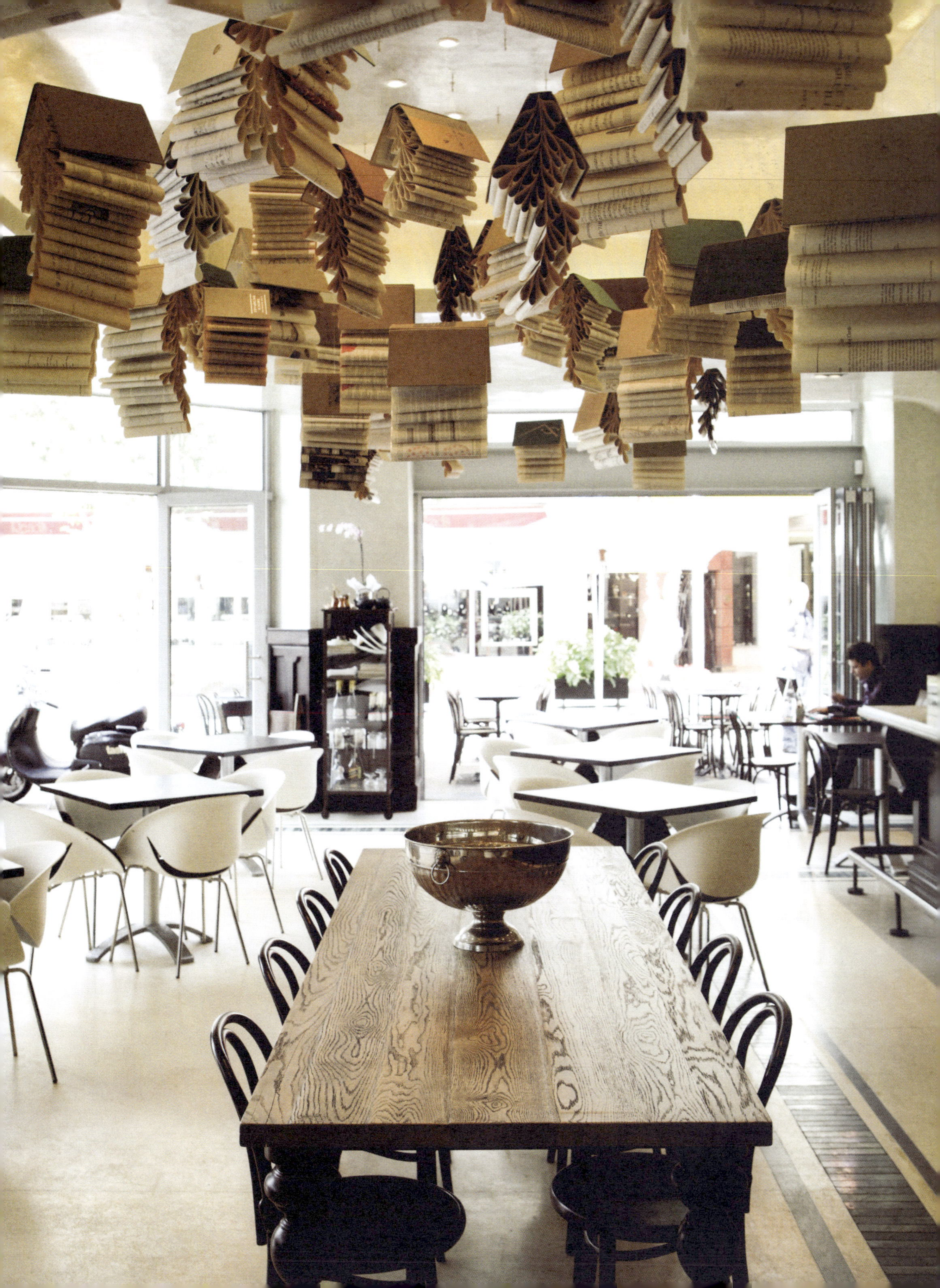

I don't have much of a sweet tooth which is probably why we don't serve a lot of desserts at tashas. We have larger dessert menus at the restaurants that are open evenings, and we do sell a lot of cakes and pastries baked for us by the best bakers in South Africa. I would love to have a bakery or a little patisserie all of our own so that we can bake for all our stores. Who knows, perhaps one day that dream will come true.

desserts

doxa's chocolate slice 167

ricotta cheese & preserved figs 169

pineapple carpaccio 171

cream victoria 173

panna cotta 175

tashas tarte tatin 177

turkish baklava 181

caramelised fruit 183

pistachio biscotti 185

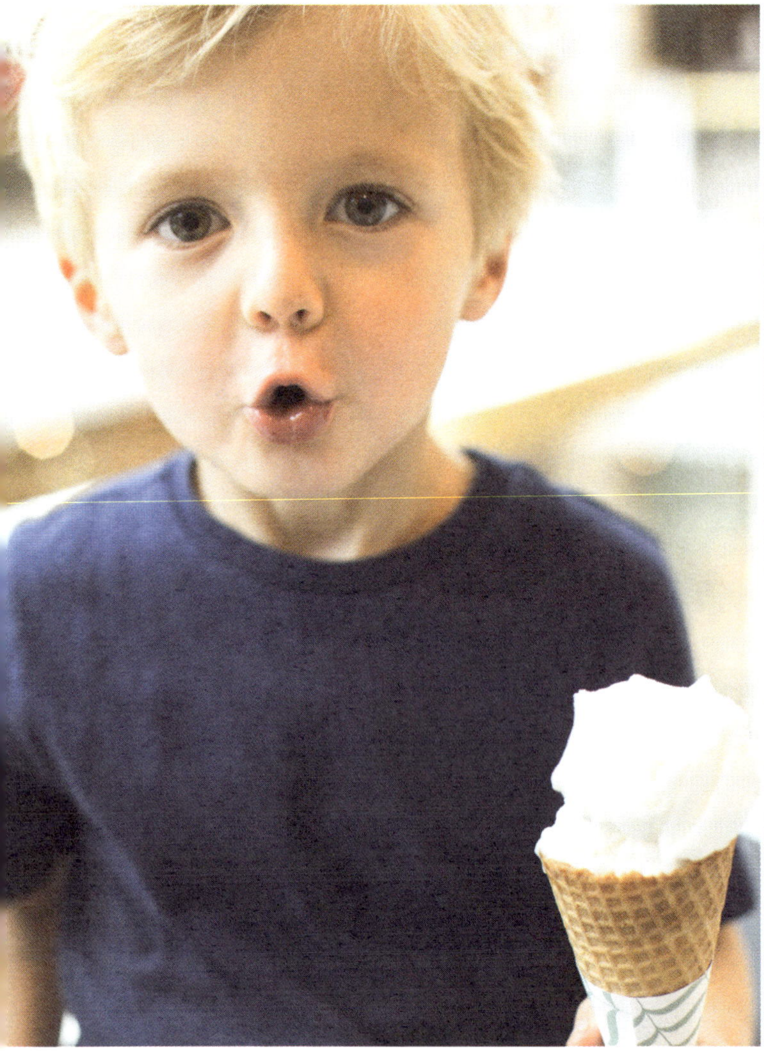

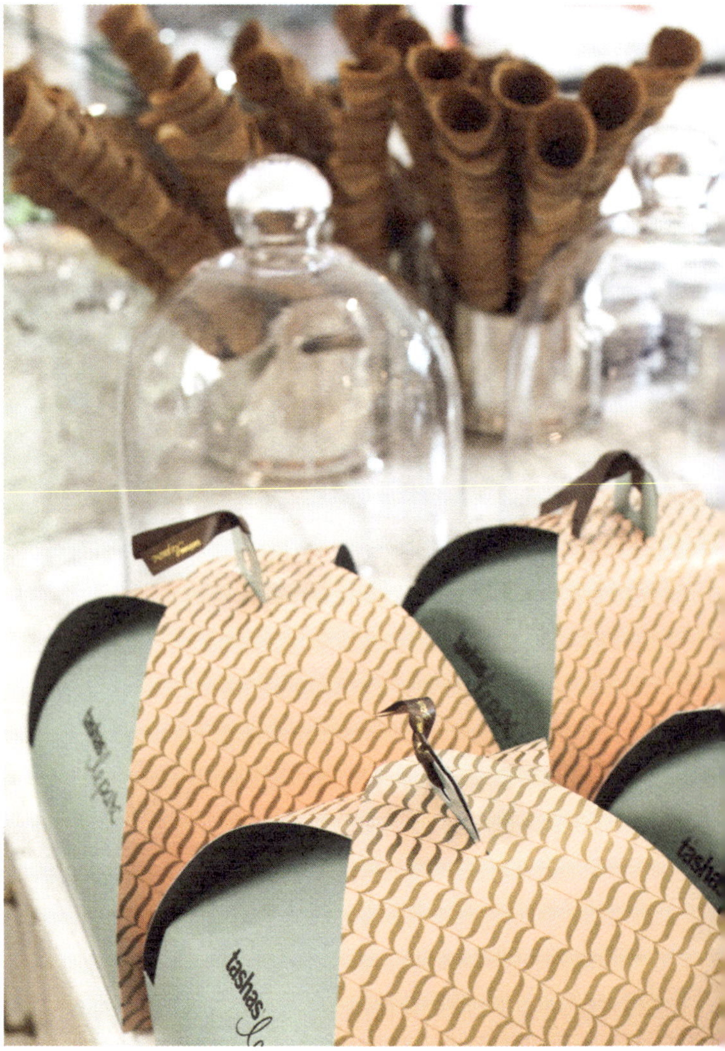
tashas

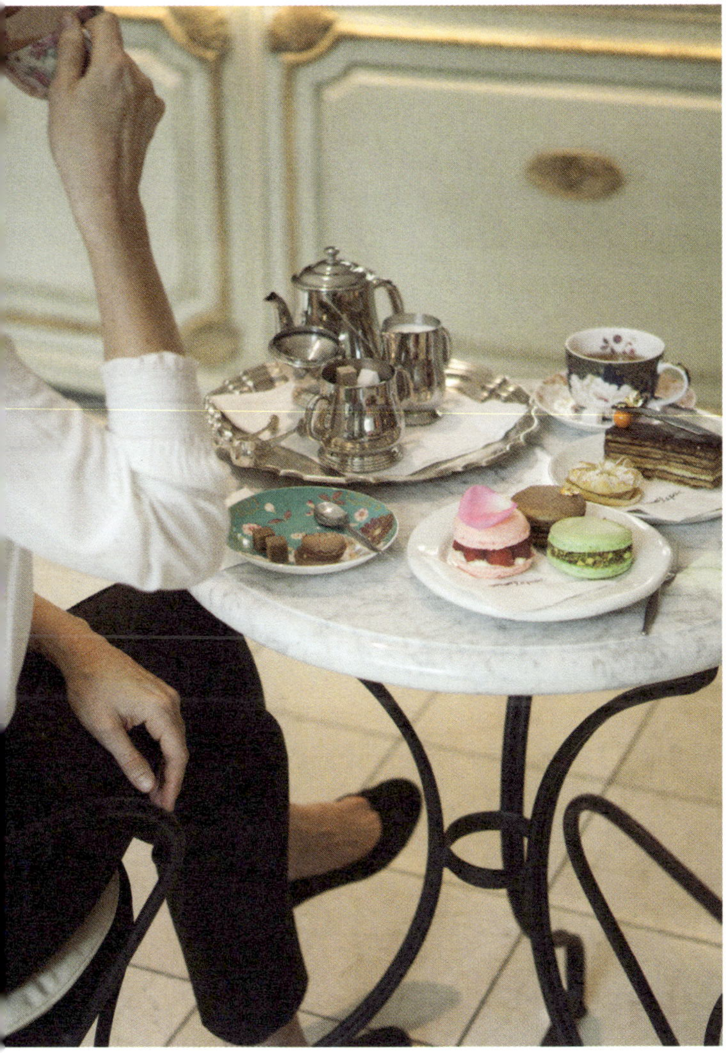

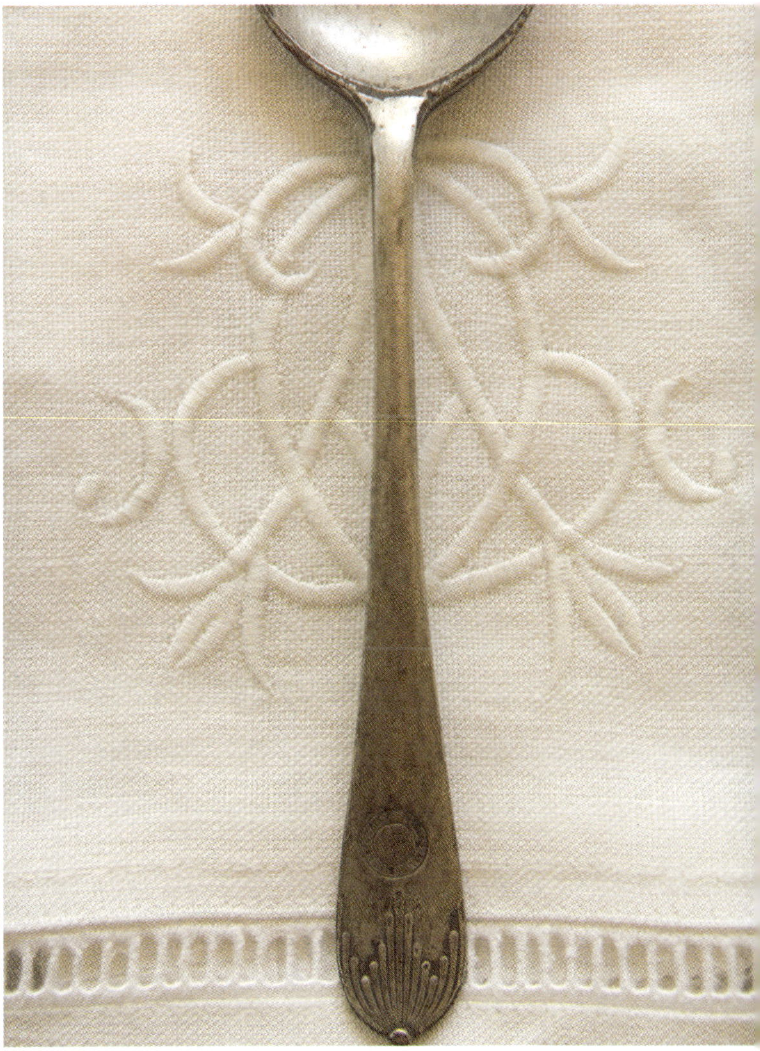

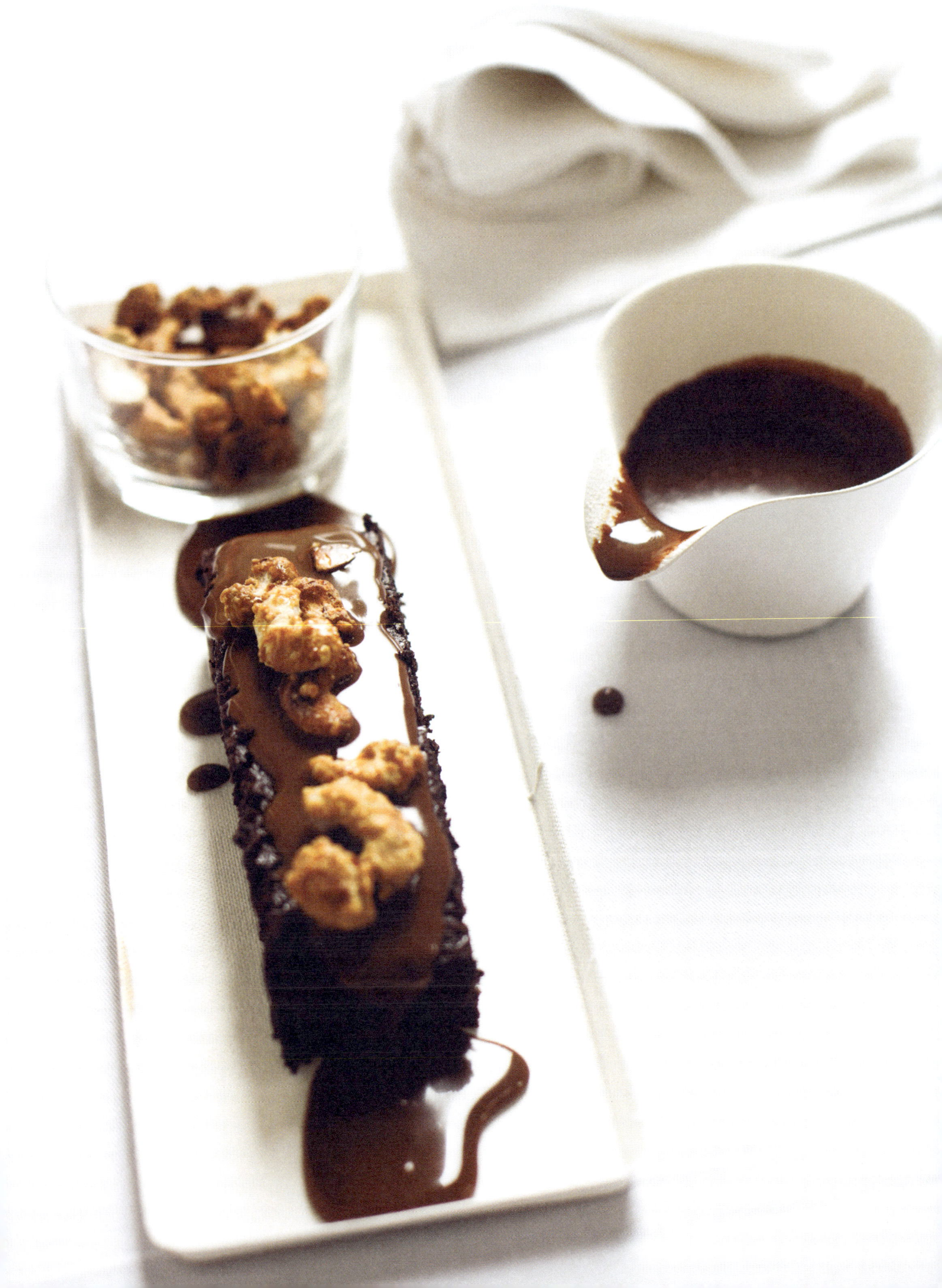

doxa's chocolate slice

I'm not a lover of cake but when my friend Melpo's mother asked me to taste-test this chocolate pudding, I couldn't refuse. Doxa's chocolate slice is rich and decadent and just about everyone, even me, finds it irresistable.

CAKE
250 ml sugar
4 eggs, separated
125 ml oil
125 ml hot water
pinch salt
2 tsp vanilla essence
60 g cocoa powder
250 ml flour
2 tsp baking powder

SYRUP
1 x 380 g tin evaporated milk
250 ml white sugar

CHOCOLATE SAUCE
1 x 380 g tin evaporated milk
300 g plain milk chocolate

Preheat the oven to 165 °C.

Line a 24–26 cm baking tin with baking paper.

To make the cake, mix the sugar, egg yolks, oil, water, salt and vanilla essence. In a separate bowl, mix the cocoa powder, flour and baking powder. Fold the two mixtures together. In a separate bowl, beat the egg whites till fluffy, then fold this into the other ingredients. Pour the mixture into the lined baking tin and bake for 30–35 minutes.

Make the syrup by bringing the first tin of evaporated milk and sugar to a boil. Stir to make sure the sugar is completely dissolved. Set aside to cool.

When the cake is ready, remove it from the oven and poke a few evenly spaced holes in it with a skewer. Allow to cool, then pour the syrup over the cake. Make sure it has all been absorbed before you slice the cake.

To make the sauce, heat the second can of evaporated milk. Once it starts steaming, add the chocolate. Stir continuously until the chocolate has melted.

The chocolate sauce can either be served on the side or as a topping. If you like, serve with caramel-coated cashew nuts and vanilla ice cream.

SERVES 4

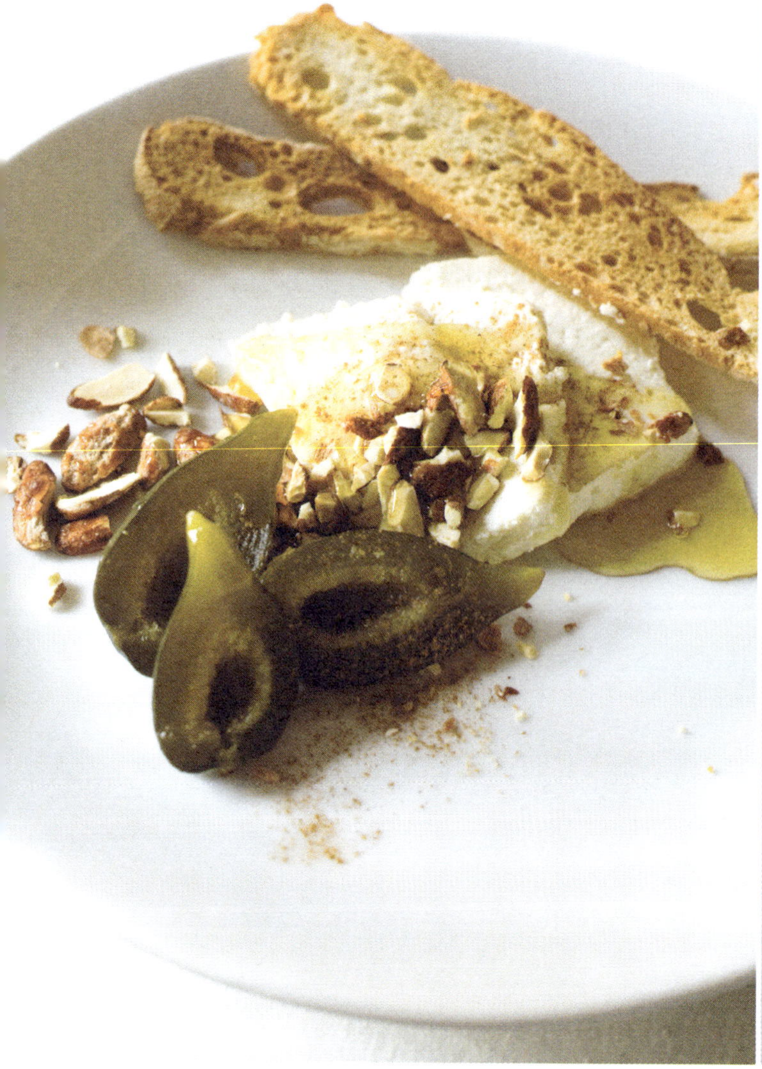
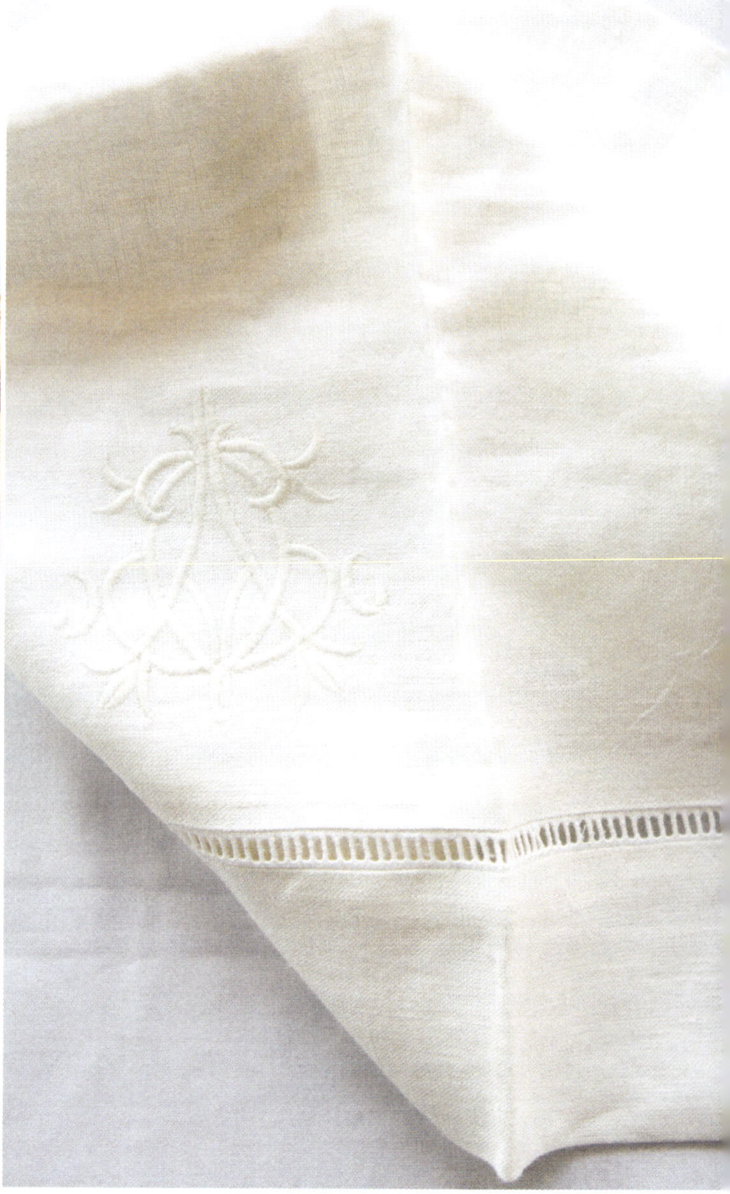

ricotta cheese & preserved figs

Ricotta works in pasta dishes, on pizza or in desserts. You can use it to make cheesecake or serve it on its own like we do with honey, nuts and preserves. This recipe is a simpler version of the traditional one, which uses real, rennet-rich whey left over from making cheeses like mozzarella. This is the recipe I like to use because it's how my Grandma made it.

2 litres full cream milk
1 tsp salt
80 ml lemon juice or white vinegar

TO SERVE
ciabatta toast
nuts: almonds, hazelnuts or pecans
preserved figs
biscotti
honey

Warm the milk in a pot over a medium heat.
After a few minutes it will begin to foam, but do not let it boil. Remove it from the stove for a bit if you need to cool it.
Let it simmer for a moment before adding the salt and the lemon juice or the vinegar. Stir well. Remove from the heat and let the milk rest for about 10 minutes, when it should begin to curdle.

Line a colander with a clean white muslin cloth or an undyed dishcloth. Strain the mixture through the cloth and squeeze out the excess fluid. Tie the cloth firmly with a piece of string and hang over a bowl to drain. Leave it in the fridge overnight until ready to serve.

Serve thick slices of the ricotta with thin slices of ciabatta toast, nuts, preserved figs, biscotti and honey.

SERVES 4

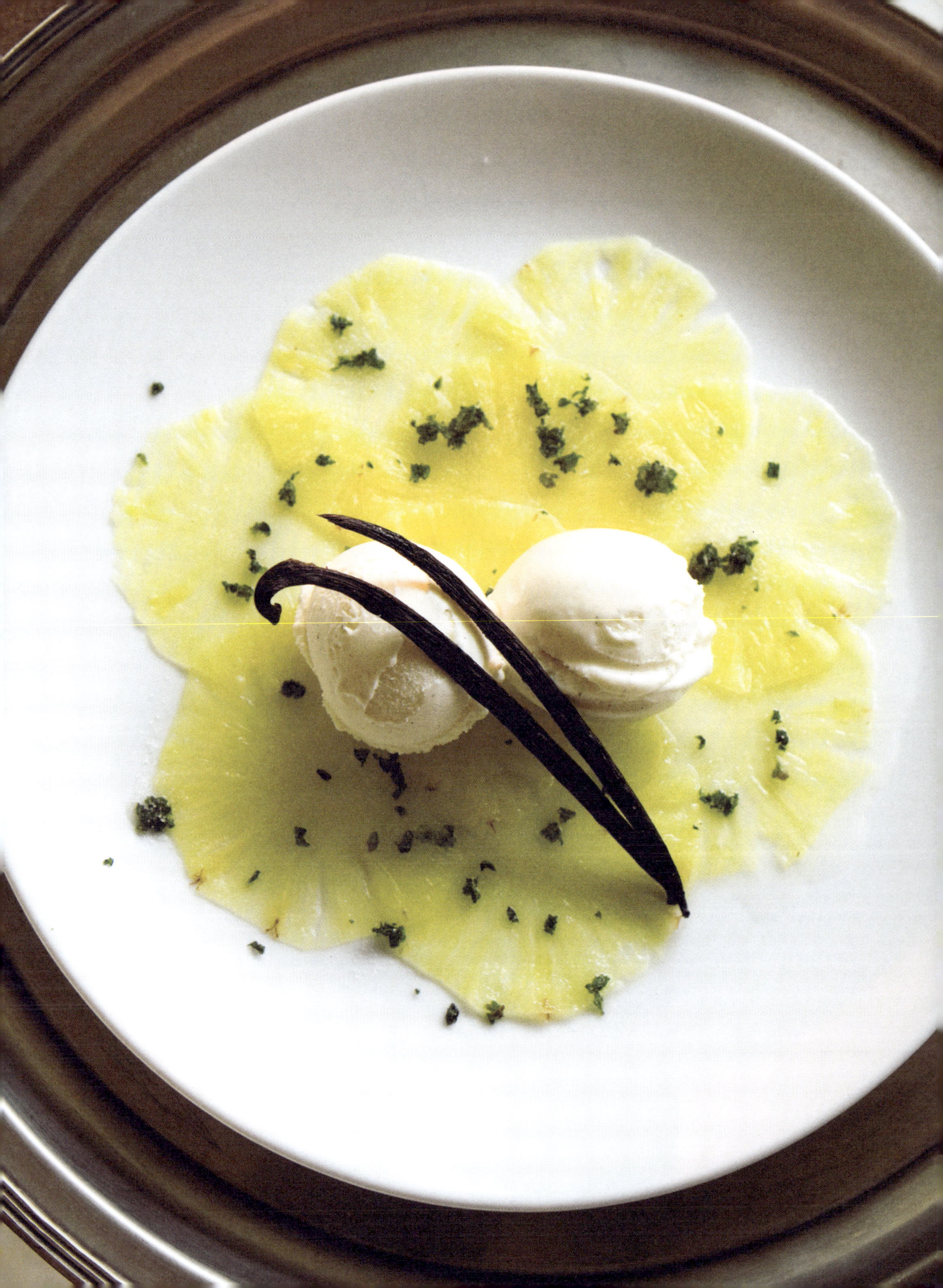

pineapple carpaccio

This is an elegant, refreshing and beautiful dessert that we serve at tashas Melrose. The best way to get the pineapple slices almost transparent is to use either a mandolin slicer, or a very sharp knife. Freeze the pineapple slices on the individual plates you're serving them on – if you freeze them in one batch, they'll break apart when you try to separate them.

2 ripe pineapples
4 vanilla pods
handful mint
1 tsp sugar
8 scoops vanilla ice cream

Peel the pineapple and slice it paper thin. Allow for about 10 slices per plate. Layer them on the individual plates, just as you would with a meat carpaccio, and then freeze.

Chop the mint together with the sugar. Score the vanilla pods lengthways and scrape out the seeds.

Sprinkle the pineapple slices with the mint and sugar and top with 2 scoops of ice cream. Garnish the ice cream with the vanilla seeds and finally, with the pods.

SERVES 4

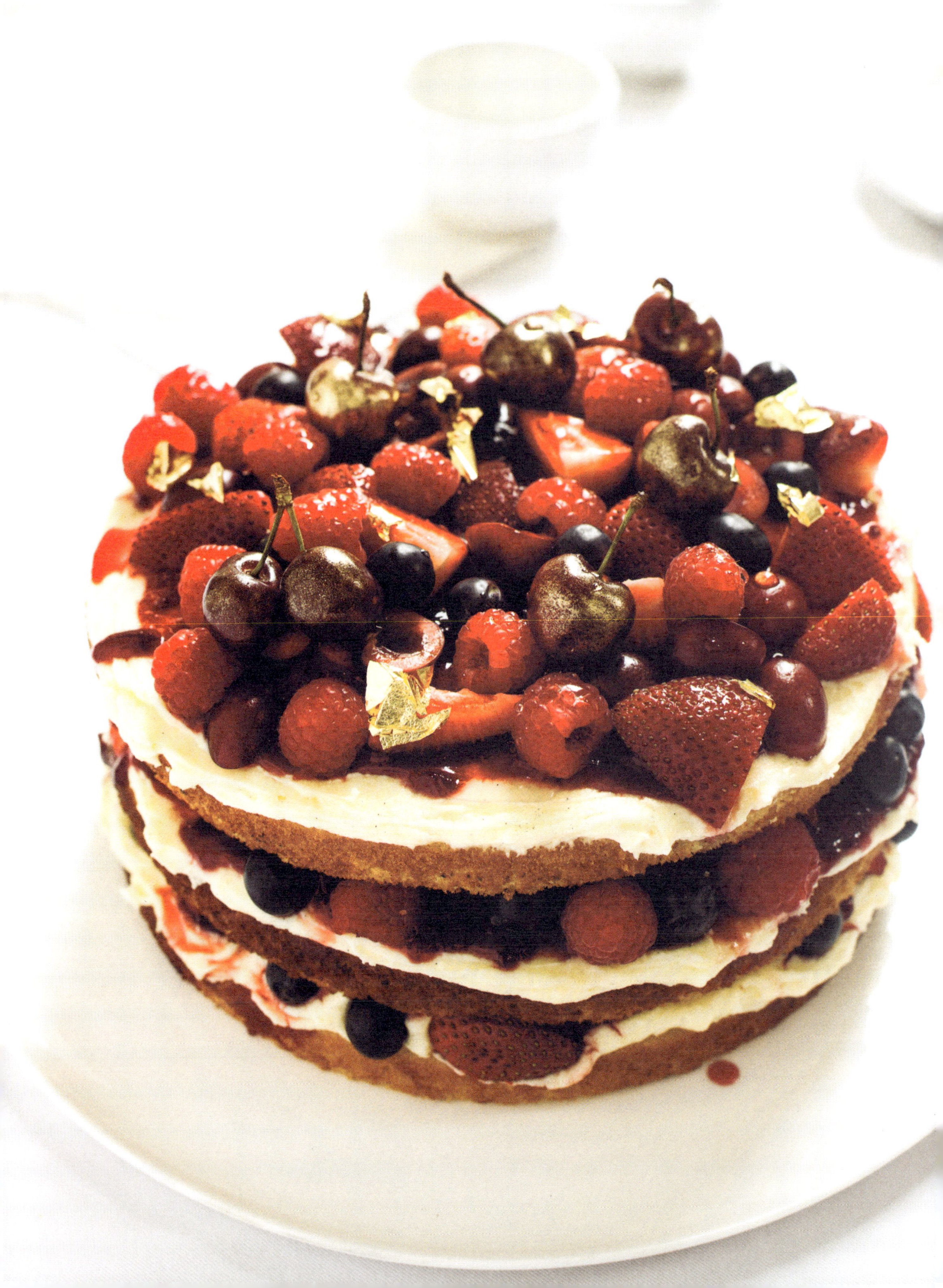

cream victoria

Extremely rich and elegant, crowned with ruby-red berries and slivers of gold leaf – this beautiful sponge cake really is the queen of cakes. This indulgent recipe comes from our wonderful pastry chef, Elze Roome.

SPONGE CAKE
500 ml flour
20 ml baking powder
5 ml salt
4 eggs, separated
250 ml sunflower oil
250 ml lukewarm water
seeds of 1 vanilla pod
375 ml sugar

CREAM CHEESE FROSTING
120 g butter
120 g cream cheese
seeds of 1 vanilla pod
2 ml salt
500 ml icing sugar

fresh mixed berries

Preheat the oven to 200 °C.
Prepare 4 x 21 cm cakes tins with baking paper and butter.

To make the sponge cake, first sift all the dry ingredients together. Whisk the egg whites to form stiff peaks. Mix the egg yolks, oil, water and vanilla seeds until the mixture is light and foamy. Add the sugar and mix well. Add the dry ingredients, then fold in the egg whites. Pour equal amounts into each of the 4 cake tins. Bake for 10 minutes at 200 °C.

Make the cream cheese frosting by beating the butter, cream cheese, vanilla seeds and salt in a mixer until smooth. Incorporate the icing sugar and mix well. The frosting should be light and fluffy.

Once the cake has cooled, ice with the frosting and decorate lavishly with a variety of fresh berries.

Serve with a pot of tea (and gloves), or a glass of chilled champagne.

SERVES 4

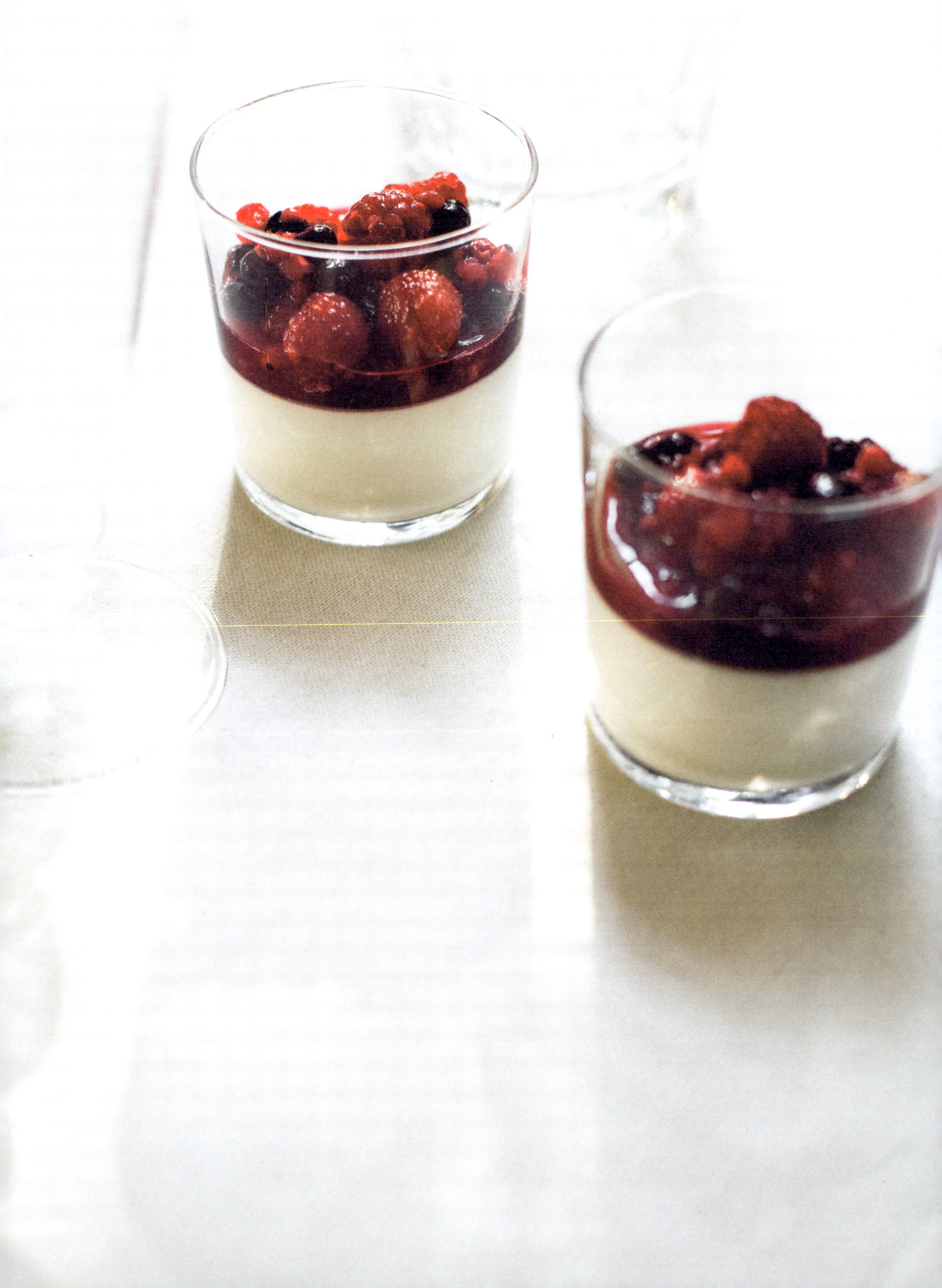

panna cotta

Not only is this is my favourite dessert, it is also the only one I really enjoy. A good panna cotta shouldn't be too sweet. Nor should it be too firm – it should have a bit of wobble. The name comes from the Italian term for 'cooked cream' but it can also be made with Greek yoghurt, which, of course, I prefer.

3 gelatine leaves
50 ml cold water
seeds of 1 vanilla pod
250 ml milk
250 ml double thick cream
60 g castor sugar
240 g mixed berries

Soak the gelatine leaves in a little cold water until soft. Open the vanilla pods lengthways and scrape out the seeds.

Warm the milk, cream, sugar, vanilla seeds and the pod in a saucepan. Bring to the boil and then remove from the heat. Take out the vanilla pod and discard. Squeeze the water out of the gelatine leaves and add them to the milk. Stir until the gelatine has dissolved.

Divide the mixture between 4 small dishes or pretty glasses and leave to cool before placing them in the fridge. Leave them in the fridge for at least an hour or until they have set.

Top with mixed berries.

SERVES 4

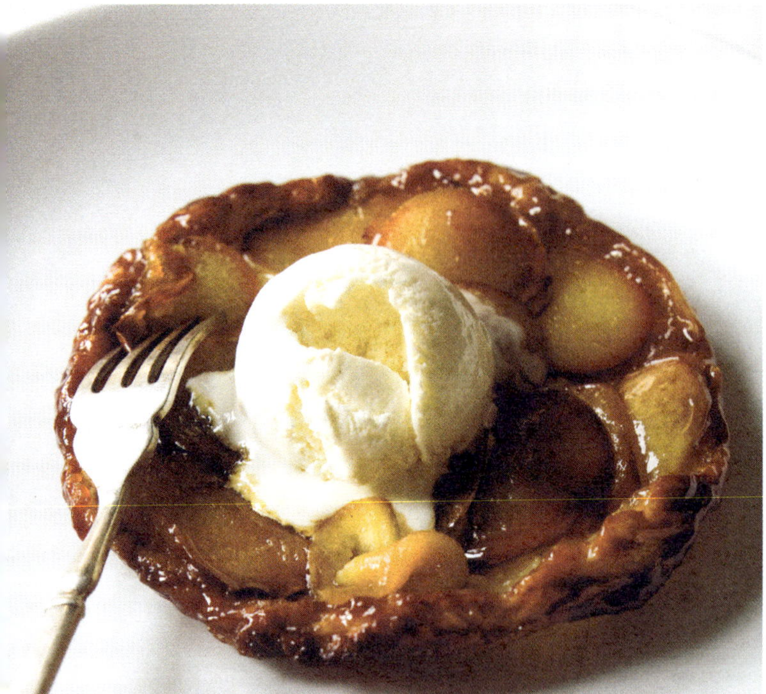
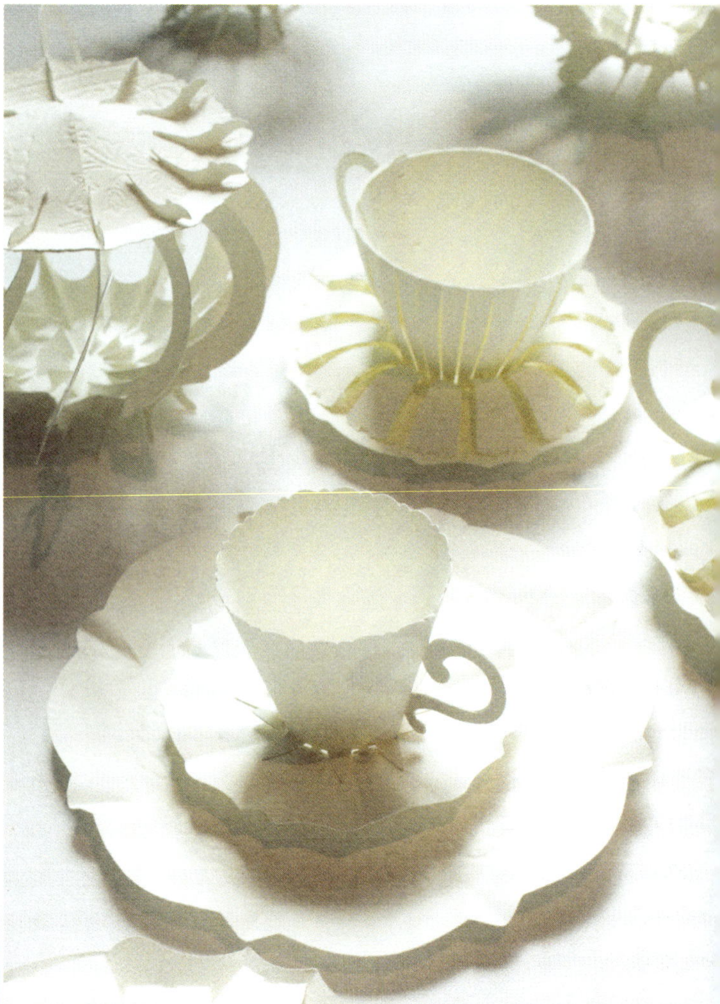

tashas tarte tatin

This is such a beautifully uncomplicated dessert and it never fails to impress. The best part is you don't even need a baking tray. It should be crisp, gooey and piping hot when you serve it. I like to make it with apples or pears, but peaches and plums are also good.

1 or 2 sheets ready-made puff pastry

200 g white sugar
40 g butter
15 ml lemon juice
pinch salt

4 apples, peeled and sliced

vanilla ice cream

You can make individual tarts if you have enough small pans, in which case you will need 2 sheets of puff pastry.

Preheat the oven to 200 °C.

Your puff pastry should be very cold so keep it in the fridge while you prepare the tart filling.

Melt the sugar over a low heat in a wide, shallow pan that can be used in the oven. Take care because it can burn very quickly and be extra careful when handling the caramel. Once the sugar has caramelised, add the butter, lemon juice and salt. Take the pan off the heat but leave the stove on.

Carefully place the fruit in the caramel. Put the pan back on the heat and allow the mixture to simmer. While it simmers, cut the puff pastry to fit over the pan. It doesn't have to be exact. This is a rustic dessert. Cover the pan with the puff pastry and place it in the preheated oven. Bake until the pastry is golden and flaky. The caramel will bubble out from under the pastry and will be very sticky.

Serve immediately. Turn the pan over onto a serving platter. Do it at the table – this is the impressive part. Cut it into slices and top with scoops of vanilla ice cream.

SERVES 4

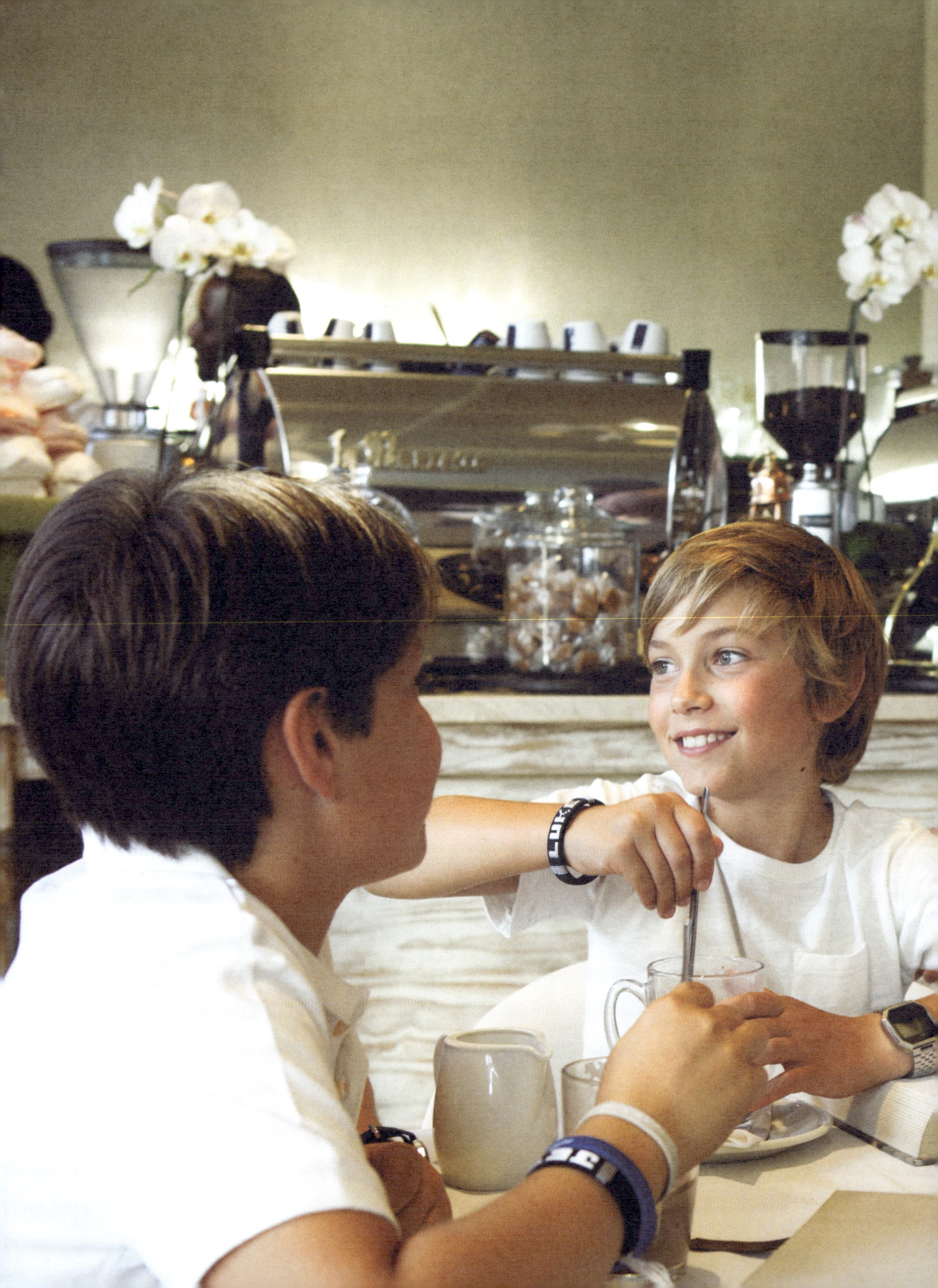

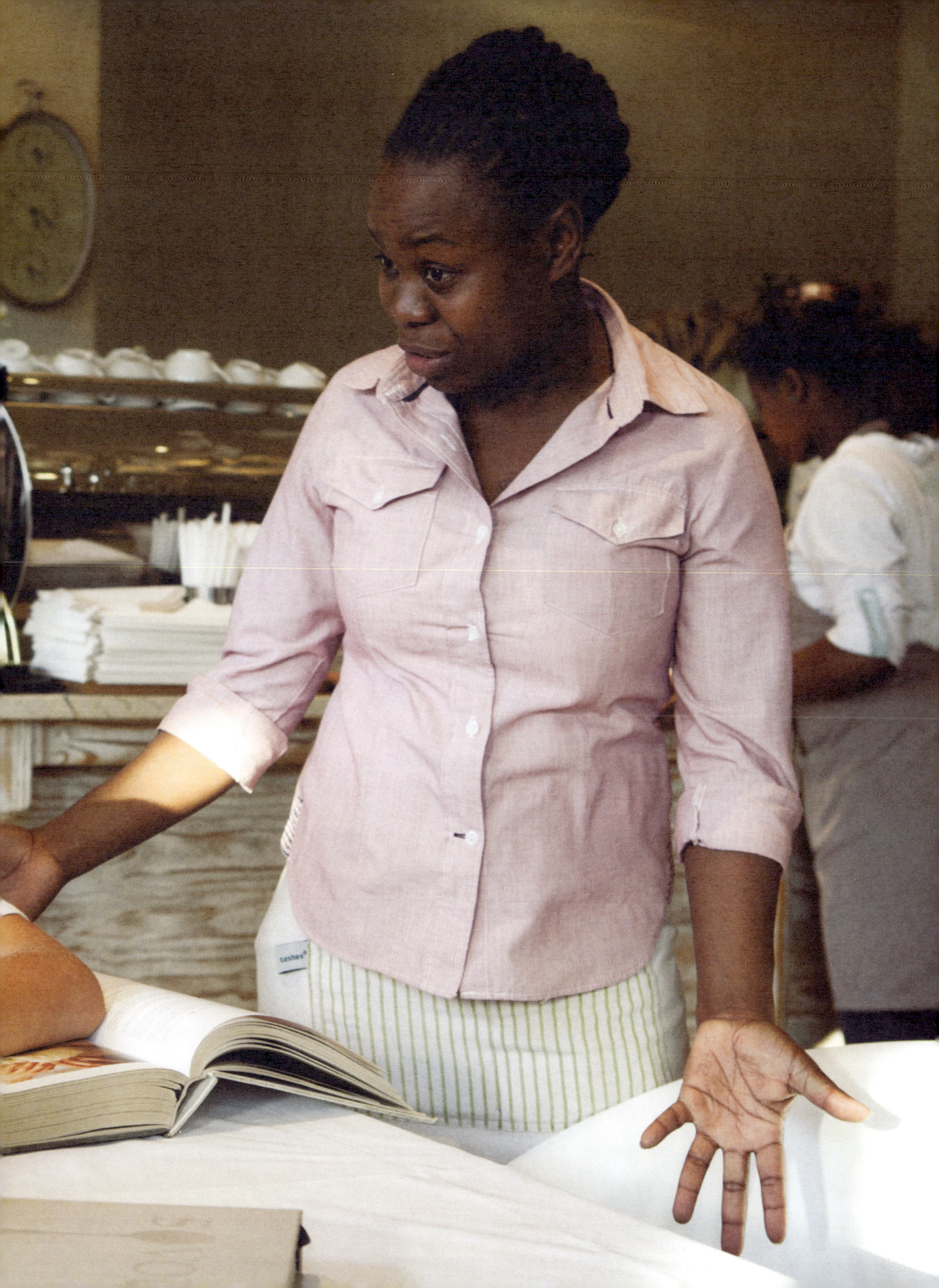

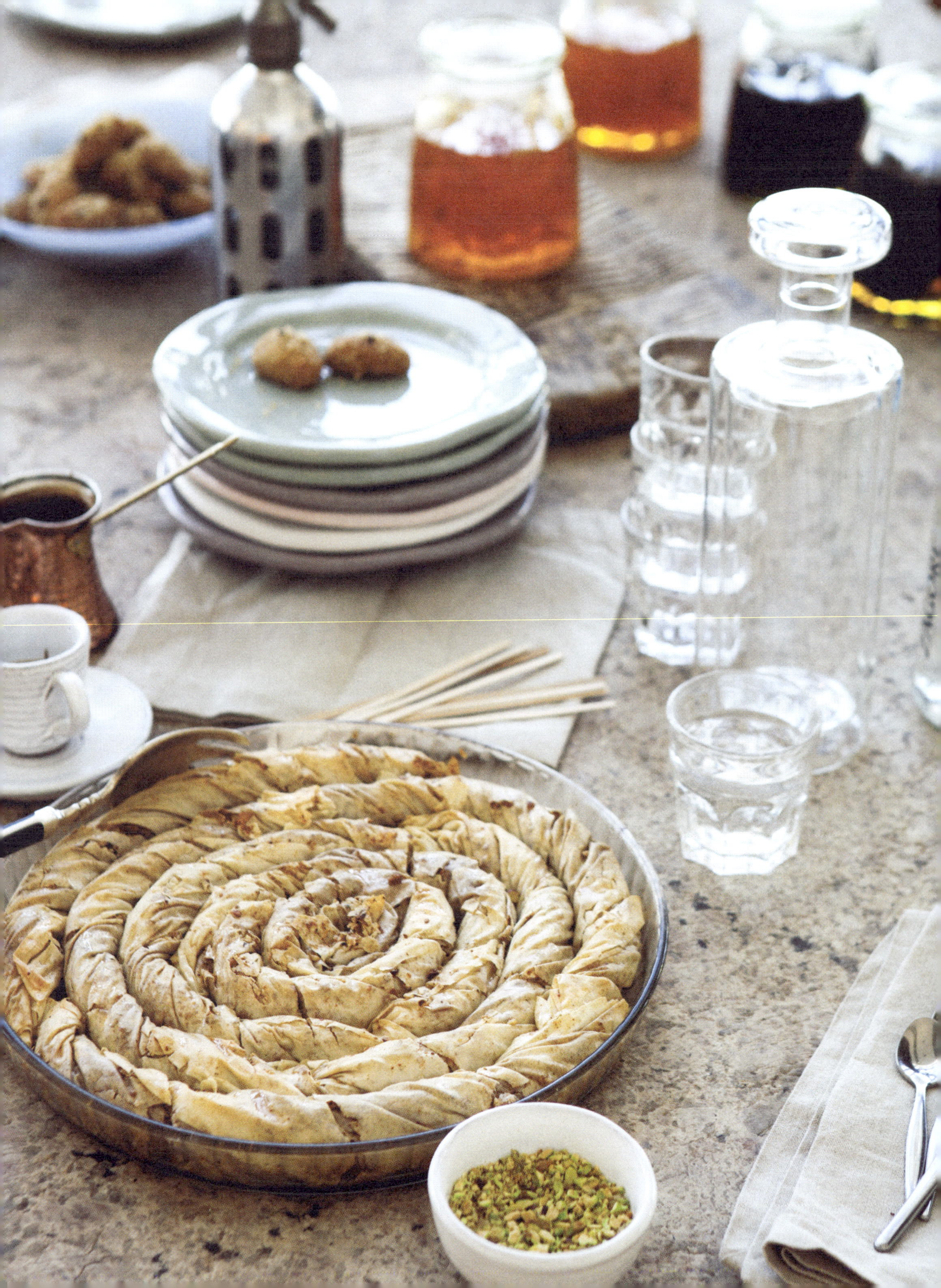

turkish baklava

The best baklava I have ever had was in Istanbul. I am so convinced of this that I'm not going to apologise to any Greeks, even if it would be safer for me to do so. The experience of this light, crispy delicacy will stay with me for a long time – despite the fact, as I said before, that I don't like sweets.

12 sheets phyllo pastry (1 box)
150 g unsalted butter, melted
200 g pistachios, roasted
200 g almonds, roasted
200 g walnuts, roasted
8 tbsp brown sugar
3 tsp cinnamon

SYRUP

750 g sugar
1 litre water
2 tsp lemon zest
2 tbsp lemon juice
2 tsp orange zest
1 cinnamon stick
2 cloves
1 tsp salt

Preheat the oven to 180 °C.
Roast the nuts until browned and then chop them finely.
Mix the nuts with the brown sugar and cinnamon.

Take 3 sheets of phyllo pastry and brush each sheet on both sides with the melted butter. Lay them on top of each other again. Scatter about a quarter of the nuts and brown sugar mixture evenly over the buttered pastry. Roll the pastry diagonally to create a long roll. Spiral it in a round baking dish about 30 cm in diameter. Repeat the process until all of the nuts and phyllo sheets have been used and the baking dish is full. Bake for 40 minutes.

While the baklava is baking, make the syrup.
Boil all the syrup ingredients together in a pot. The liquid will reduce. When it becomes thick and syrupy, remove from the heat and set aside.

When the baklava is ready, remove it from the oven and pour half of the hot syrup over it. Allow it to rest and absorb all the syrup. Pour the remaining syrup over the baklava once the first half has been completely absorbed. Leave the baklava to cool to room temperature and serve with Greek coffee (page 201).

SERVES 4

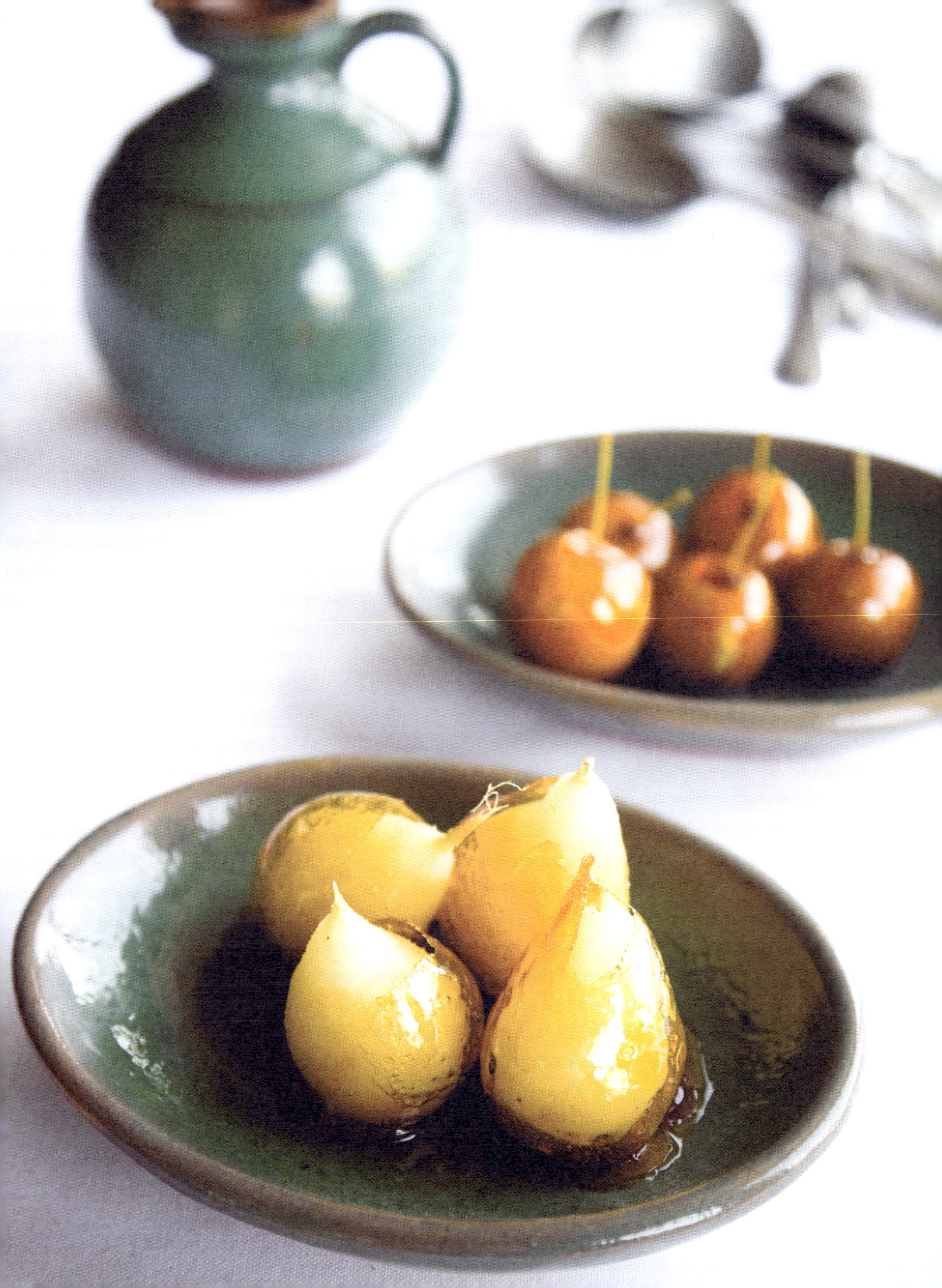

caramelised fruit

These are like toffee apples for grown-ups. They make a delicious change from preserves on a cheeseboard or they can be served on their own as a dessert. You can use fresh fruit such as figs and strawberries, or tinned fruit, as we have.

20 tinned baby apples
16 tinned baby pears
500 g white sugar
12 scoops vanilla ice cream

Drain the tinned apples and pears well – you can pat them dry with a kitchen towel, if needed.

In a heavy pot, melt the sugar over a low heat. Do not stir it with a spoon; rather shake the pot gently as the sugar melts. Don't let the sugar burn – remove the pot from the heat as soon as it has melted. Tilt the pot and dunk the apples and the pears in the caramel. Place the fruit on a non-stick tray or wax paper and allow to set.

Serve with ice cream as a dessert or as part of a cheeseboard with a variety of cheeses.

SERVES 4

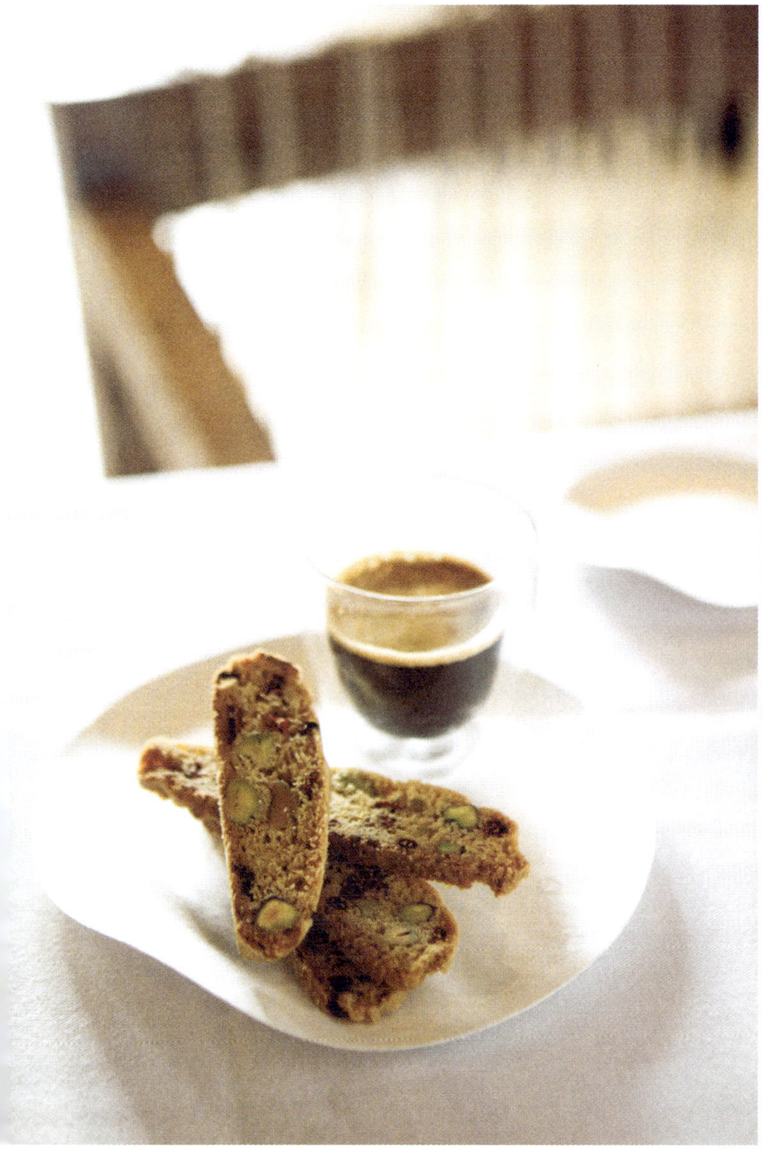
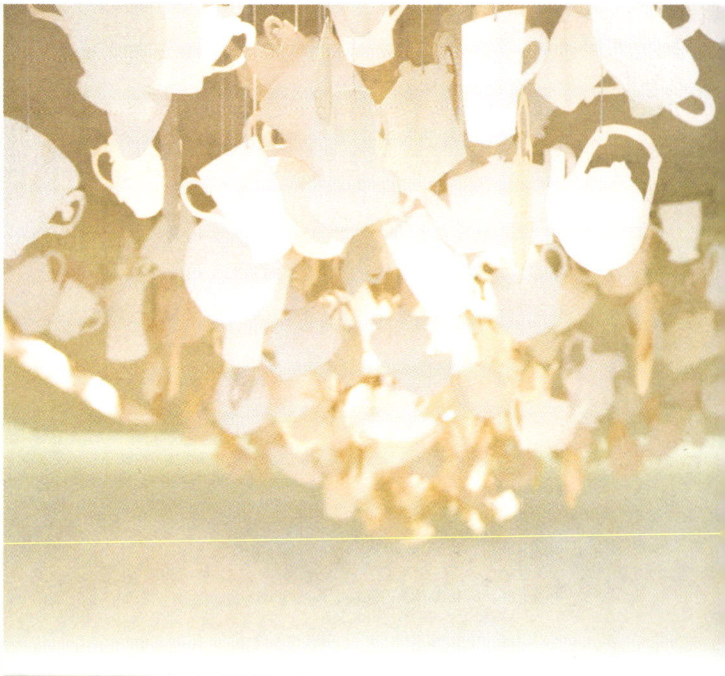
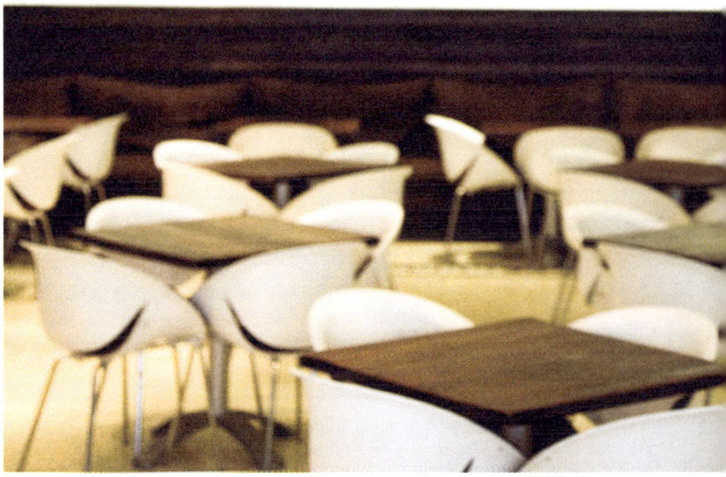

pistachio biscotti

Biscotti are twice-baked biscuits, which is why they are so time-consuming to make. But they keep very well and the method is not difficult. They are wonderful served with a single shot of strong espresso or a small glass of dessert wine after dinner. If you can't get hold of goji berries, dried cranberries are also lovely.

560 g flour
1 tsp bicarbonate of soda
1 tsp baking powder
pinch salt
250 g butter, softened
450 g sugar
120 ml orange zest, about 4 oranges
seeds of 2 vanilla pods
4 eggs
200 g pistachios
100 g goji berries

Preheat the oven to 180 °C.

Sift together the flour, bicarbonate of soda, baking powder and salt. In a separate bowl, cream the butter, sugar, orange zest and vanilla seeds until light and fluffy. Add the eggs to the butter mixture one at a time, mixing thoroughly after adding each one. Fold the dry ingredients into this mixture. Crush the pistachios. Gently mix them and the goji berries into the dough. Let the dough rest in the fridge for an hour.

Butter, then dust the baking sheet with flour. Divide the dough in half. Lightly flour your hands and roll the dough into 2 log shapes of about 4 cm diameter. Arrange the logs on the prepared baking sheet. Bake for 30 minutes or until light brown and firm to the touch. The logs will spread during cooking. Remove from the oven and let them cool.

Turn the oven down to 150 °C. Carefully transfer the logs to a cutting board. Using a serrated knife, cut slices about 2 cm thick. Arrange them cut-side down on the baking sheet. Bake again for 15 minutes or until nicely browned. Transfer the biscotti to wire racks to cool. You can store them in an airtight container at room temperature for up to 2 weeks.

Serve after dinner with coffee and liqueur.

MAKES 35-40 BISCOTTI

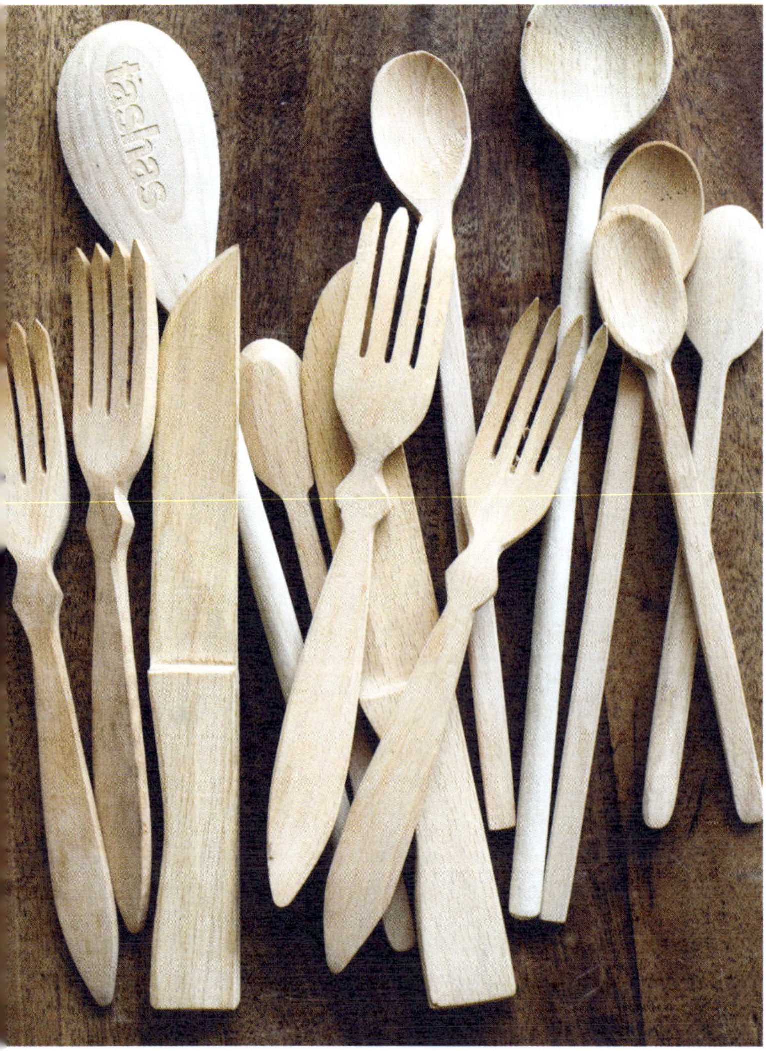
tashas

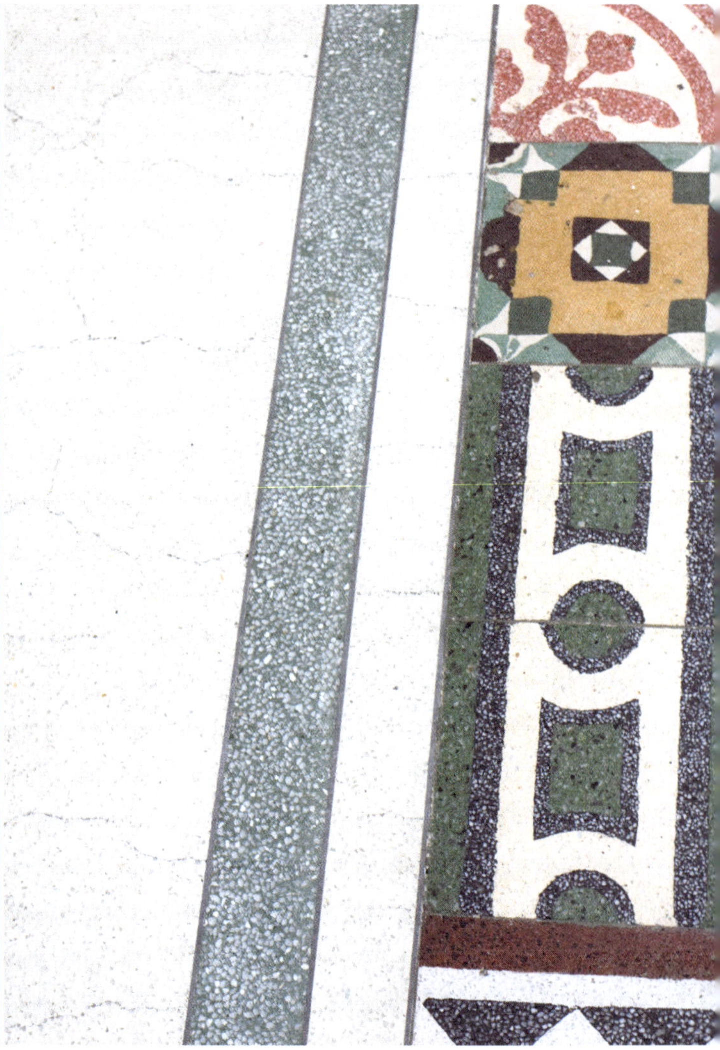

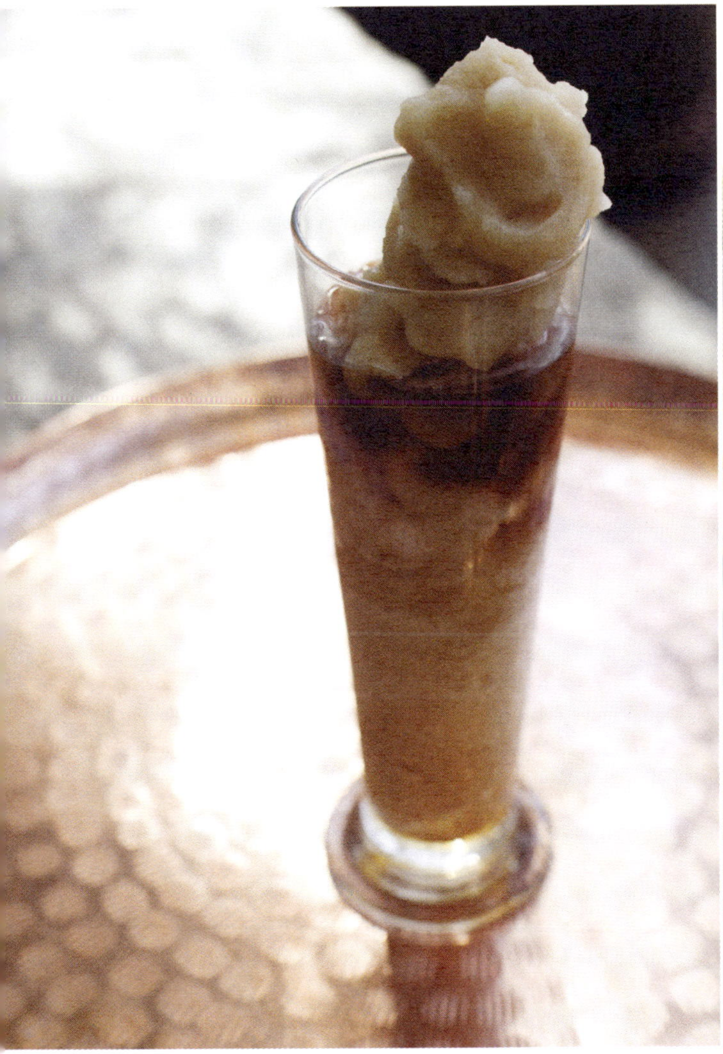

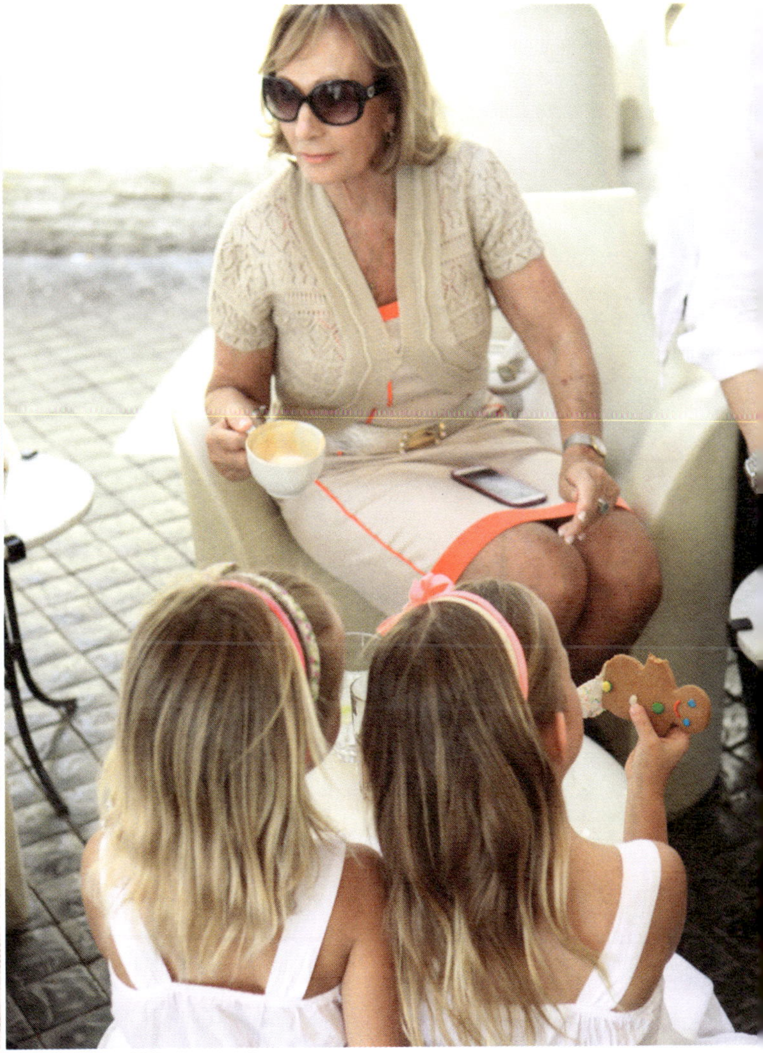

I like to think the drinks we serve are another point of difference for us.
We serve drinks that are unique, alternative and diverse. Drinks are an opportunity for something exciting. Have fun with them and take a moment to think about your presentation. Don't just put them in any old glass – make the glass and the garnish part of the experience.

drinks

the big squeeze	193
granitas	195
frullato	197
oreo cookie milkshake	199
greek coffee	201

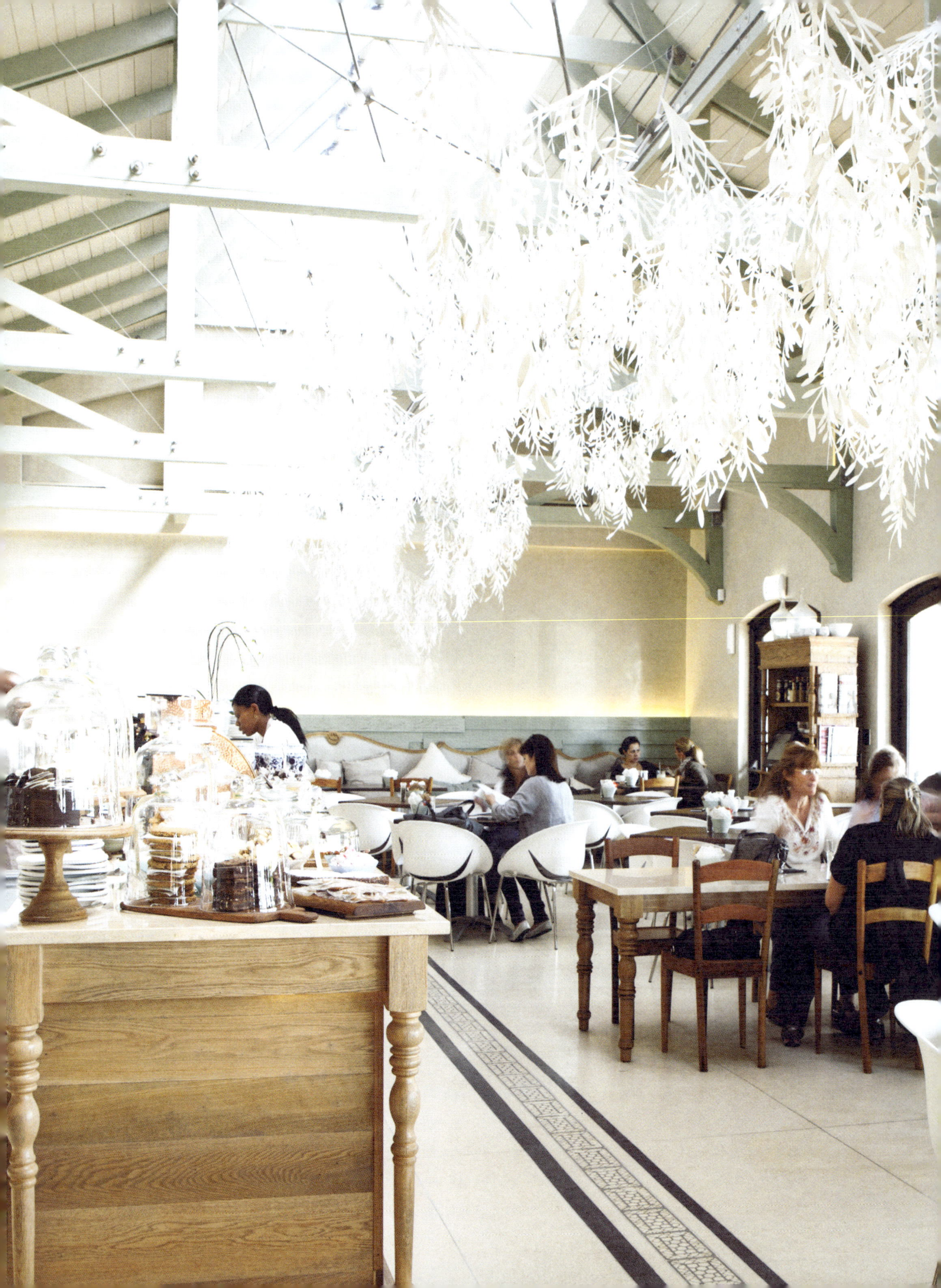

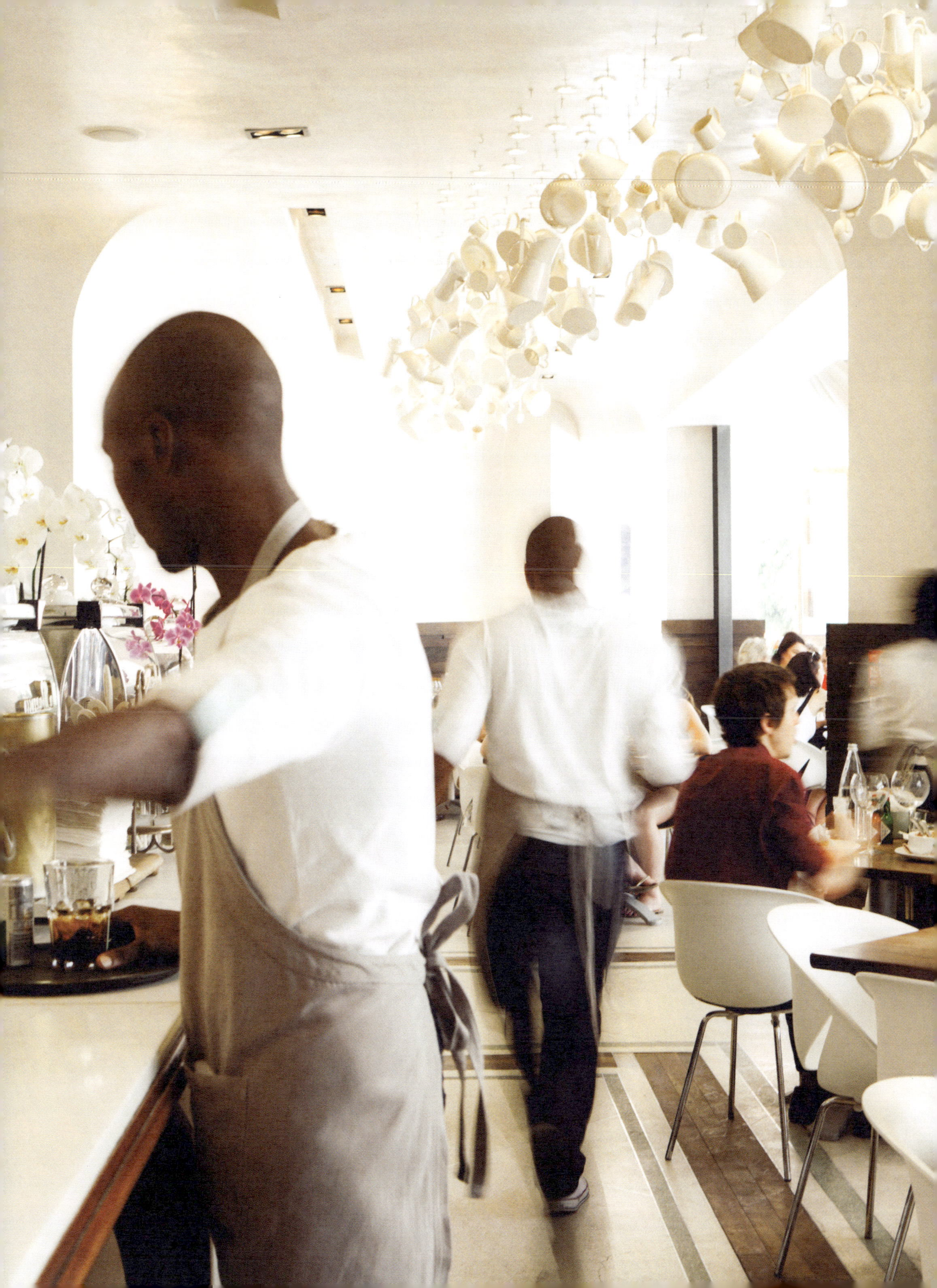

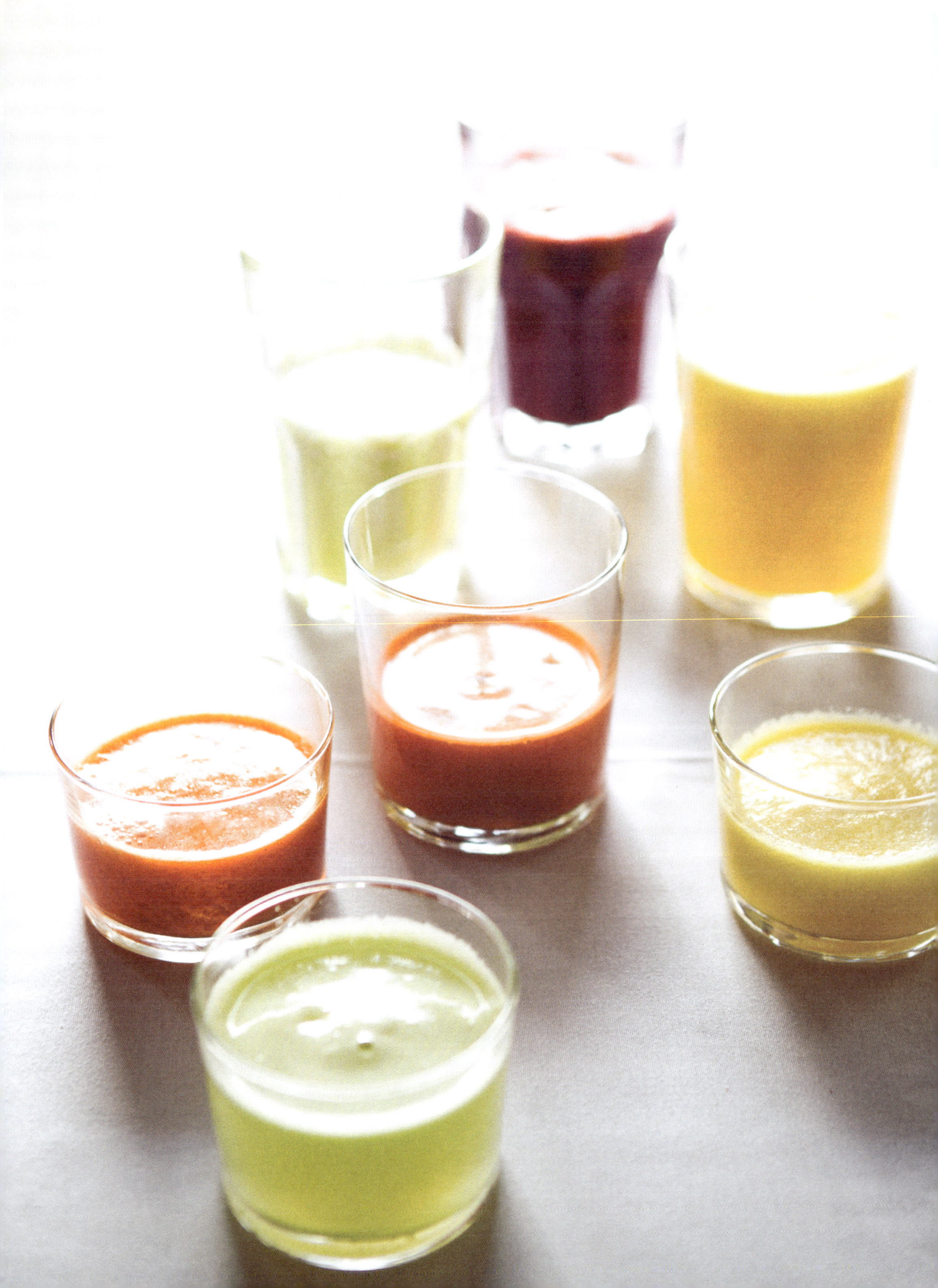

the big squeeze

We serve a lot of freshly squeezed juices and we have a variety of mixes, both savoury and sweet. These are just a few of our most popular combinations.

CARROT, BEETROOT, APPLE & LIME
5 carrots
1 beetroot
3 apples
1 lime

PINEAPPLE, GINGER, MELON & MINT
1 pineapple
5 cm piece ginger root
a quarter melon
10 mint leaves

GRAPEFRUIT & PEAR
2 grapefruits
2 pears

APPLE, LIME & GINGER
4 apples
1 lime
5 cm piece ginger root

CITRUS BLAST
2 grapefruits
3 oranges

GREEN MELON, CANTALOUPE, LEMON & MINT
one-quarter green melon
half a spanspek
1 lemon
15–20 mint leaves

Wash the fruit and vegetables for your juice. There's no need to peel them – the juicer will sort it out. You should be able to make about 300 ml of juice with these quantities, enough for one large glass. Juice and enjoy.

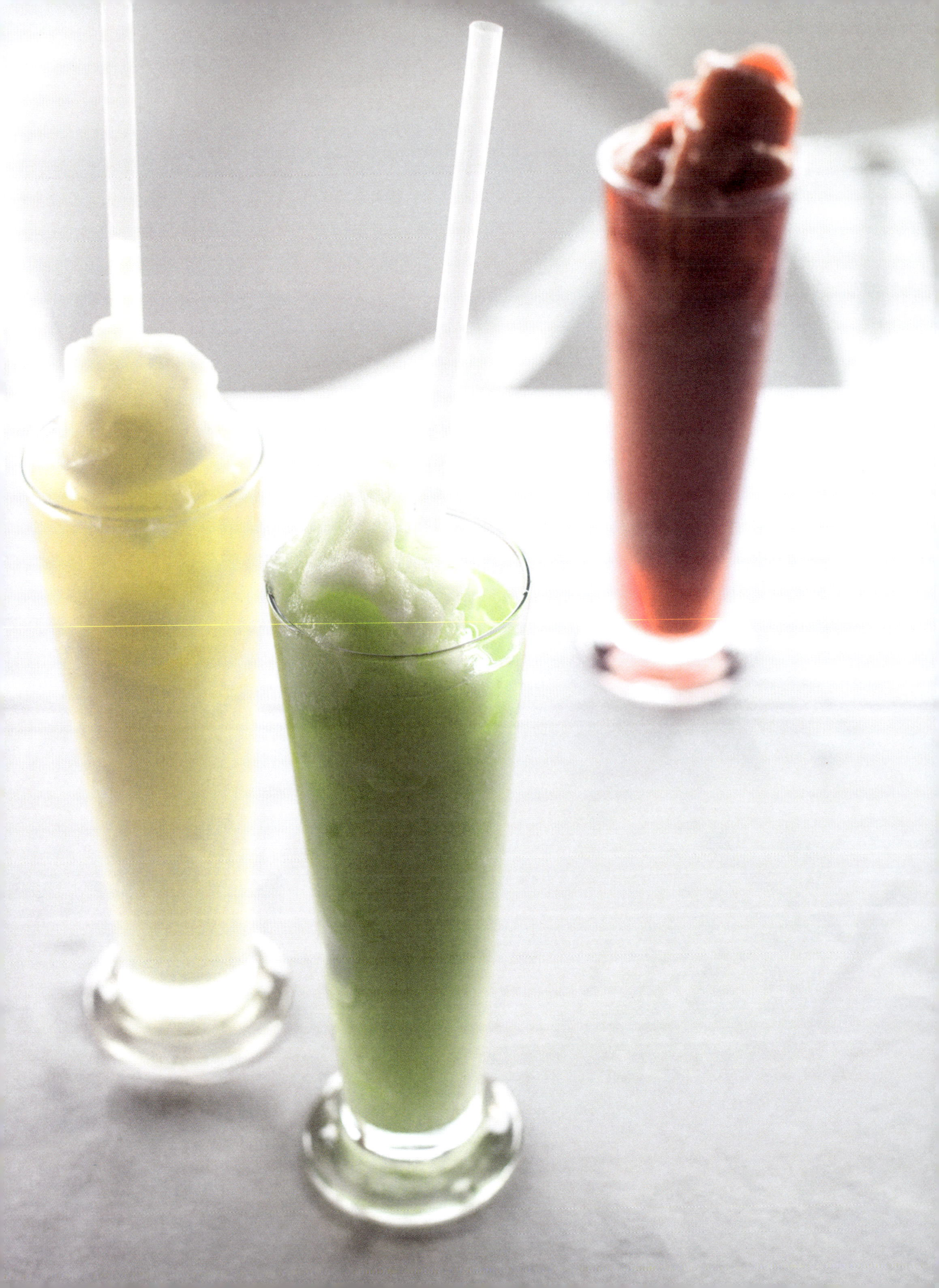

granitas

Granitas are the cool and sophisticated version of the slush puppy and they make a wonderfully refreshing summer drink. The secret to a good granita lies in the addition of the sugar syrup. It not only sweetens the granita but, more importantly, it's what prevents the fruit juice and the ice from splitting. This recipe is for an apple granita but you can make them with any of your favourite fruit.

80 ml boiling water
80 ml sugar
8 mint leaves, torn
1 green apple, cored and cut
500 ml ice

To make the syrup, heat the water and sugar in a pot. Let it boil for 2 minutes or until it has reduced to half and has the consistency of a runny syrup. Set aside to cool.

To make the granita, blend the mint, fruit, ice and cold sugar syrup in a blender.

Serve the granita in a tall, ice-cold glass with a thick straw or a long spoon.

MAKES 1

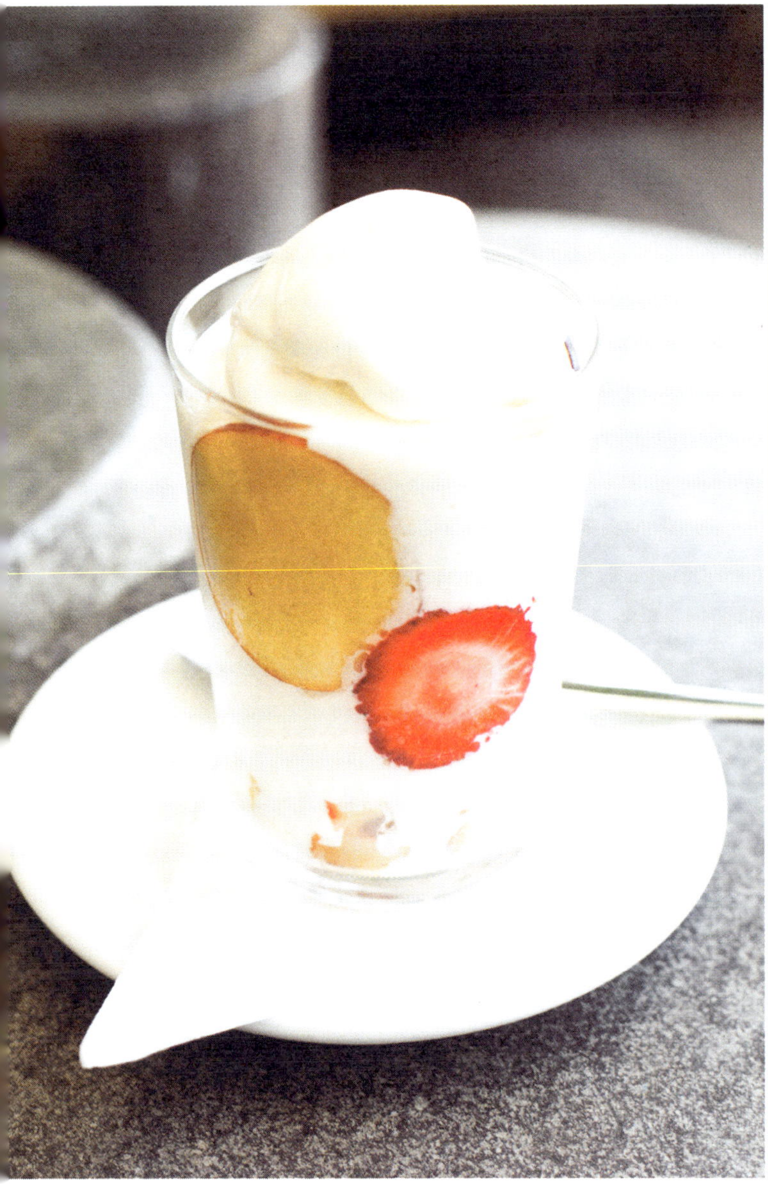

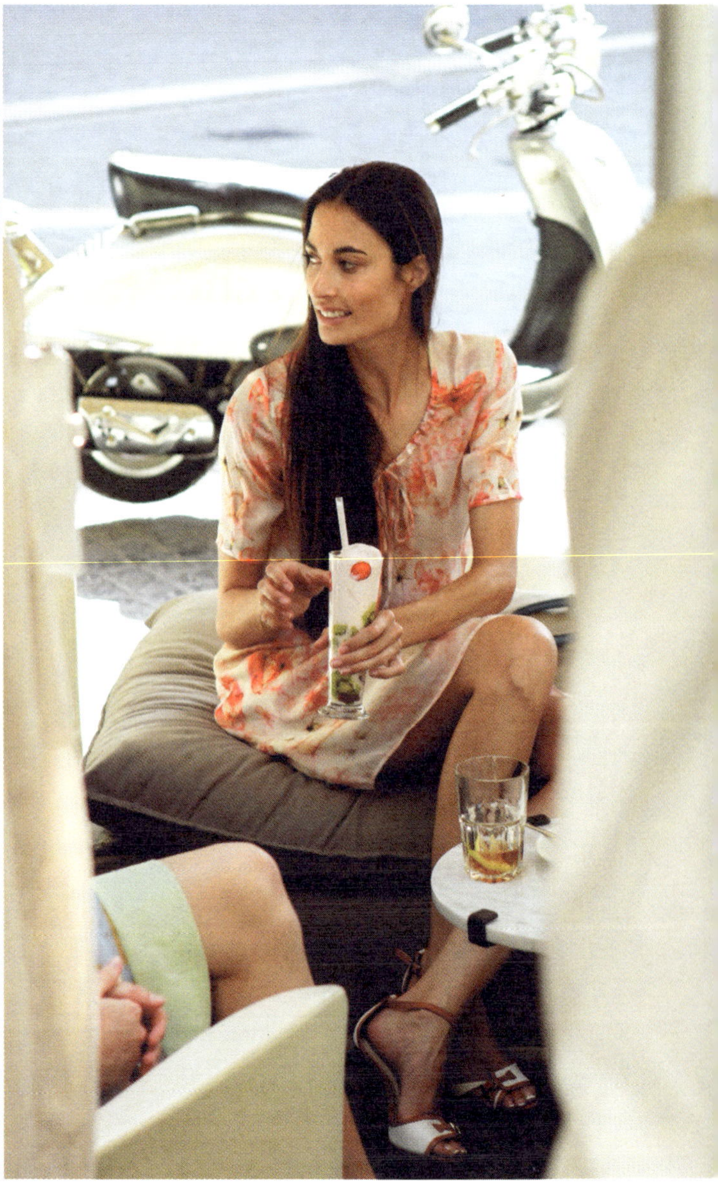

frullato

A frullato is a fruity milkshake or a creamy fruit juice. We use a rich ice cream but you can substitute with frozen yoghurt for a healthier alternative that still has all the flavour only without the calories. Serve your frullato in a tall glass and decorate the sides with slices of fresh fruit. This is only one idea for a very versatile recipe, so be creative and experiment with other juices and fruit.

5 scoops vanilla ice cream or frozen yoghurt
200 ml fruit cocktail juice
2 strawberries, sliced
1 kiwifruit, sliced

Blend the ice cream or frozen yoghurt and the fruit juice in a blender.

Take a few slices of fruit and arrange them on the insides of the glass. If they're not cut too thick, they should stick long enough for you to pour the frullato mix into the glass.

Serve with a long spoon.

MAKES 1

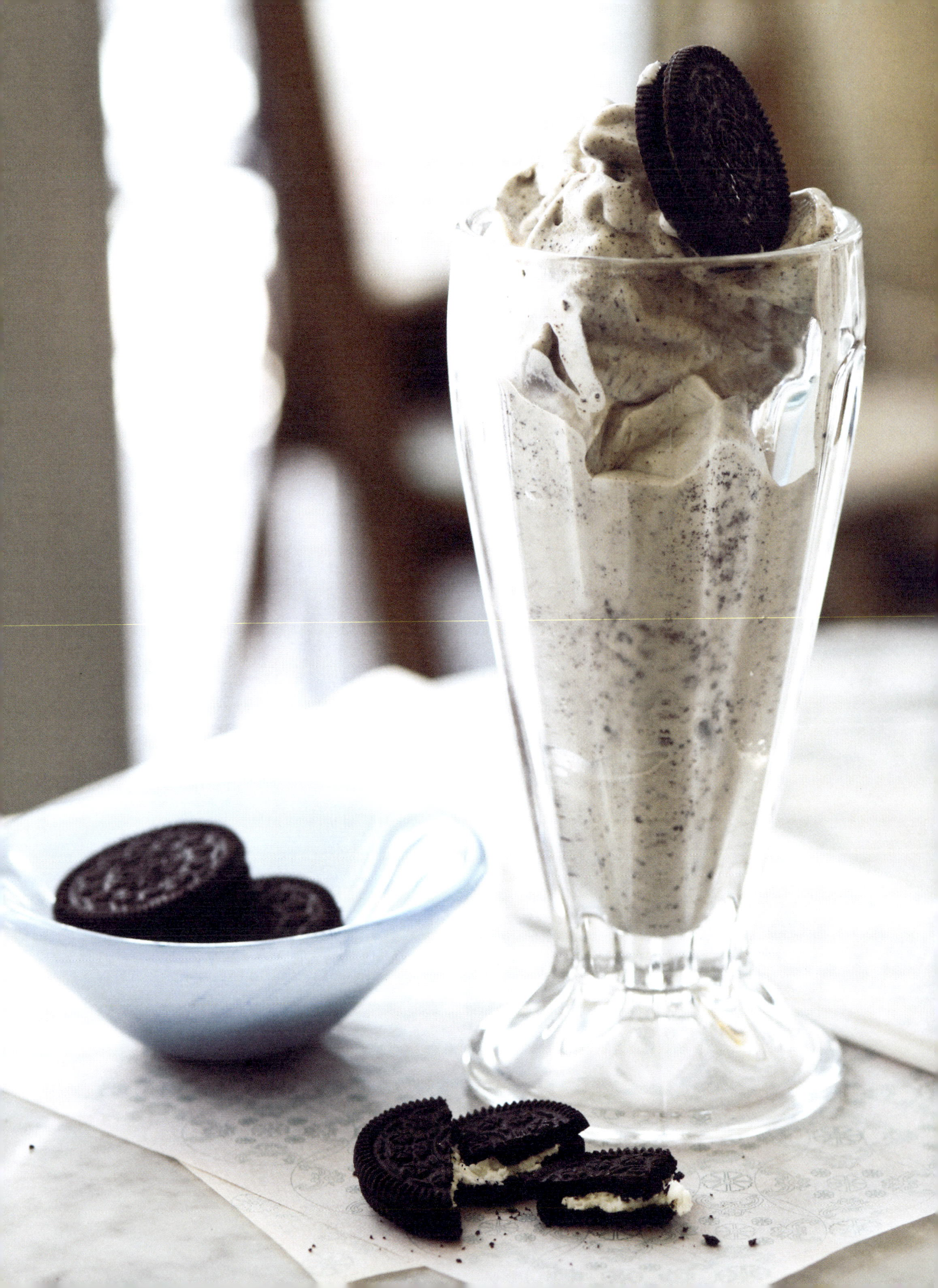

oreo cookie milkshake

In my world, milkshakes and Mondays will always go together. We serve this milkshake at tashas Rosebank along with a selection of our Paparazzi Shakes, Mondays and every other day of the week. If you can get your hands on some double thick straws, you're going to need them because it's fabulous when the chewy Oreo bits make their way up the straw.

4 scoops vanilla ice cream
60 ml milk
4 Oreo cookies

Blend the ice cream, milk and 3 Oreo cookies in a blender. Pour into a tall milkshake glass and put an Oreo cookie on top of the shake. Serve with a straw and a long spoon.

MAKES 1

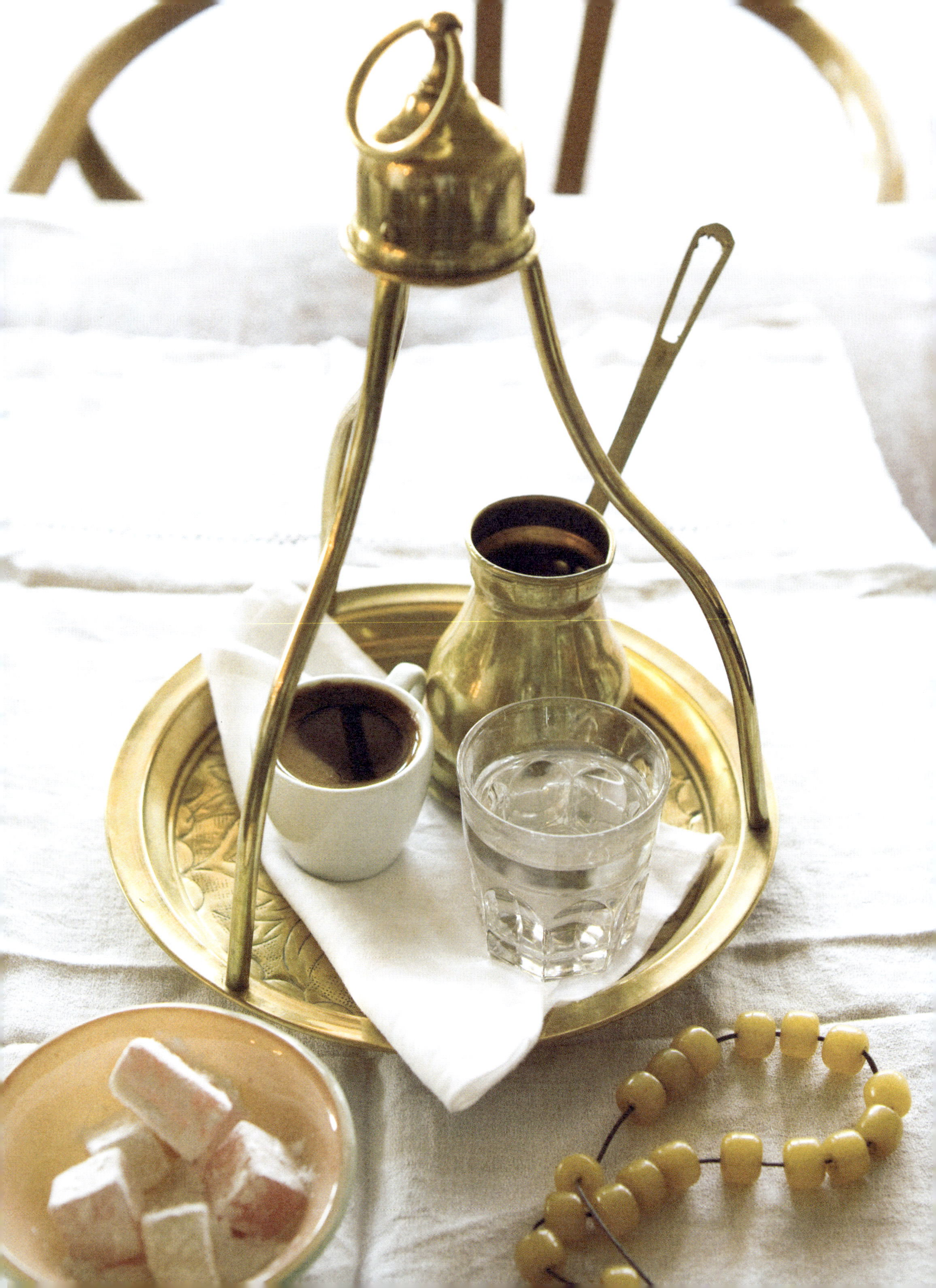

greek coffee

If anyone ever tells you that the Turks invented coffee, sever all ties with them immediately. The Greeks invented slow-brewed coffee. Ask any one of us, we'll tell you. You need a Greek coffee pot to make this properly. It's called a *briki*.

about 100 ml water, depending on cup size

Greek coffee

PLAIN / SKETOS
1,5 tsp coffee, no sugar

STRONG / VARIS
2–3 tsp coffee
1 tsp sugar

LIGHT / ELAFRIS
1 tsp coffee
1 tsp sugar

SWEET / GLYKOS
1 tsp coffee
2 tsp sugar

Fill your cup with water, then pour the water into the *briki*. The *briki* must be big enough for the coffee to steam, bubble and foam. Decide how strong and sweet you want your coffee and add the amount, shown in the ingredients, to the water. Stir, then put the *briki* on the stove. Keep the heat low. The coffee should heat slowly. Keep an eye on it but allow it to simmer.

Once it starts to foam, remove it from the heat and let the foam settle. Repeat this process. When the coffee has foamed again, remove it from the heat once more. Don't over-boil the coffee, you will not have enough foam if you do, but also, if you don't boil it enough you will taste the grounds.

Use a coffee cup, with a saucer. Pour the coffee into the cups and divide the foam evenly between each if you are making more than one. Serve with a glass of cold water on the side.

Savour every sip as you drink your coffee. This is not an espresso to drink on the run. And do not drink the grounds, you'll not like yourself afterwards.

SERVES 1

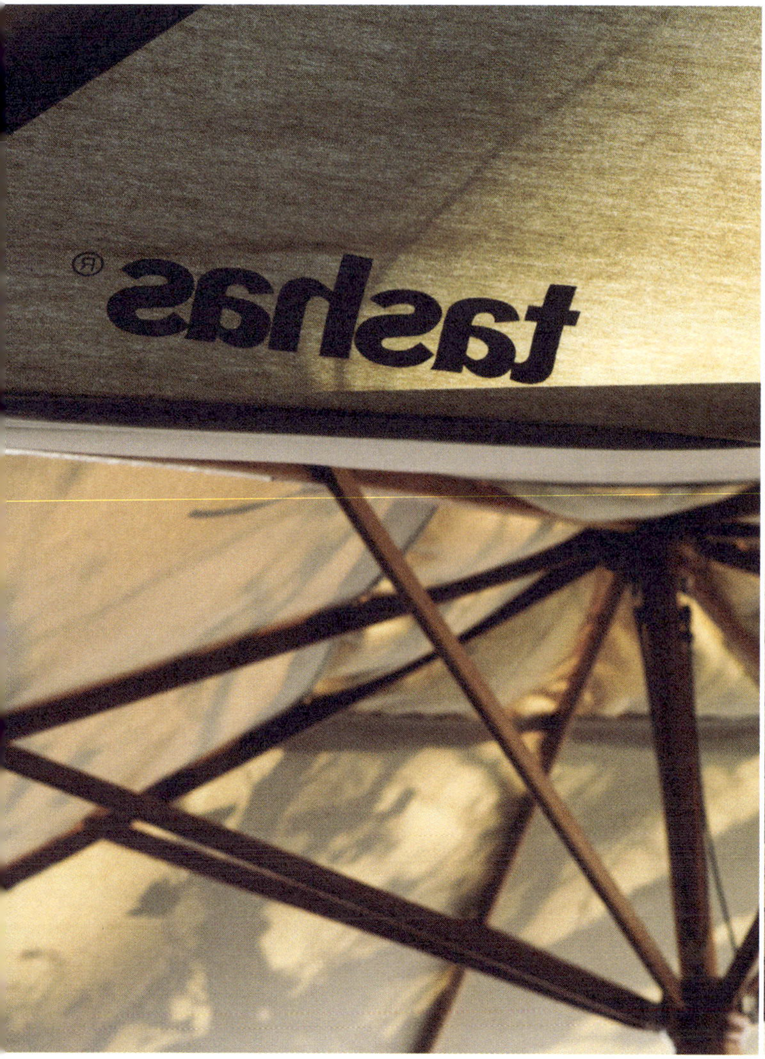
tashas

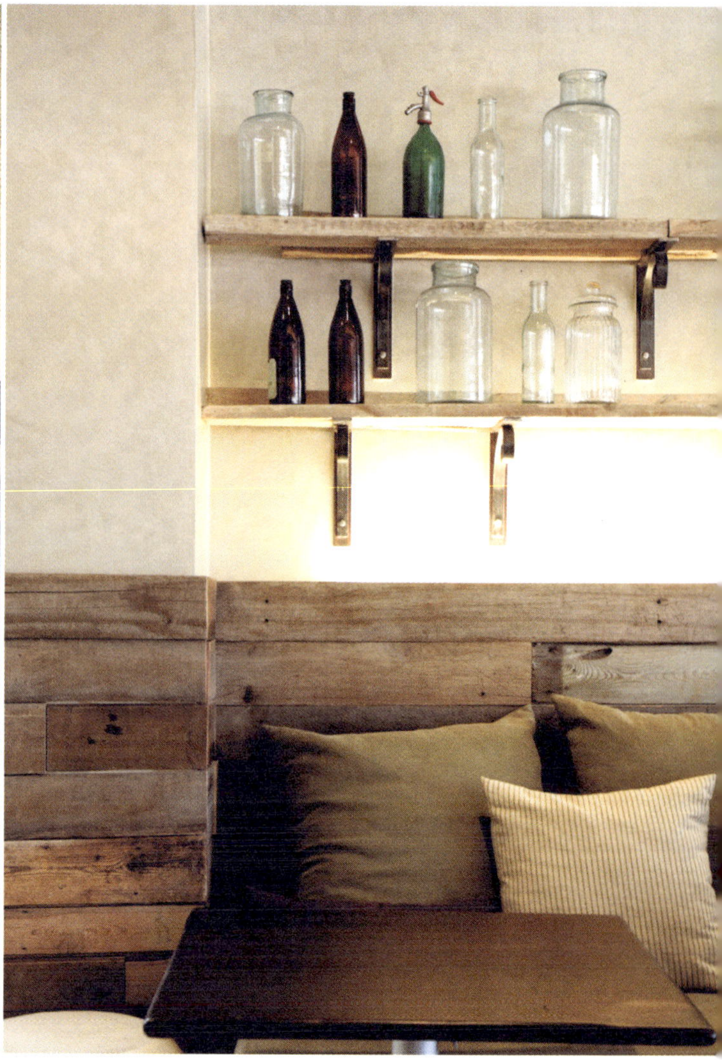

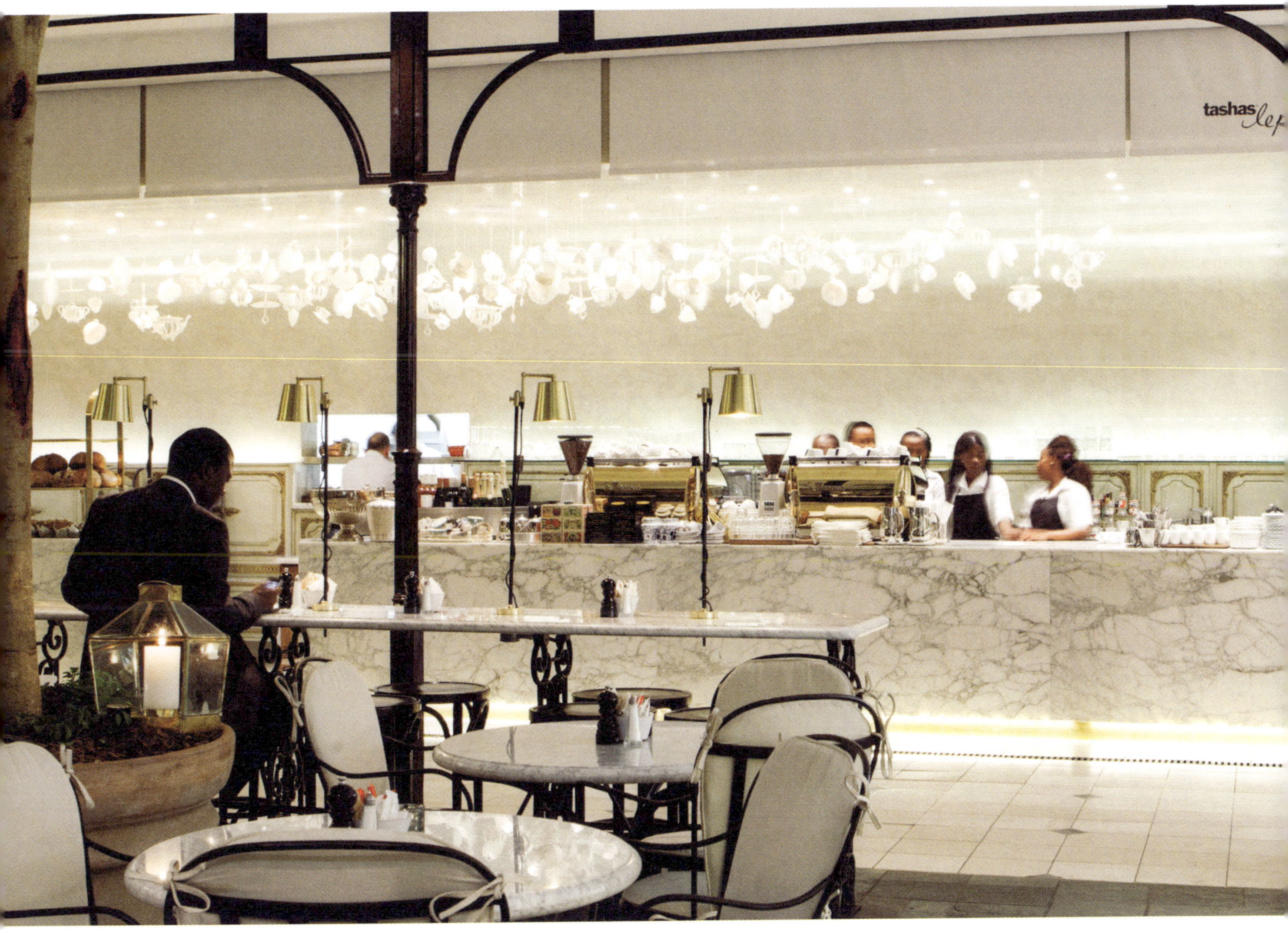
tashas

I am not an umbrella, straw or hollow-pineapple cocktail drinker.
The closest I'll get to a cocktail umbrella is a long, leafy celery stick. I prefer my cocktails old-school. These recipes are all classics, except for the Turkish delight cocktail, which is as pink as it is sweet, but you'll like it, I'm sure.

cocktails

negroni 207

whiskey sour 209

gin gimlet 211

bloody ross 213

turkish delight cocktail 215

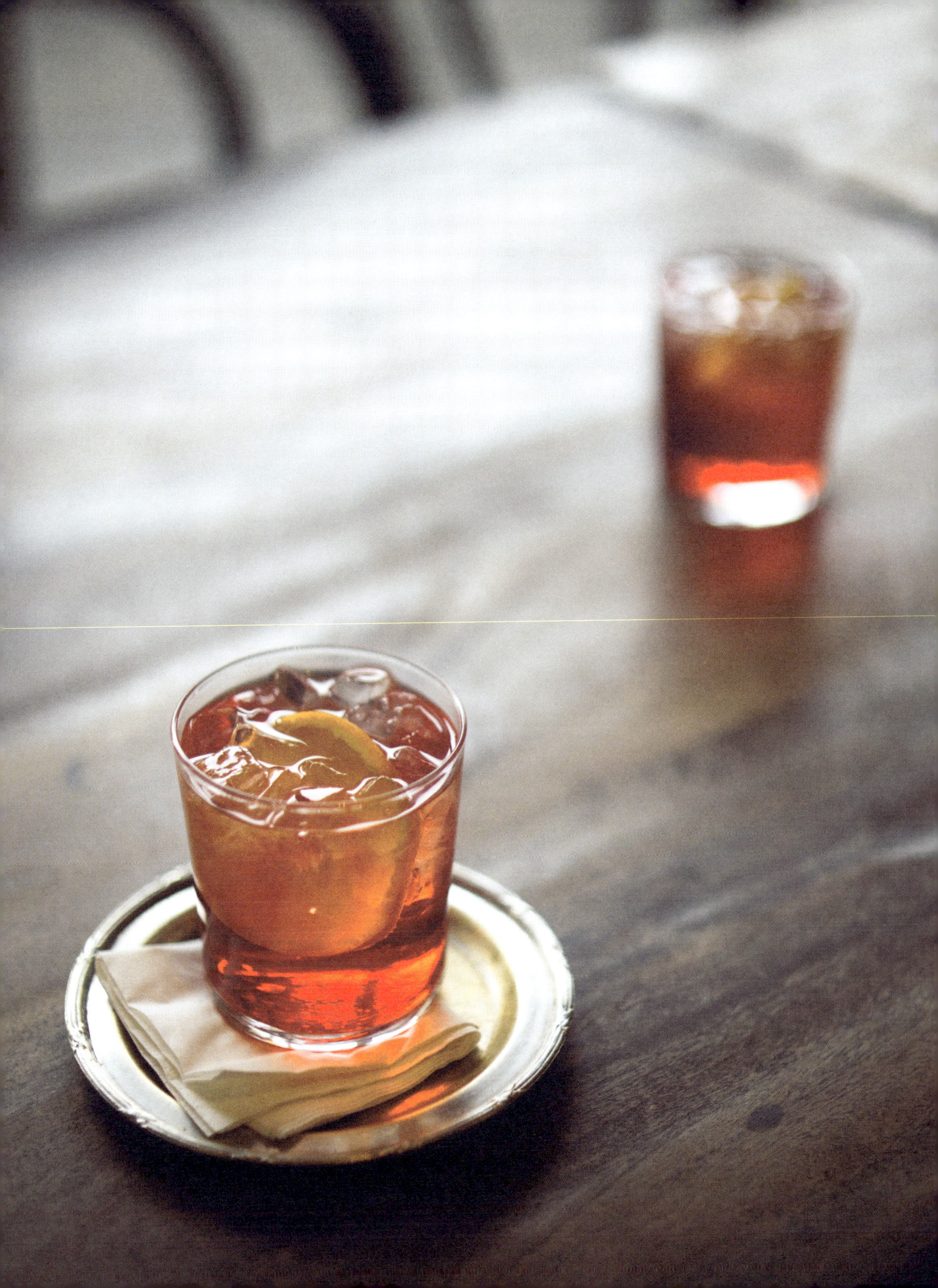

negroni

Orson Welles' famous description of the negroni pretty much sums it up: "The bitters are excellent for your liver, the gin is bad for you. They balance each other." You can balance it further by getting the ice-to-cocktail ratio right – use a short glass and not too much ice. Garnish with a slice of orange or a twist of burnt orange peel.

30 ml gin
30 ml Martini Rosso
30 ml Campari
180 ml crushed ice
sparkling water (optional)
dash bitters
half a slice of orange

Combine the gin, Martini Rosso and Campari in a shaker with ice and shake. Strain into a chilled tumbler that is about three-quarters filled with crushed ice. Add a splash of sparkling water and a dash of bitters.

Garnish with half a slice of orange.

MAKES 1

tashas le parc

whiskey sour

The whiskey sour is as classic as old-fashioned cocktails get and it definitely goes down smoother if you dress up for it. You can leave out the traditional maraschino cherry and orange slice if they're a bit dated for your style, but it's just not the same without the egg white topping.

60 ml whiskey
60 ml lemon juice
2 tbsp castor sugar
ice cubes

TOPPING
1 egg white
1 tsp castor sugar

lemon zest to garnish

Blend the whiskey, lemon juice and castor sugar in a shaker with a few ice cubes until the sugar has dissolved. Strain into a whiskey tumbler.

Whisk the egg white with the castor sugar until foamy. Spoon on top of the drink and sprinkle with lemon zest.

MAKES 1

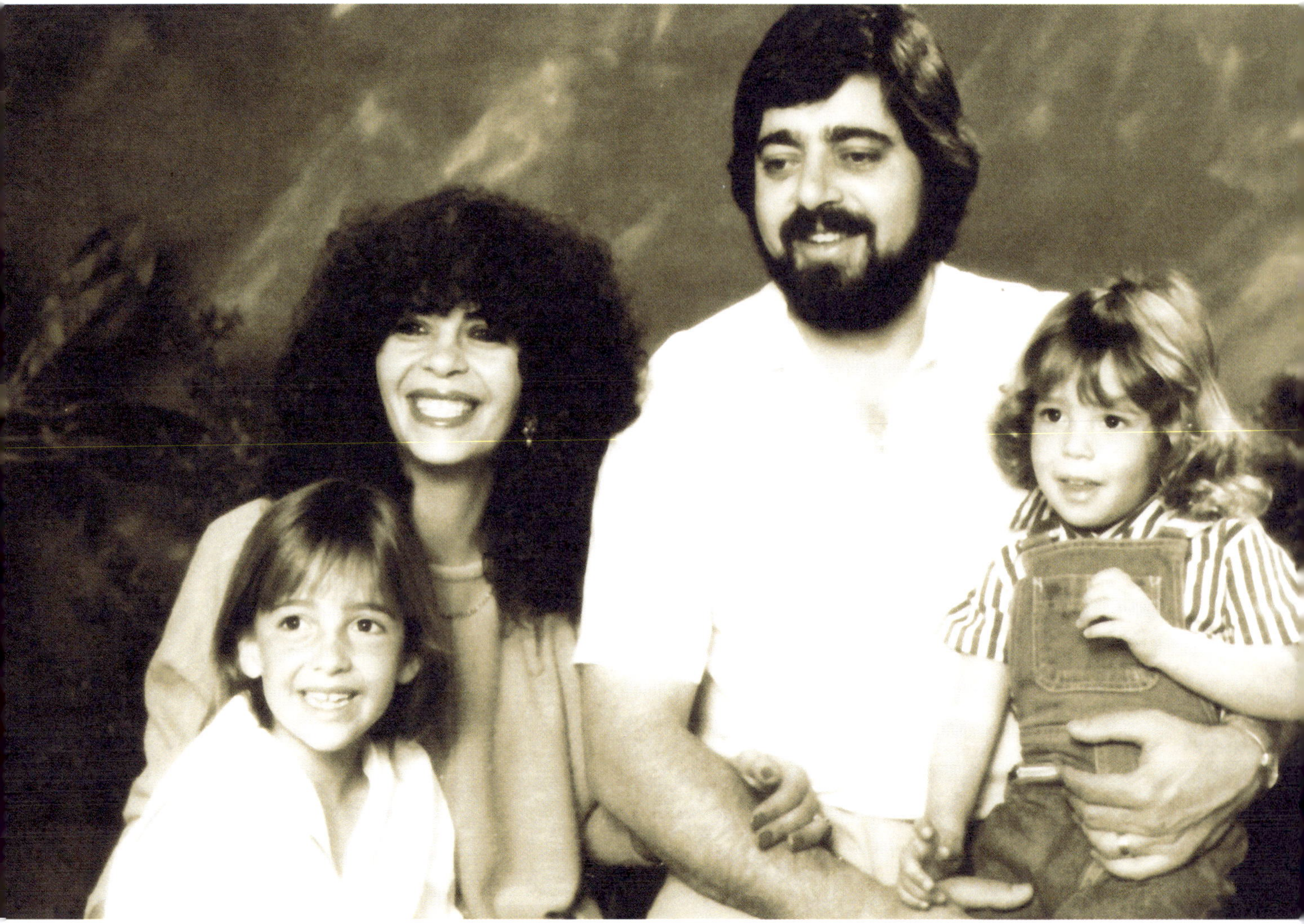

gin gimlet

In the 70s the only thing bigger than a mirror ball was my dad's hair. My mom's, of course, trumped that. But back then, even bigger than that were the Avo Ritz and the Gin Gimlet.

SUGAR SYRUP
80 ml water, boiling
80 ml sugar

60 ml gin
30 ml fresh lime juice
15 ml lime cordial
ice
small wedge lime

To make the syrup, heat the water and sugar in a pot. Let it boil for 2 minutes or until it has reduced to half and has the consistency of a runny syrup. Leave the syrup to cool. This is more than the recipe for one cocktail calls for but it's always good to have some syrup in the fridge.

Combine 30 ml of the sugar syrup with the gin, lime juice and cordial in a shaker filled with ice. Shake vigorously. Strain into a tumbler with ice. Rub a lime wedge along the rim of the glass before dropping it into the drink.

Serve with a classic 70s track.

MAKES 1

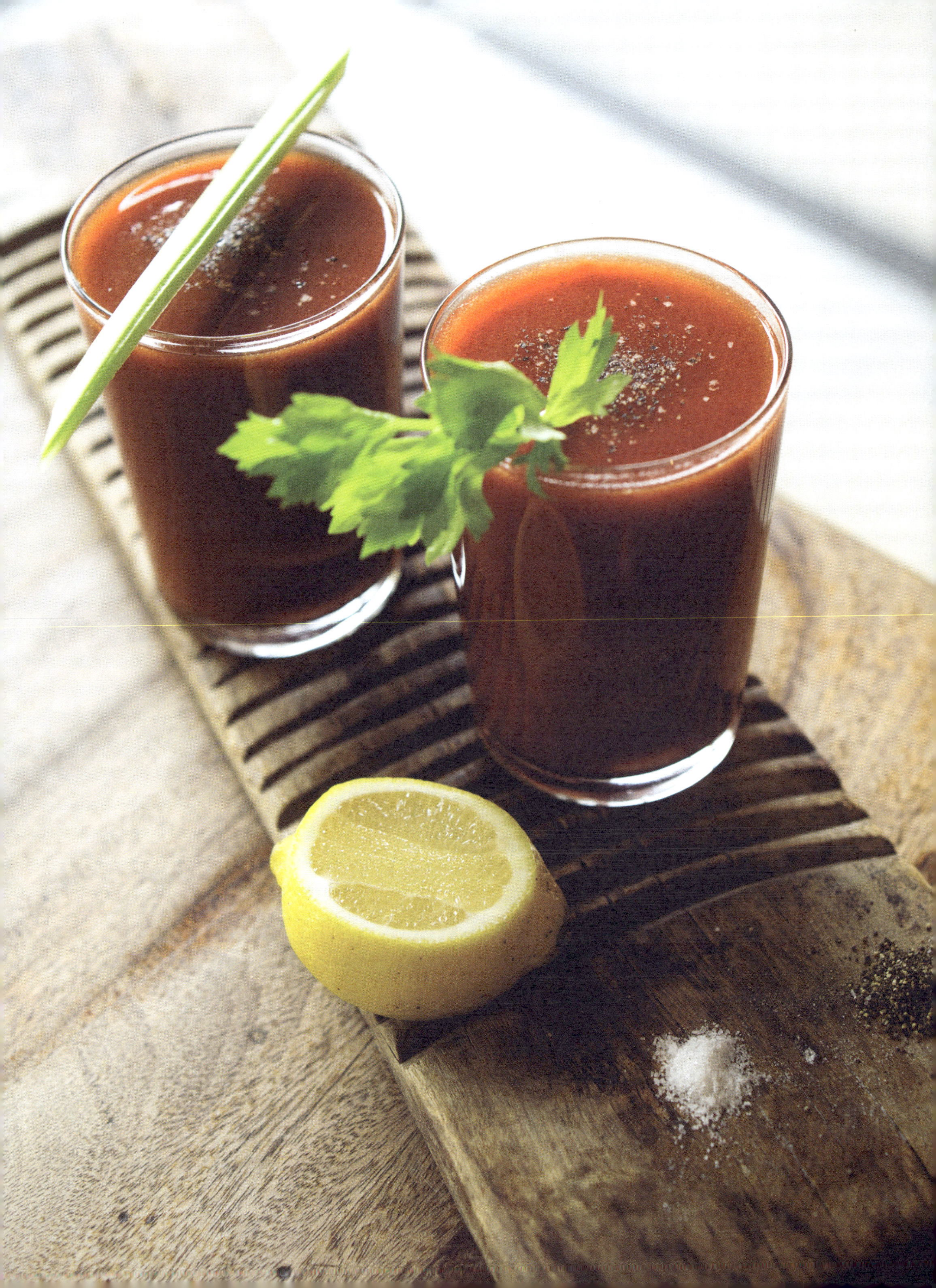

bloody ross

Originally, the Bloody Mary was made with equal measures of tomato juice and vodka, which is probably why it was called the Red Hammer. This version, given to us by brother and sister David Ross and Alexandra Ross, is far less potent, but it still packs a punch. The secret ingredients are fresh, grated horseradish, which you can get at a Chinese supermarket, and a dash of sherry, which cuts the acidity. The Rosses insist on a spicy cocktail – you can't chicken out and have a mild one. And the celery stalk must have leaves.

30 ml vodka
15 ml medium-dry sherry
250 ml tomato cocktail
Tabasco sauce, to taste
dash Worcestershire sauce
pinch fresh grated horseradish
squeeze lemon juice
ice

celery stalk for garnish
salt and pepper

Shake all the ingredients apart from the celery, salt and pepper, in a cocktail shaker with a few ice cubes. Pour into a tall glass. Garnish with the leafy celery and season with salt and pepper. If you're using a flavoured tomato cocktail go easy on the Worcestershire sauce and the salt.

MAKES 1

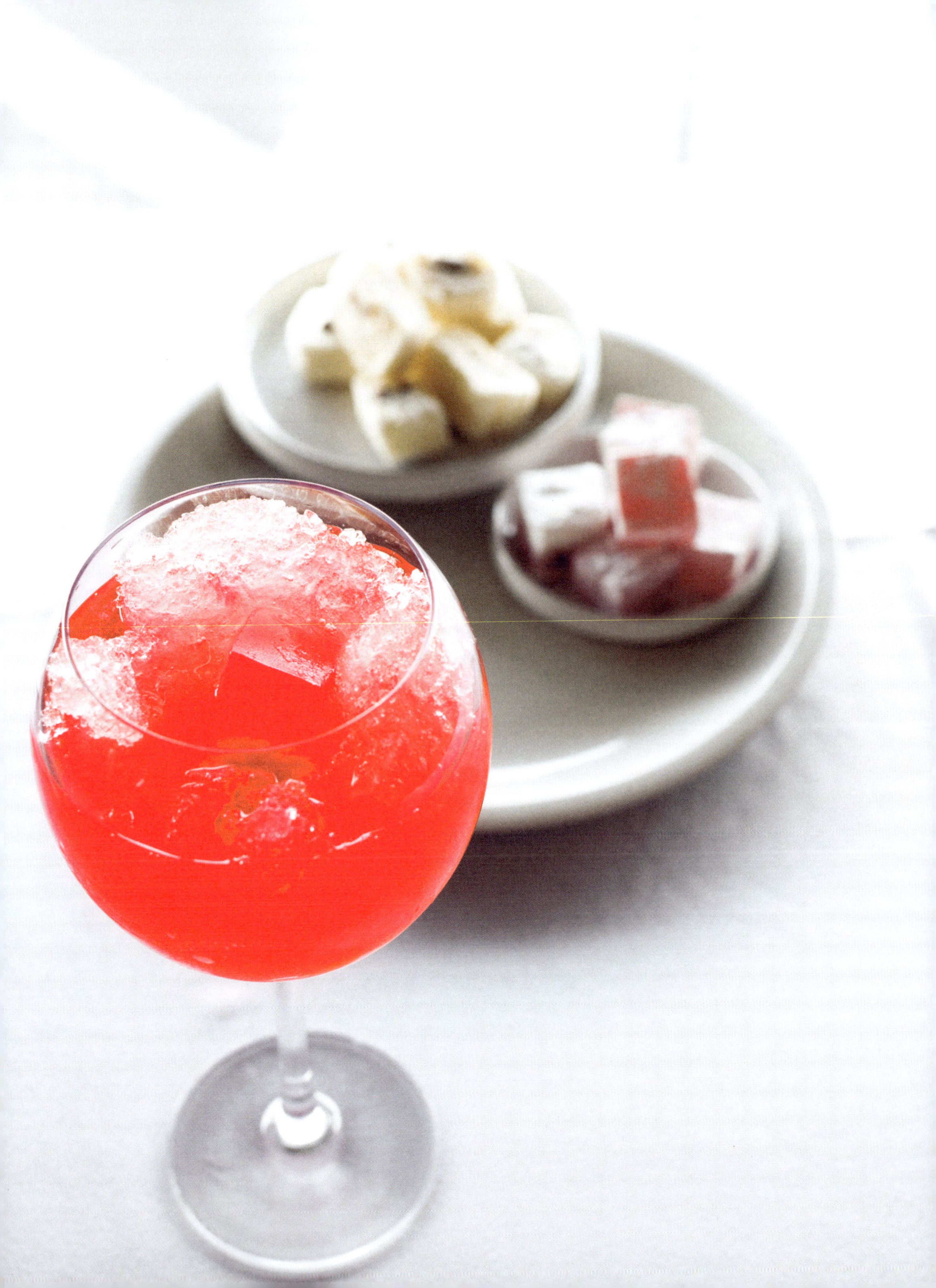

turkish delight cocktail

The best part of this cocktail is watching people try to get to the pieces of Turkish delight. They start off by trying to manoeuvre the chunks up the side of the glass with the straw but soon give up and then just fish them out with their fingers. This is a very sweet cocktail and makes a great grown-up dessert.

60 ml vodka
30 ml rose syrup
juice of 1 lime wedge
150 ml cranberry juice
2 pieces Turkish delight, powder rinsed off

Combine all the ingredients except the Turkish delight in a shaker. Shake well and pour over crushed ice.

Drop in the 2 pieces of Turkish delight.

SERVES 1

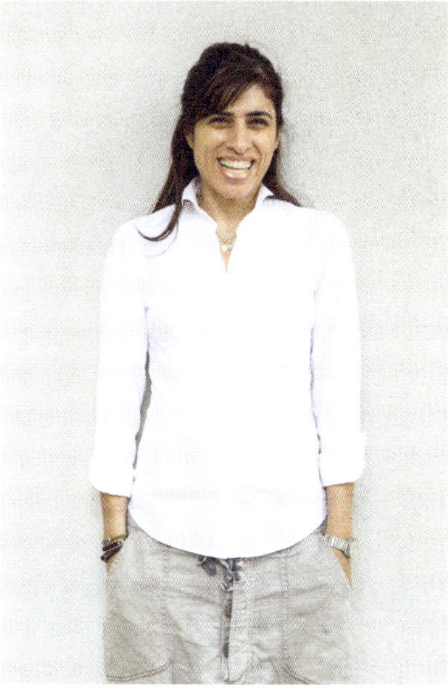
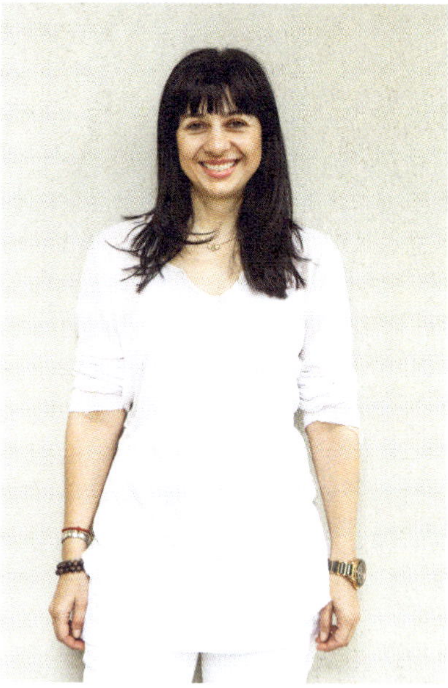
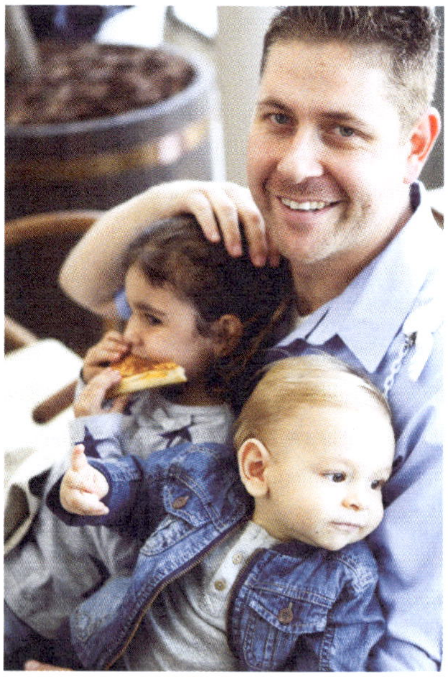
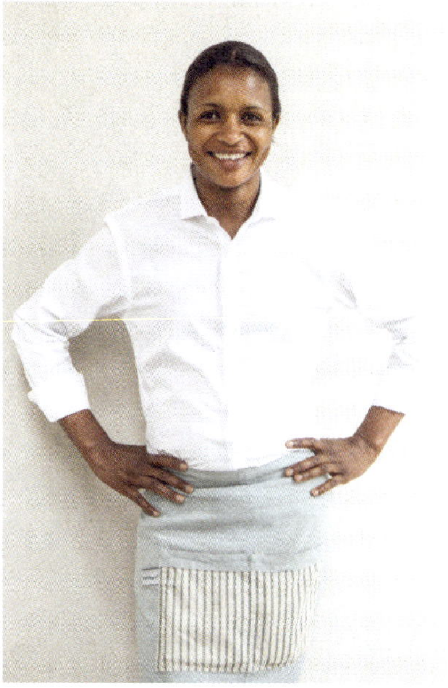
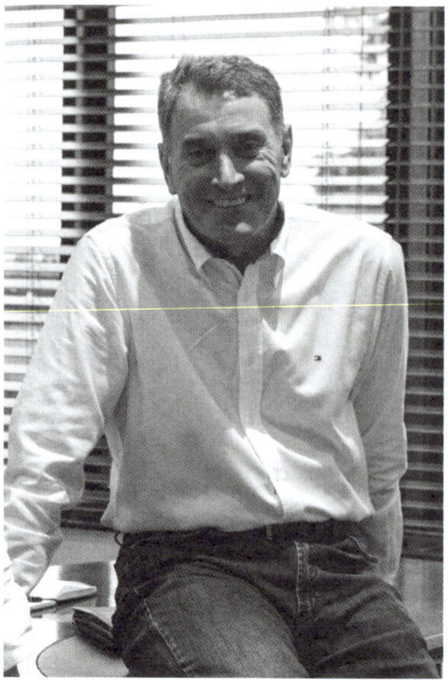
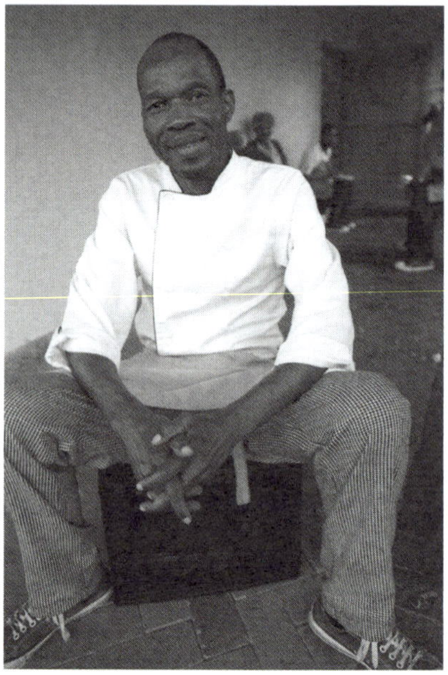
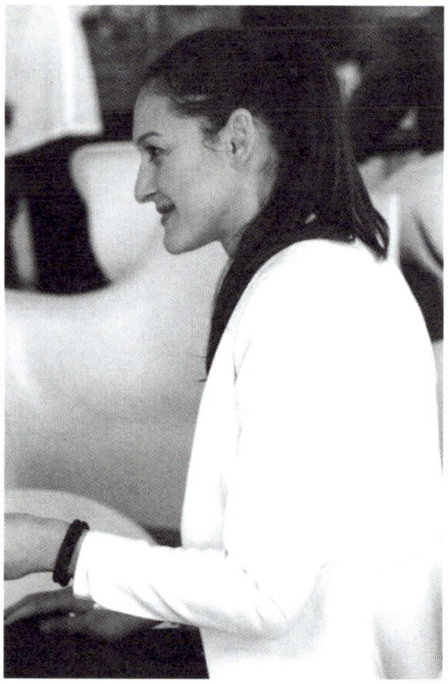
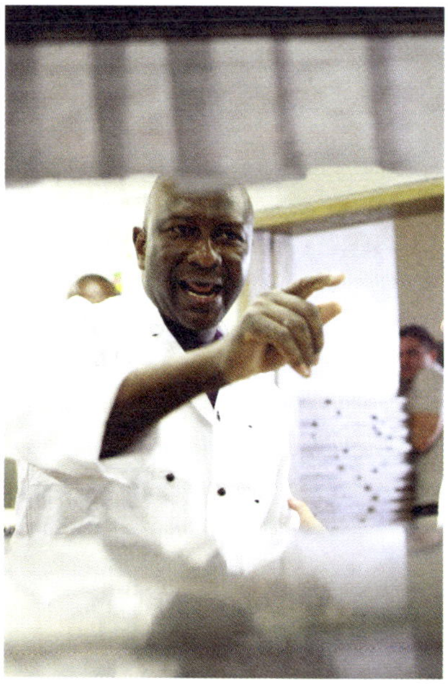
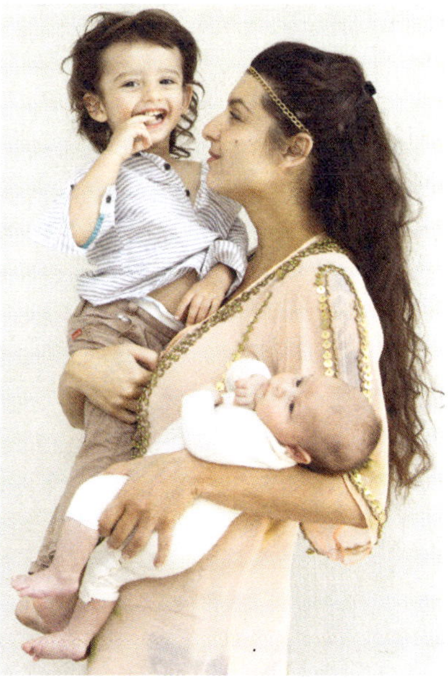

acknowledgements

I often go up to the second floor of the Atholl Centre in Johannesburg and look down on the first tashas. It never fails to amaze me how far we have come. I am so blessed. My dreams have not only come true, they have been far exceeded. The restaurants and this book, would not exist if it weren't for the support of so many people, business partners, franchisees, managers, chefs, kitchen and front-of-house teams, suppliers, family and friends. Without your passion and dedication, your patience and support, without your willingness to always do better, I would not have been inspired to do the same. And to the people who eat and play at tashas everyday, my sincere thanks to all of you too. You are why I do what I do.

Special thanks to...

My family: My father Harry, for being my mentor and best friend. My mother, Sophie, for teaching me how to cook with love. My aunt Maroulla and my cousin Maya, for getting me started and my sister Letiwe, for always standing by me. Savva, my brother, for being my driving force, for never letting me give up and for always being there, I love you more than you know. Tina Sideris for being my life mentor in the times when I needed her most.

My partners, Famous Brands: Kevin Hedderwick and the Halamandaris family for giving Savva and me free rein, for providing much-needed structure and for putting up with our 'Mediterranean natures'. Thank you for being the partners I never knew I needed.

The head office team: Melissa Broodryk, Gerard Southey and Elze Roome for your ongoing pursuit of perfection.

The franchisees: Each and every one of you for bringing the tashas experience to life in your stores. And for putting up with my relentless attention to detail. Peter Otto, deserves a special mention for letting me pretend tashas Atholl is still mine when I'm there.

The brand design team: My friends of 20 years, Alexandra Avgitidis and Melpo Theodorou, for all of your passion and expertise in developing the brand and for countless hours debating recipes and putting the menus together.

The design team: My interior architect and designer, Neydine Bak, for your innovation and inspiration in turning my creative vision into tactile, tangible and beautiful spaces. To the many designers that I have had the privilege of collaborating with – Lisa Occhipinti, Gregor Jenkins, Elonah O'Neil, Anthony Shapiro and Andrea Kleinloog.

My staff: There are so many of you that have been on this journey with me that I would like to thank, but a special thanks to Memory, Jimmy, Maggie and Luckiness for putting up with me for all of these years and for your dedication.

My friends: Lidija for supporting me through all of it, for allowing me to use your flat as my office in the early days, and for believing in me every day. Vasili for being like a second brother and for all of the punts you give me. There are too many of you to mention but I thank you all.

The book team: Tessa Graham, for pushing me to make this dream a reality. David Ross, for nine years of exceptional photography. Alexandra Ross for her styling and for pulling out all the stops to design this beautiful book. Mia Botha, for writing it all down. Chefs Elze Roome and Tanith for meticulously testing all the recipes, and the team at my publishers, Jonathan Ball – Jeremy Boraine, Ingeborg Pelser, Ceri Prenter, Marius Roux and Kathy Sutton – for your invaluable support and help in getting this book onto the shelves and into your hands.

Thank you all, from tasha, with love.

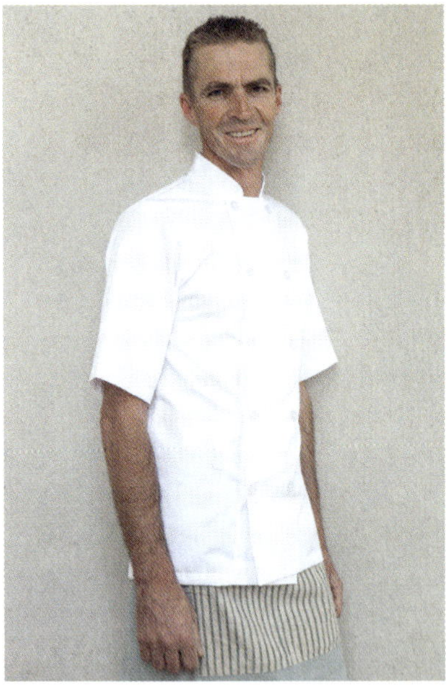
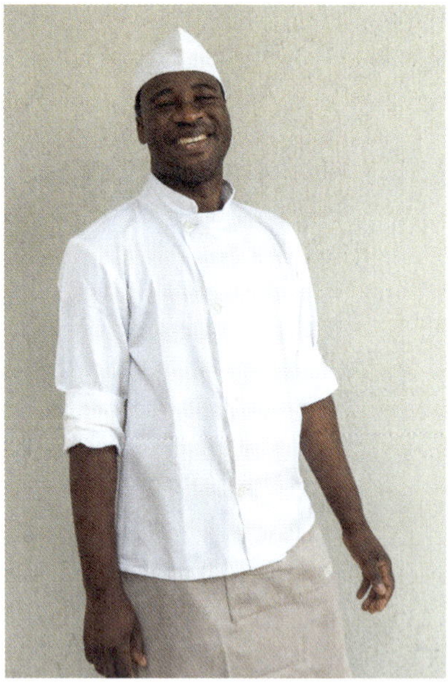
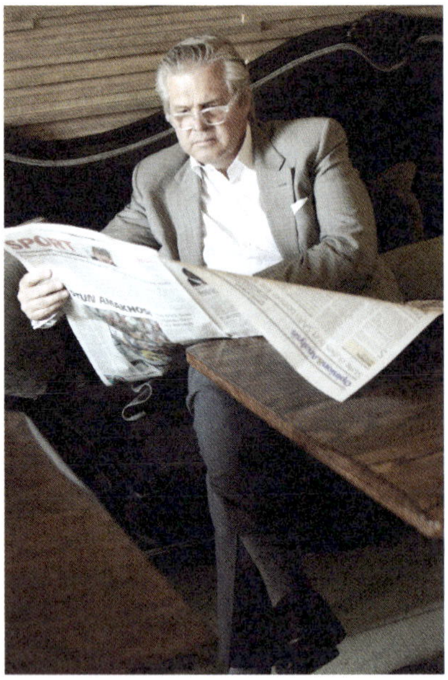
SPORT
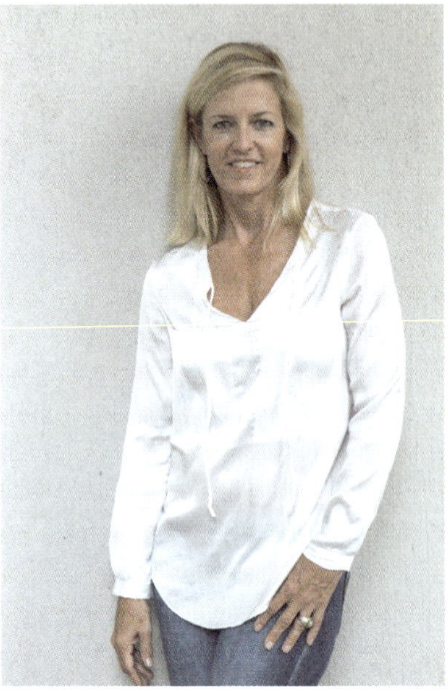
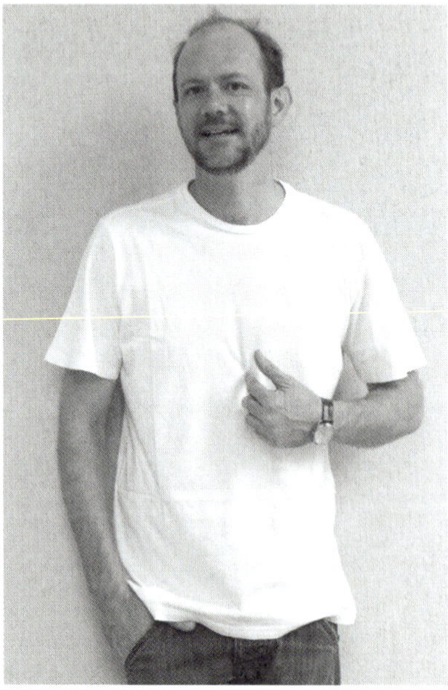
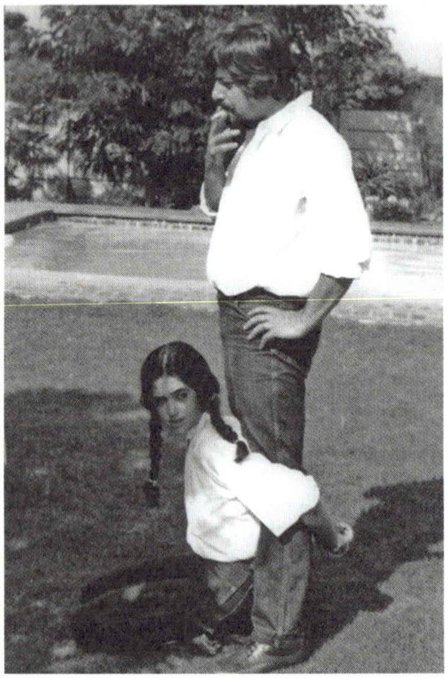
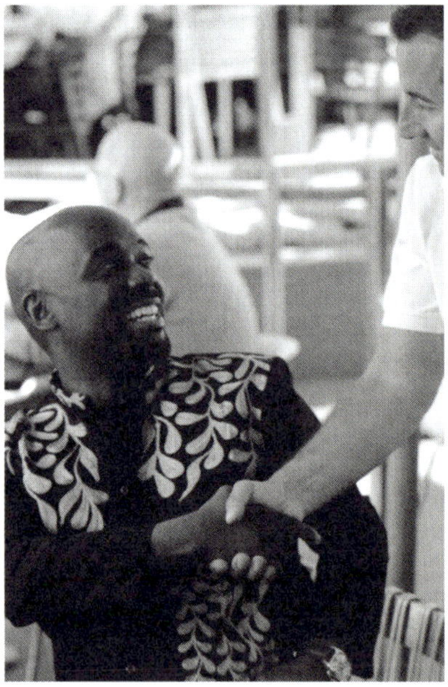
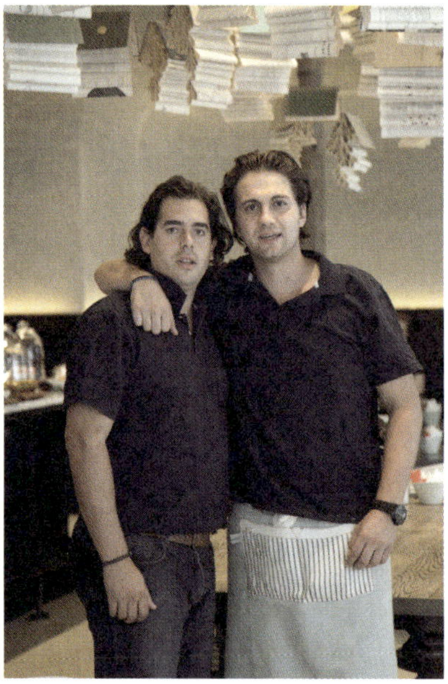
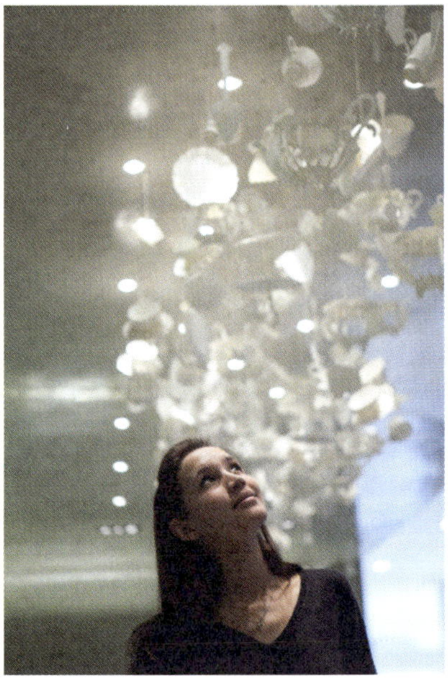

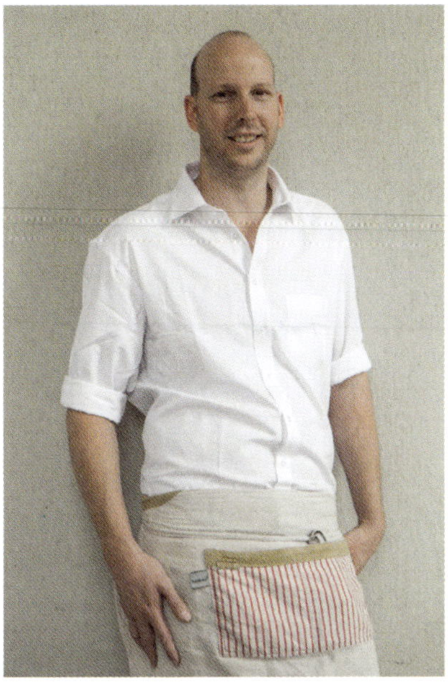
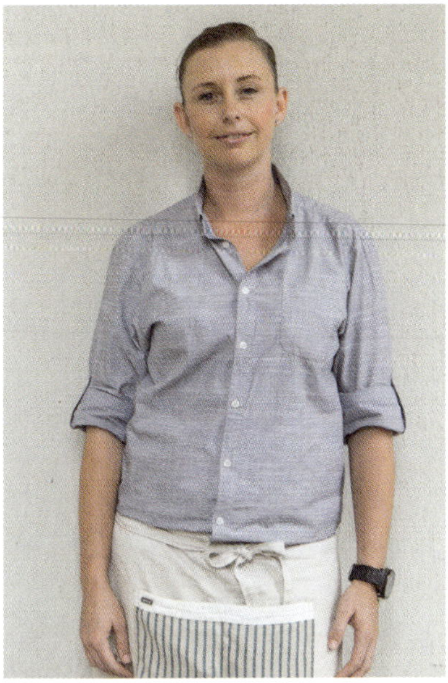
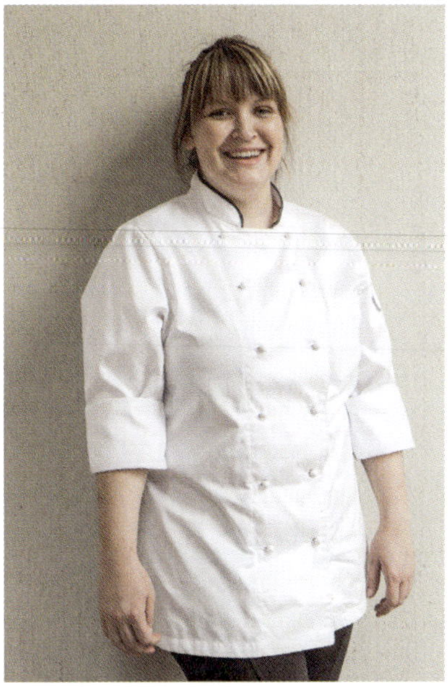
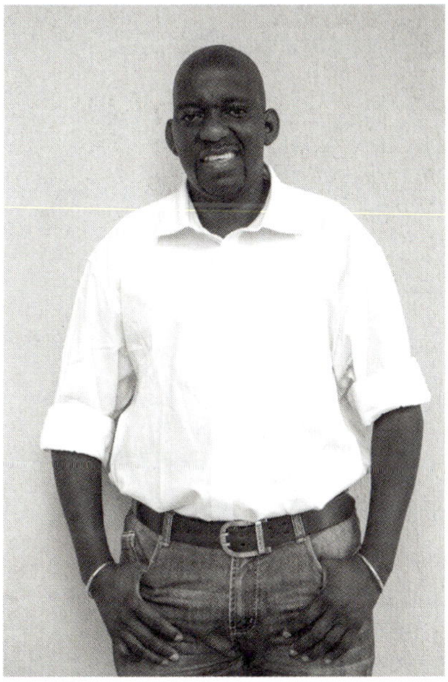
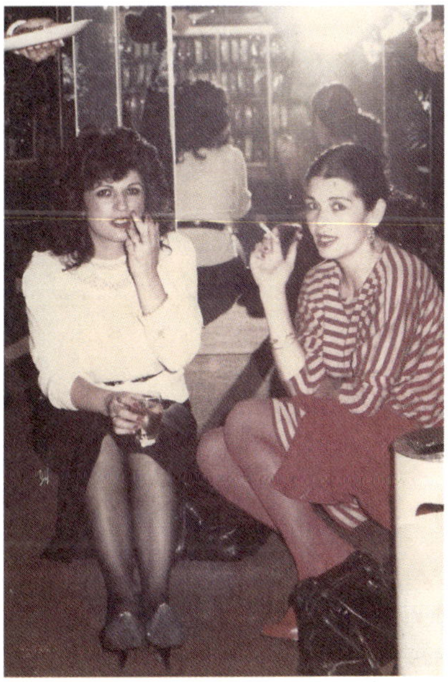
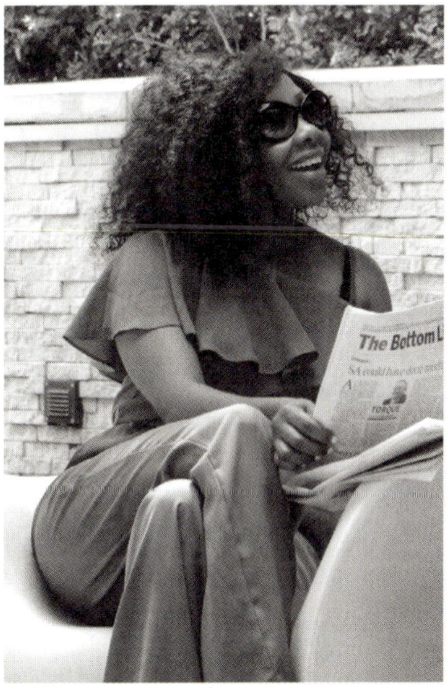
The Bottom
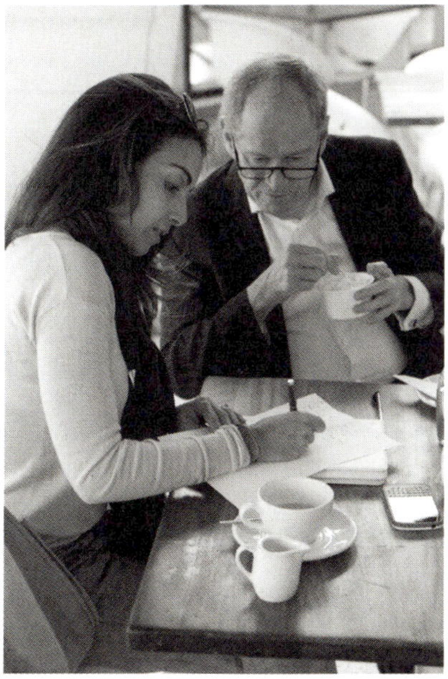
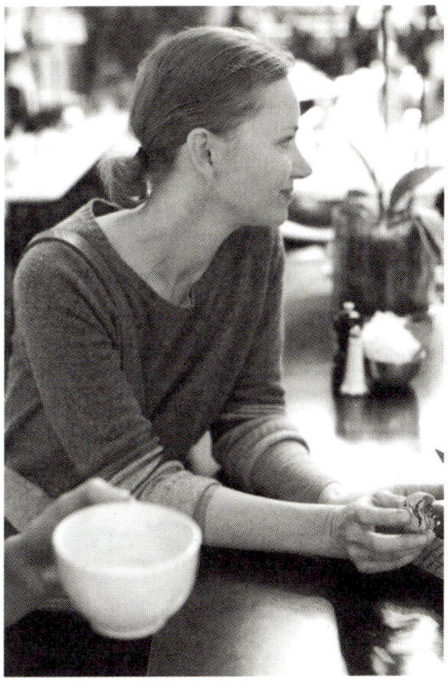
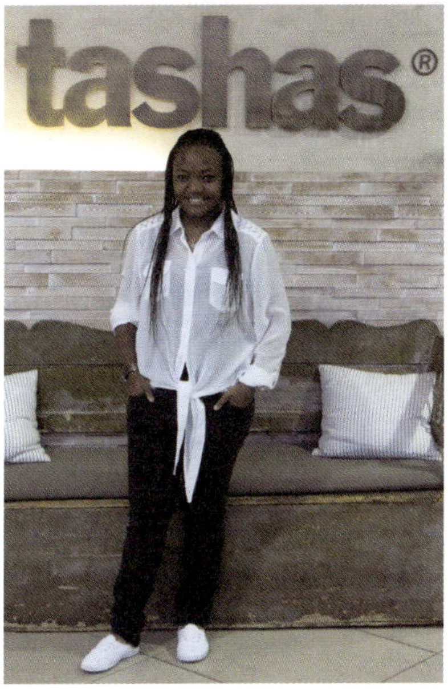
tashas®

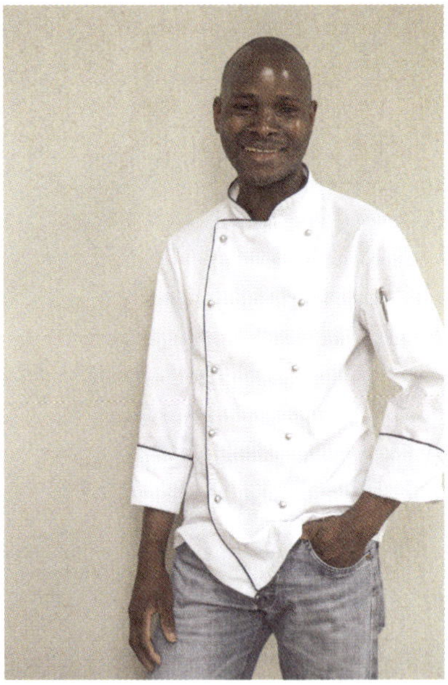
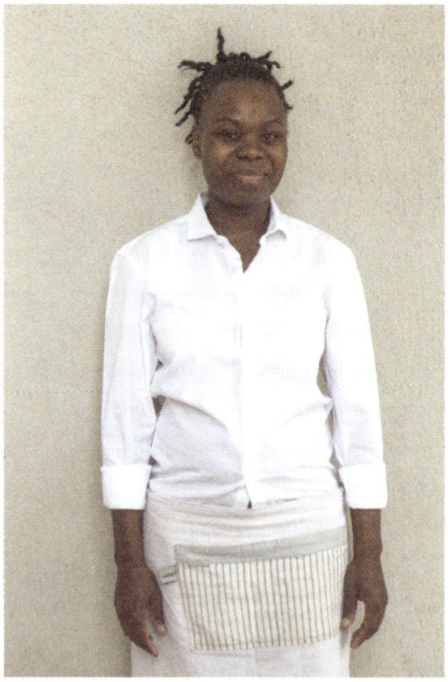
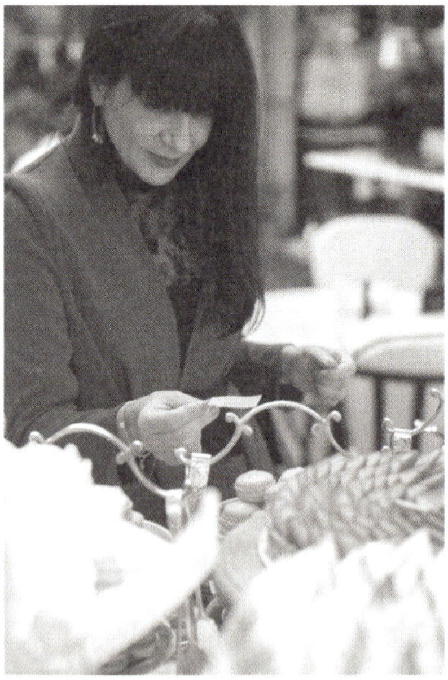
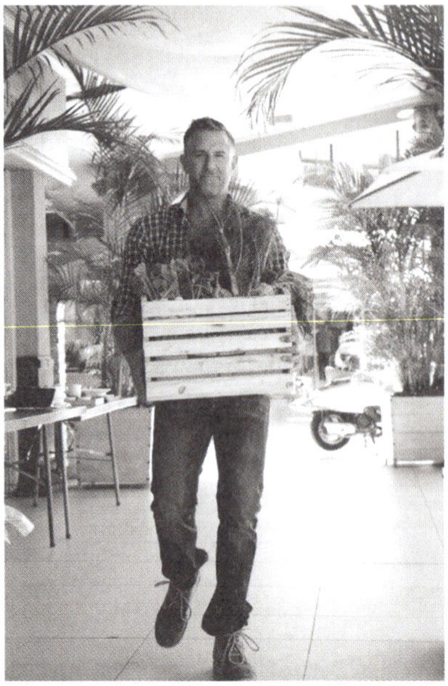
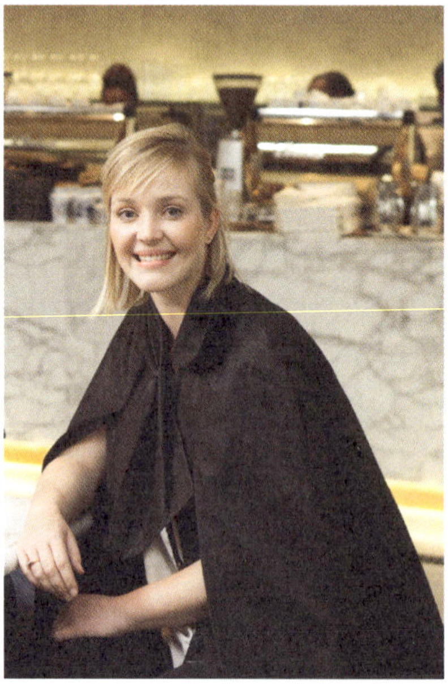
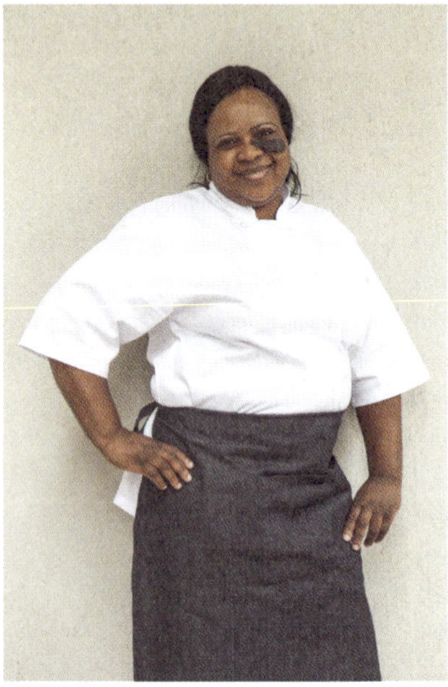
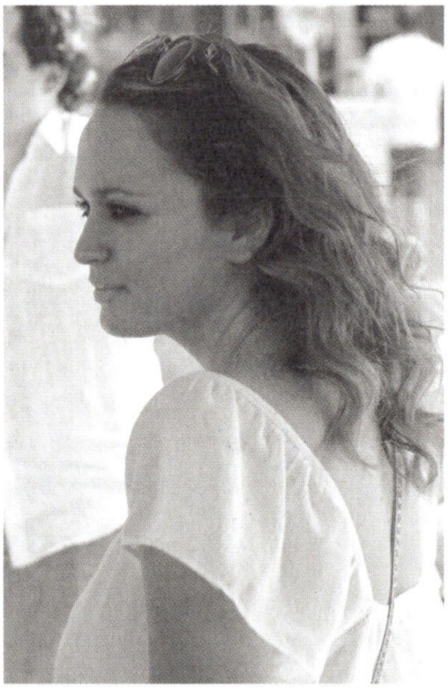
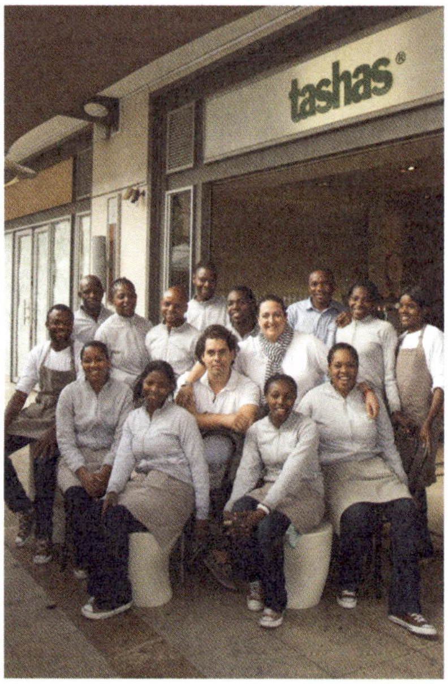
tashas
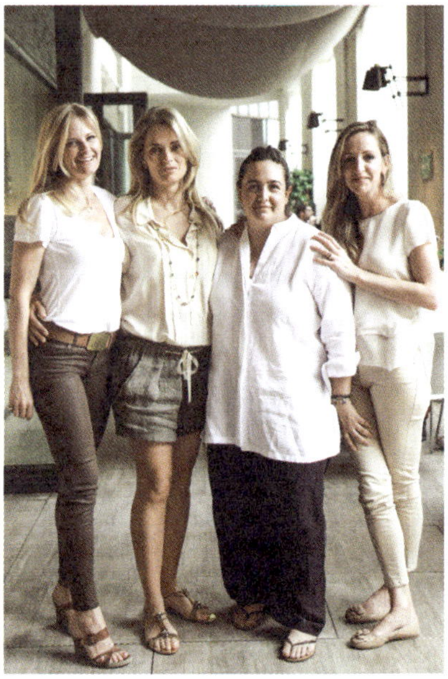

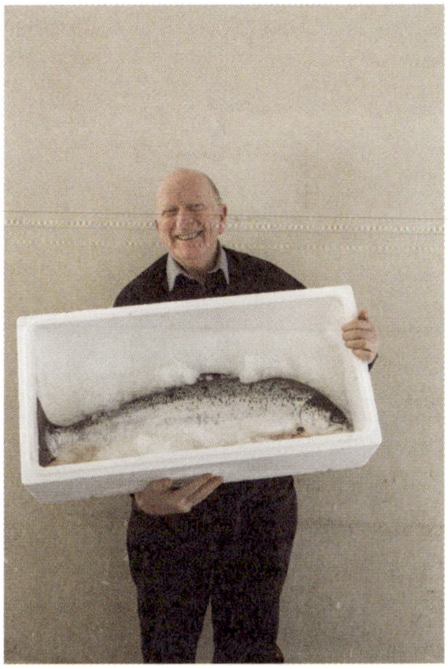
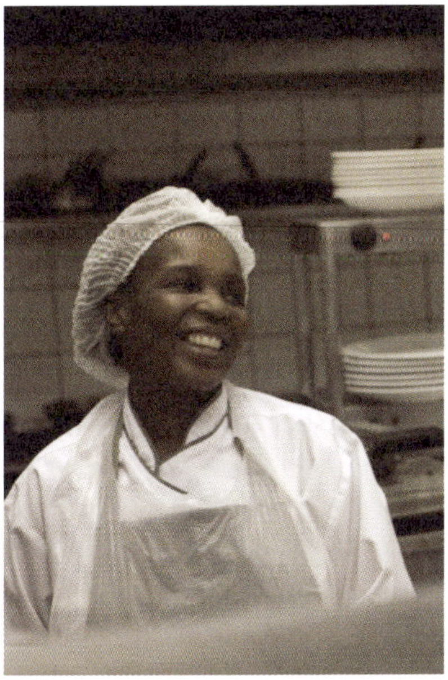
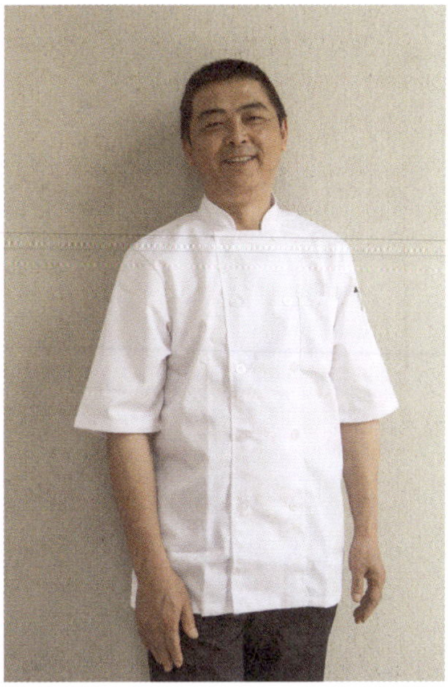
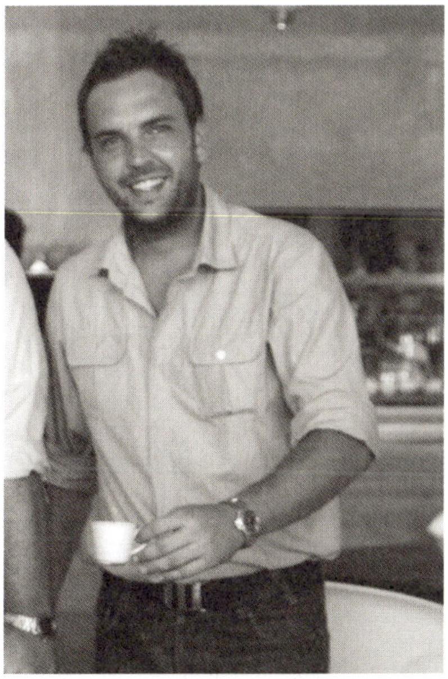
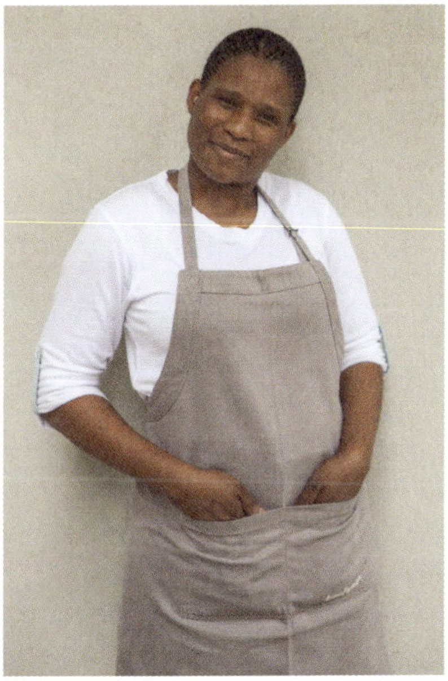
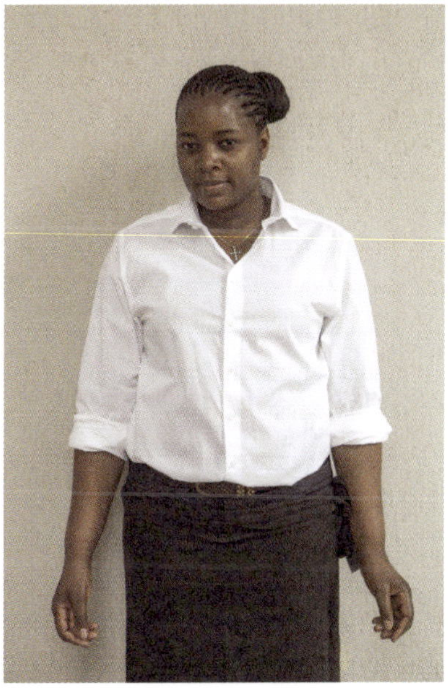
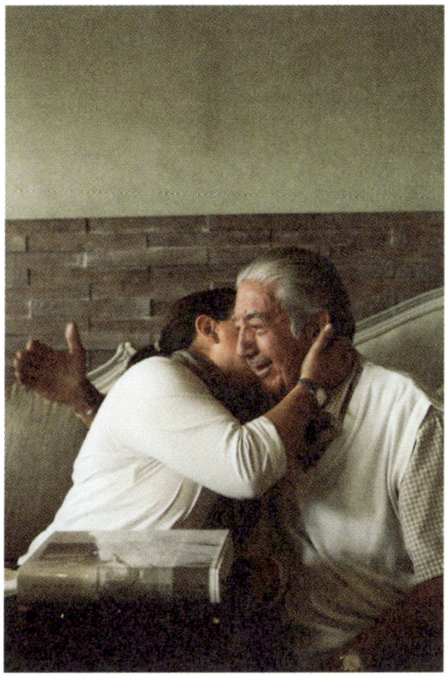
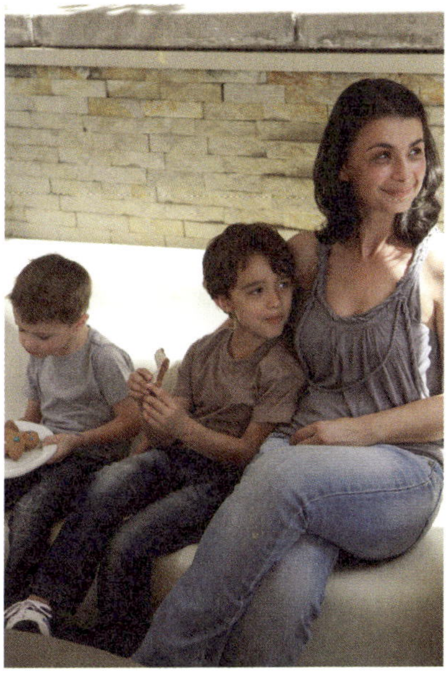
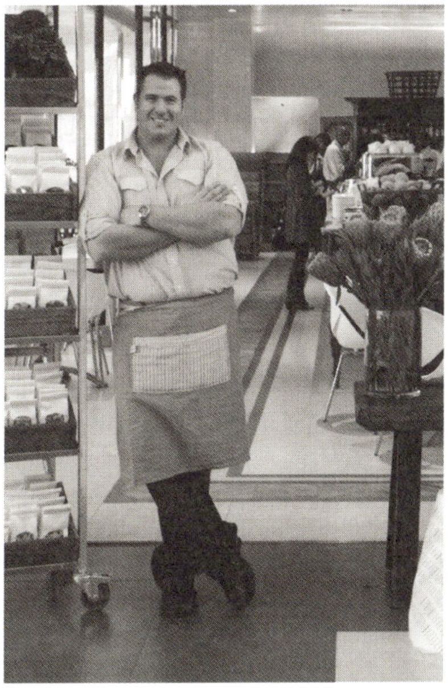

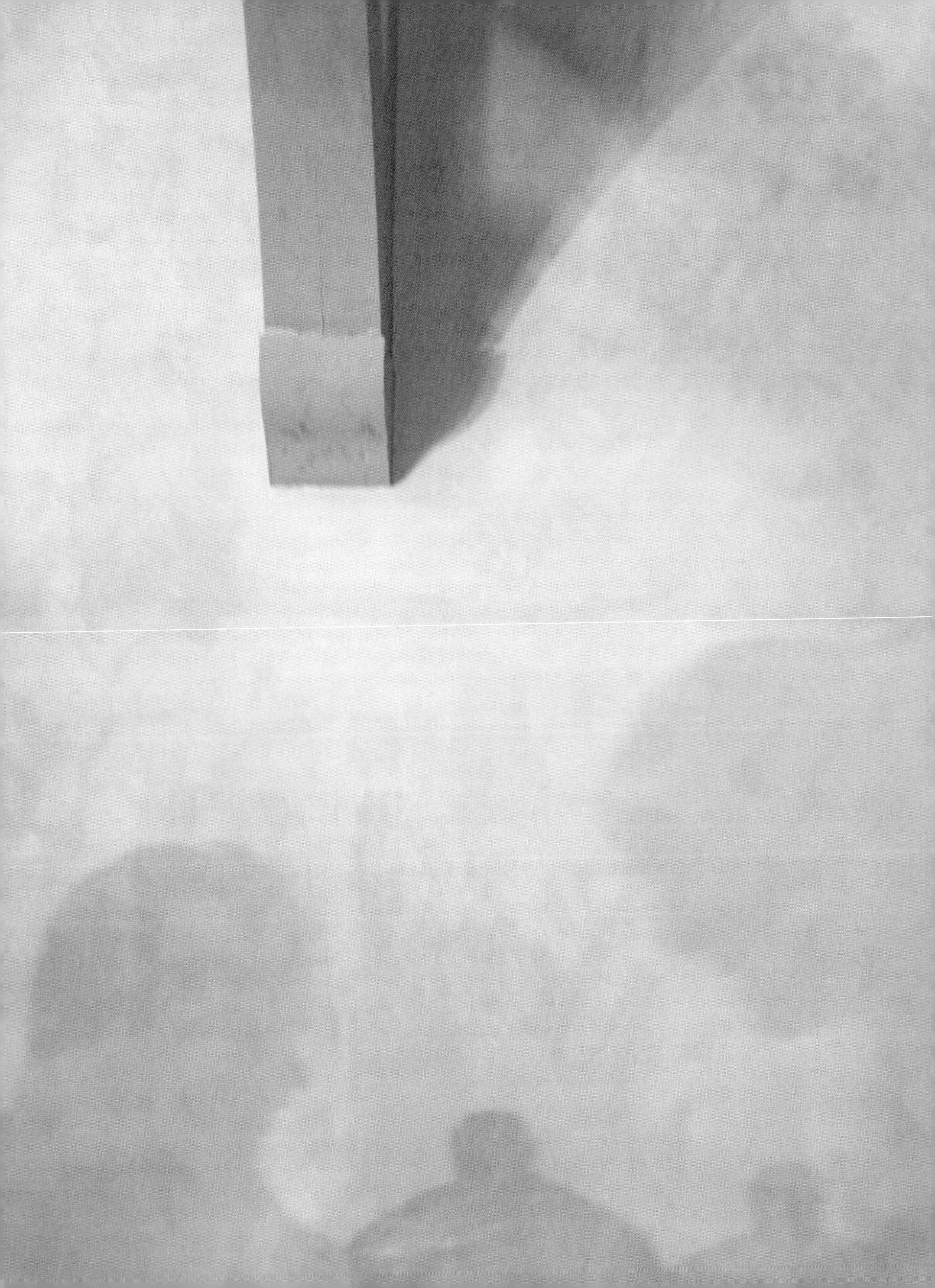

index

12 o'clock breakfast 47

a

apples
apple, lime & ginger juice 193
caramelised fruit 183
carrot, beetroot, apple & lime juice 193
granny smith 25
tashas tarte tatin 177

asparagus
breakfast royale 31
king, queen & i 61
labne lentil salad 95
prawn & asparagus sandwich 61

avocado
avocado salsa 73

b

bacon
bacon rösti 37
baked pasta 125
golden pear salad 97
jett & luke's breakfast 35
pea & fennel bruschetta 33
baked pasta 125
baklava syrup 181
baklava, turkish 181
balsamic toffee dressing 97
barbecue, *see* bbq
barley & bocconcini salad 89
bbq sauce 65

beef
baked pasta 125
harry's roadhouse steak sarmie 65
mini beef burgers 69
spaghetti bolognaise 113
steak tagliata 153
steak tartare 159
beer batter fish & chips 137

beetroot
carrot, beetroot, apple & lime juice 193
jimmy's lamb sandwich 59
labne lentil salad 95
quinoa & edamame salad 91
big squeeze, the 193
biscotti 185
bloody ross 213
bocconcini cheese 89
bolognaise sauce 113, 125
box of prawns 141
brazilian, the 79

berries
cream victoria 173
grandma goes french 53
health breakfast 27
panna cotta 175

breakfast
12 o'clock breakfast 47
bacon rösti 37
breakfast royale 31
good intentions 23
grandma goes french 53
granny smith 25
health breakfast 27
jett & luke's breakfast 35
lazy smoked salmon frittata 51
livers on toast 45
millionaire's breakfast 49
mushroom ciabatta 41
pea & fennel bruschetta 33
pimp my toast 39

burgers
   burger patties 69
   mini beef burgers 69
   mini salmon burger 73

c

caesar dressing 77
caesar salad, traditional 87
caesar sarmie, classic 77
campari 207
caramelised fruit 183
carrot, beetroot, apple & lime juice 193
caviar 49
cheese sauce 63
chicken
   brazilian, the 79
   chicken pot pie 149
   classic caesar sarmie 77
   creamy chicken pesto 121
   livers on toast 45
   parmesan chicken couscous 143
   texas salad 93
   traditional caesar, the 87
chocolate slice, doxa's 167
citrus blast juice 193
cocktails
   bloody ross 213
   gin gimlet 211
   negroni 207
   turkish delight cocktail 215
   whiskey sour 209
coffee, greek 201
cream cheese frosting 173
cream victoria 173
creamy chicken pesto 121

d

dakos salad 99
desserts
   caramelised fruit 183
   cream victoria 173
   doxa's chocolate slice 167
   panna cotta 175
   pineapple carpaccio 171
   pistachio biscotti 185
   ricotta cheese & preserved figs 169
   tashas tarte tatin 177
   turkish baklava 181
dressing
   balsamic toffee dressing 97
   caesar dressing 77, 87
   fruit salad dressing 27
   lemon basil dressing 89, 93
   niçoise dressing 103
   tomato salad vinaigrette 151
   vinaigrette 91
drinks
   big squeeze, the 193
   frullato 197
   granitas 195
   greek coffee 201
   oreo cookie milkshake 199

e

easy eats
   beer batter fish & chips 137
   box of prawns 141
   chicken pot pie 149
   easy tart 145
   fish goujons 135
   greek lamb cutlets 151
   linefish with sauce vierge 139

    minestrone 147
    parmesan chicken couscous 143
    salmon fish cakes 133
    steak tagliata 153
    steak tartare 159
    sticky apricot ribs 155
easy tart 145
edamame beans
    quinoa & edamame salad 91
eggs
    12 o'clock breakfast 47
    breakfast royale 31
    cooking methods 18
    egg mayonnaise sandwich 61
    grandma goes french 53
    jett & luke's breakfast 35
    lazy smoked salmon frittata 51
    madame & monsieur 63
    millionaire's breakfast 49
    mushroom ciabatta 41
    pea & fennel bruschetta 33
    steak tartare 159

f

falafel pockets 81
fennel
    fennel salad 141
    pea & fennel bruschetta 33
    rocket, fennel & herb salad 133
feta spread 91, 99
figs, ricotta cheese & preserved 169
fish
    beer batter fish & chips 137
    box of prawns 141
    breakfast royale 31
    cucumber & salmon sandwich 61
    fish goujons 135
    healthy salmon bite 75
    king, queen & i 61
    lazy smoked salmon frittata 51
    linefish with sauce vierge 139
    mini salmon burger 73
    prawn & asparagus sandwich 61
    prawn & pea linguine 117
    salmon fish cakes 133
    savva's seafood pasta 119
forestiere sauce 37
frittata, salmon 51
fruit
    big squeeze, the 193
    caramelised fruit 183
    cream victoria 173
    fruit salad 27
    fruit salad dressing 28
    golden pear salad 97
    good intentions 23
    grandma goes french 53
    granitas 195
    granny smith 25
    health breakfast 27
    panna cotta 175
frullato 197

g

gin
    gin gimlet 211
    negroni cocktail 207
golden pear salad 97
good intentions 23
goujons, fish 135
grandma goes french 53
granitas 195

granny smith 25
granola 27
grapefruit & pear juice 193
greek coffee 201
greek lamb cutlets 151
green melon, cantaloupe, lemon & mint juice 193

h

hake
   beer batter fish & chips 137
   fish goujons 135

ham
   breakfast royale 31
   madame & monsieur 63
   traditional caesar, the 87
hamburgers, *see* burgers
harry's burger basting sauce 70
harry's roadhouse steak sarmie 65
health breakfast 27
healthy salmon bite 75

j

jett & luke's breakfast 35
jimmy's lamb sandwich 59
juices, freshly squeezed 193

k

king, queen & i 61

l

labne lentil salad 95

lamb
   greek lamb cutlets 151
   jimmy's lamb sandwich 59
   pulled lamb pasta 111

lemon
   lemon basil dressing 93
   lemon butter sauce 141
   lemon sauce 31
lemongrass, lime & ginger syrup 28

lentils
   labne lentil salad 95
linefish with sauce vierge 139
livers on toast 45

m

madame & monsieur 63
martini rosso 207
mascarpone & roast tomato penne 115
milkshake, oreo cookie 199
millionaire's breakfast 49

mince
   baked pasta 125
   mini beef burgers 69
   spaghetti bolognaise 113
   steak tartare 159
minestrone soup 147
mini beef burgers 69
mini salmon burger 73
mint & sesame seed syrup 28
mushroom ciabatta 41

mushrooms
   12 o'clock breakfast 47
   mushroom ciabatta 41
   mushroom sauce 37, 41, 123

pimp my toast 39
wild mushroom linguine 123

n

napolitana sauce 106
negroni cocktail 207
niçoise salad 103

nuts
   good intentions 23
   health breakfast 27

o

oats
   granny smith 25
   health breakfast 27
   orange zest syrup 28
   oreo cookie milkshake 199

p

panna cotta 175
parmesan chicken couscous 143

pasta
   baked pasta 125
   creamy chicken pesto 121
   mascarpone & roast tomato penne 115
   prawn & pea linguine 117
   pulled lamb pasta 111
   savva's seafood pasta 119
   spaghetti bolognaise 113
   wild mushroom linguine 123

pears
   caramelised fruit 183
   golden pear salad 97
   grapefruit & pear juice 193

peas
   pea & fennel bruschetta 33
   prawn & pea linguine 117

pesto sauce 121
pie, chicken pot 149
pimp my toast 39
pineapple carpaccio 171
pineapple, ginger, melon & mint juice 193
pistachio biscotti 185
pita pockets 81

pork
   apricot ribs 155

potatoes
   bacon rösti 37
   jett & luke's breakfast 35
   potato salad 133

prawns
   box of prawns 141
   king, queen & i 61
   prawn & asparagus sandwich 61
   prawn & pea linguine 117
   savva's seafood pasta 119
   see also fish

pulled lamb pasta 111

q

quinoa & edamame salad 91

r

ribs, apricot 155
ricotta cheese & preserved figs 169
rocket, fennel & herb salad 133
rösti 37

S

salad dressing, *see* dressing

salads
    barley & bocconcini salad 89
    dakos salad 99
    fennel salad 141
    golden pear salad 97
    labne lentil salad 95
    potato salad 133
    quinoa & edamame salad 91
    rocket, fennel & herb salad 133
    salad niçoise 103
    texas salad 93
    tomato salad 151
    traditional caesar, the 87

salmon
    breakfast royale 31
    cucumber & salmon sandwich 61
    healthy salmon bite 75
    lazy smoked salmon frittata 51
    mini salmon burger 73
    salmon fish cakes 133

sandwiches
    brazilian, the 79
    classic caesar sarmie 77
    cucumber & salmon 61
    egg mayonnaise 61
    falafel pockets 81
    harry's roadhouse steak sarmie 65
    healthy salmon bite 75
    jimmy's lamb sandwich 59
    king, queen & i 61
    madame & monsieur 63
    prawn & asparagus 61

sauces
    basting sauce, greek lamb cutlets 151
    bbq sauce 65
    bolognaise sauce 113, 125
    cheese sauce 63
    chocolate sauce 167
    forestiere sauce 37
    harry's burger basting sauce 70
    lemon butter sauce 141
    lemon mayonnaise sauce 135
    lemon sauce 31
    mushroom sauce 37, 41, 123
    napolitana sauce 106
    pulled lamb pasta sauce 111
    pesto 121
    rib basting sauce 155
    steak tagliata sauce 153
    tartar sauce 137
    vierge sauce 139

seafood
    seafood pasta, savva's 119
    see also fish, prawns

seeds
    good intentions 23
    granny smith 25
    health breakfast 27
    mint & sesame seed syrup 28

sherry 213
smoked salmon frittata 51
spaghetti bolognaise 113
sponge cake 173
sugar syrup 211

syrups
    baklava syrup 181
    fruit salad syrups 28
    granita syrup 195
    lemongrass, lime & ginger syrup 28
    mint & sesame seed syrup 28
    orange zest syrup 28
    sugar syrup 211

t

tartar sauce 137
tart, easy 145
tarte tatin, tashas 177
texas salad 93
tomatoes
    bloody ross 213
    mascarpone & roast tomato penne 115
    napolitana sauce 106
    oven-roasted 37, 39, 111, 115, 119
    savva's seafood pasta 119
    tomato salad 151
truffles 49
turkish baklava 181
turkish delight cocktail 215
tzatziki 59, 69, 81

V

vegetarian
    12 o'clock breakfast 47
    barley & bocconcini salad 89
    big squeeze, the 193
    caramelised fruit 183
    cream victoria 173
    dakos salad 99
    doxa's chocolate slice 167
    easy tart 145
    falafel pockets 81
    frullato 197
    good intentions 23
    grandma goes french 53
    granitas 195
    granny smith 25
    health breakfast 27
    mascarpone & roast tomato penne 115
    minestrone 147
    mushroom ciabatta 41
    oreo cookie milkshake 199
    panna cotta 175
    pimp my toast 39
    pineapple carpaccio 171
    pistachio biscotti 185
    quinoa & edamame salad 91
    ricotta cheese & preserved figs 169
    tashas tarte tatin 177
    turkish baklava 181
    wild mushroom linguine 123
vierge sauce 139
vinaigrette 91
vodka
    bloody ross 213
    turkish delight cocktail 215

W

whiskey sour 209
wild mushroom linguine 123

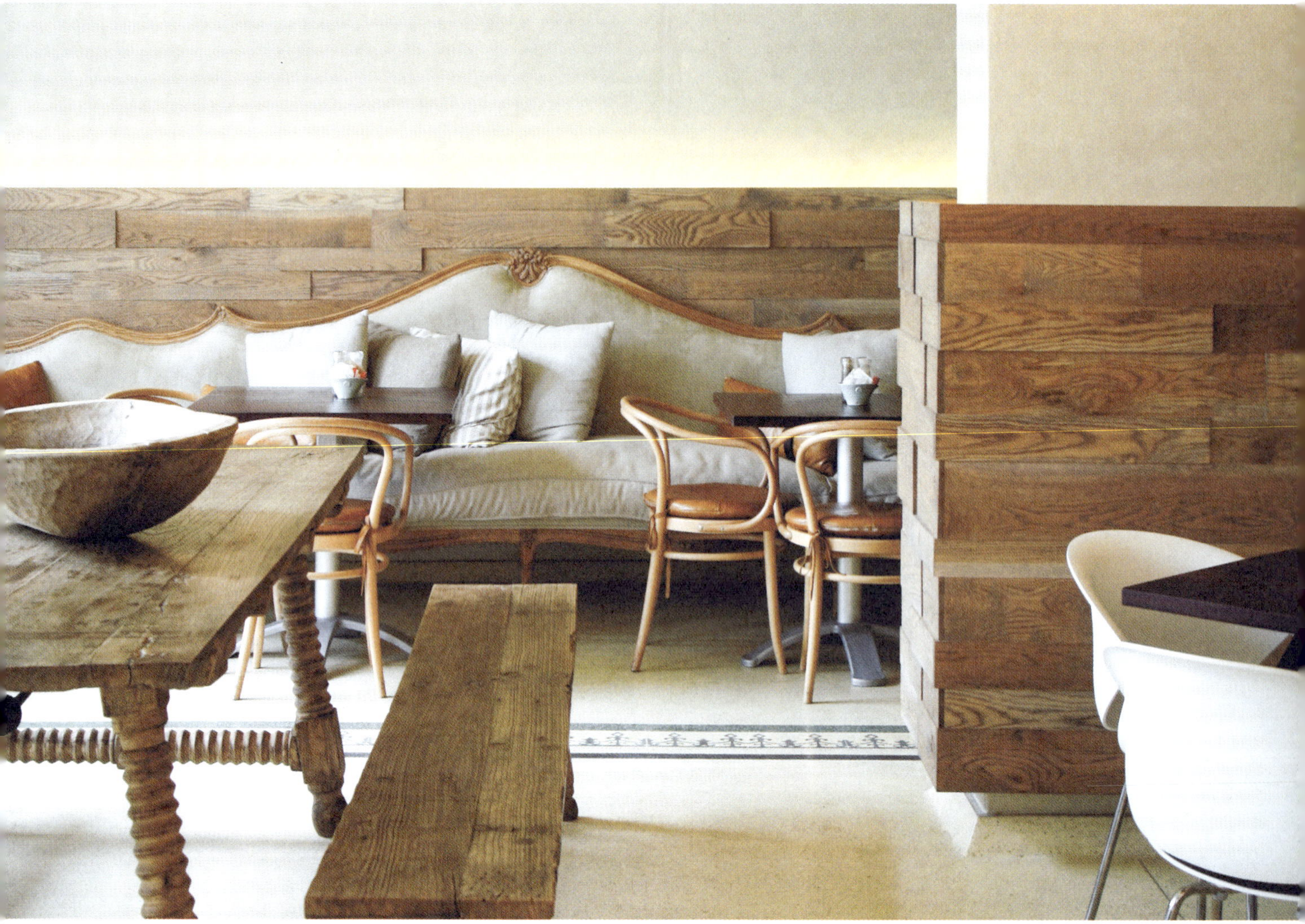

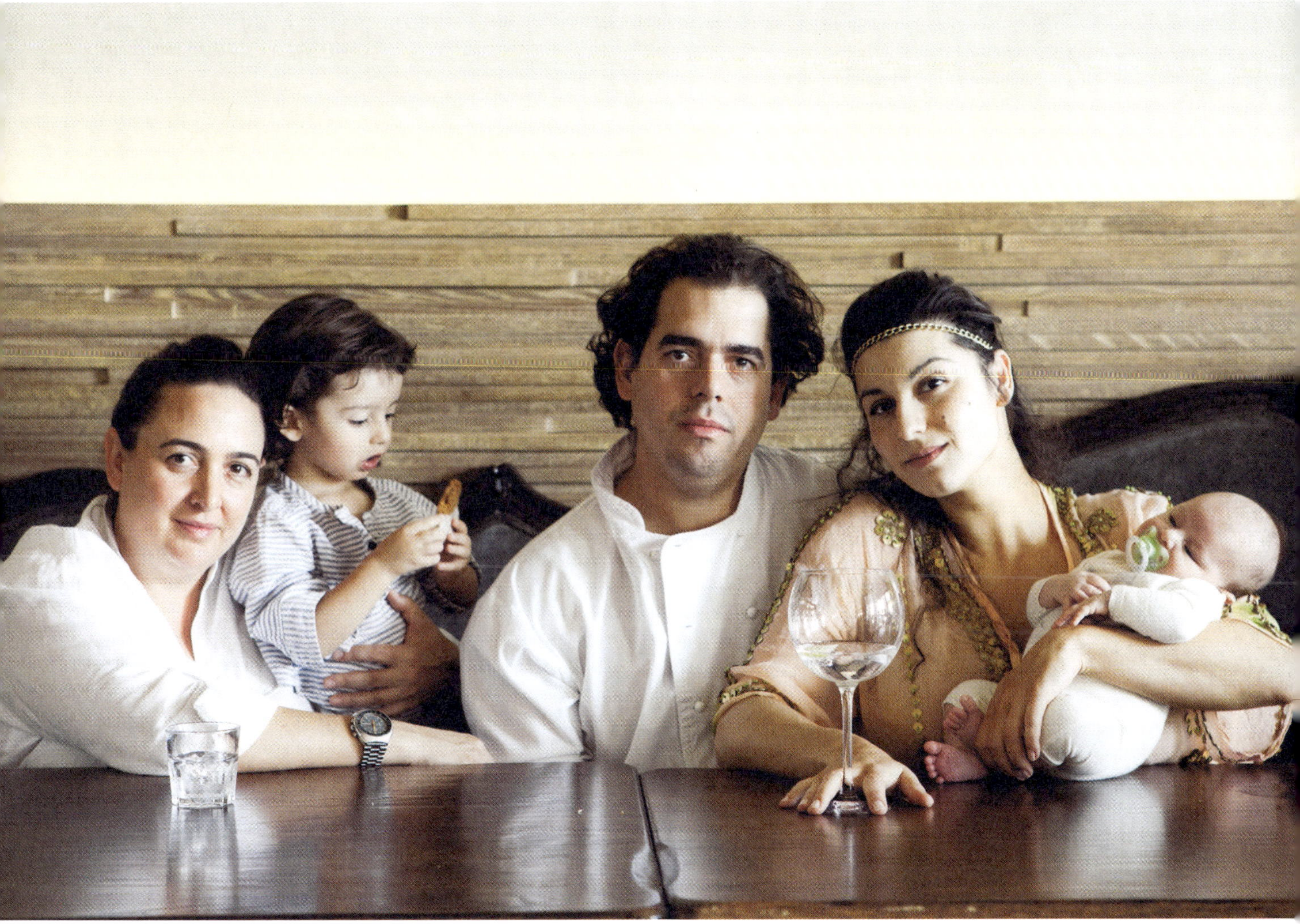

JOHANNESBURG

Inspired by the City
Atholl Square Shopping Centre, Sandton

Inspired by the Suburbs
Village View Shopping Centre, Bedfordview

tashas Melrose
Inspired by Salmon, Champagne and Oysters
The Piazza, Melrose Arch, Melrose

tashas Morningside
Inspired by the Market
Morningside Shopping Centre, Morningside

tashas le Parc, Hyde Park
Inspired by Paris
Hyde Park Shopping Mall, Hyde Park

tashas Nicolway
Inspired by the Mediterranean
Nicolway Shopping Centre, Bryanston

tashas Rosebank
Inspired by New York
The Zone Rosebank

PRETORIA

tashas Brooklyn
Inspired by Dutch Huguenot
Design Square, Brooklyn

CAPE TOWN

tashas Canal Walk
Inspired by Art Deco
Canal Walk Shopping Centre

tashas Constantia
Inspired by Country French
Constantia Village, Constantia

tashas Waterfront
Inspired by Spain
Victoria & Alfred Waterfront

DURBAN

tashas Umhlanga
Inspired by the Explorers
Gateway Shopping Centre

DUBAI

tashas Jumeirah
Inspired by Africa
The Galleria, Jumeirah